LIBERIAN
DREAMS

LIBERIAN DREAMS

Back-to-Africa Narratives from the 1850s

Edited by
Wilson Jeremiah Moses

The Pennsylvania State University Press
University Park, Pennsylvania

Library of Congress Cataloging-in-Publication Data

Liberian dreams : back-to-Africa narratives from the 1850s / edited by
    Wilson Jeremiah Moses.

    p. cm.
    Includes bibliographical references and index.
    Contents: The looking-glass : being a true report and narrative of the
life, travels, and labors of the Rev. Daniel H. Peterson / Daniel H.
Peterson—Four months in Liberia, or, African colonization exposed /
William Nesbit—Four years in Liberia : a sketch of the life of Rev.
Samuel Williams, with remarks on the missions, manners, and customs
of the natives of western Africa ; Together with an Answer to Nesbit's
book / Samuel Williams—Five letters on Liberian colonization /
Augustus Washington.
    ISBN 0-271-01710-4 (cloth : alk. paper)
    ISBN 0-271-01711-2 (pbk. : alk. paper)
    1. Liberia—History—1849–1944—Sources. 2. Back to Africa
movement—History—Sources. 3. Liberia—Description and travel.
I. Moses, Wilson Jeremiah, 1942—   .
DT634.L53   1997
966.62'02—dc21   97-37112
                                                                         CIP

It is the policy of The Pennsylvania State University Press to use acid-free
paper for the first printing of all clothbound books. Publications on
uncoated stock satisfy the minimum requirements of American National
Standard for Information Sciences—Permanence of Paper for Printed
Library Materials, ANSI Z39.48-1992.

For Maureen

Contents

Preface

On November 10, 1853, the barque *Isla de Cuba* sailed from New York Harbor for the West African Republic of Liberia with a company of fifty-three emigrants. They reached the Liberian capital, Monrovia, on December 18. Ironic counterparts of the tired, poor, and tempest-tossed Europeans who were no doubt arriving in New York at that same moment, they too were willing to brave the uncertainties of life in an unfamiliar environment.

This volume brings together, for the first time, four documents written by black Americans and relating to that voyage of the *Isla de Cuba*. (Actually, there are five documents, if we count Dr. Martin R. Delany's blistering "Introduction" to William Nesbit's *African Colonization Exposed.*) In addition to Nesbit's narrative are Samuel Williams's more positive reflections in *Four Years in Liberia;* Daniel Peterson's *The Looking-Glass;* and several letters by the well-educated and enterprising Augustus Washington.

Why this particular set of documents? Allow me to share an anecdote by way of explanation. During African American History Month 1997, I was contacted by the host of a radio talk show in State College, Pennsylvania—a very nice white fellow—asking if I would be willing to grant him an interview on the subject of slavery. We chatted amiably for a few minutes, and then I suggested that a novel approach might be to focus on the Free African population in the antebellum United States. The concept elicited mild surprise, but my flexible host was intrigued by the idea, and we scheduled a telephone interview for later that week. As I had anticipated, the opening questions were directed at the dismal legal and social status of Free African communities in the nineteenth-century United States. I explained that although those issues have attracted a portion of my interest, my principal interests have been focused otherwise. The topic of antebellum racism was diligently studied by the generation of scholars before me. These included historians, who like John Hope Franklin reached maturity in the 1940s and whose work was rightly dedicated to the crusade against *de jure* segregation in America. The times then dictated more pressing concerns than researching the Back-to-Africa movement and the history of black nationalism.

Anyone interested in the harrowing experiences of nonenslaved black people in the antebellum United States is referred to the chapter title "Quasi-Free Blacks" in John Hope Franklin's *From Slavery to Freedom* and to his model study, *The Free Negro in North Carolina: 1719–1860*. These works describe the legal and social status of free black people, who numbered 59,000 at the time of the first federal census in 1790, and 488,000 by the Civil War—roughly 10 percent of the African American population. These people, who referred to themselves as "Free Africans" at the end of the eighteenth century, and "Free Colored People" in the 1850s, were constantly the targets of childish and petty insults, and almost universally confronted by smirking viciousness, mean-spirited discrimination, and gratuitous violence.

But that is an old story. Often during my interview, as I attempted to focus on what African Americans had attempted to do for themselves during the antebellum era, the interviewer sought to return to the theme of the mistreatment and discrimination faced by the antebellum Free Africans. The topic is undoubtedly important, but equally significant is the topic of the attempts of blacks to take control of their own destinies during these years.

I have expended a great deal of energy on the study of black middle-class separatism over the past quarter-century. In 1978 I published a book on the subject called *The Golden Age of Black Nationalism, 1850–1925,* in which I focused on the traditions of self-reliance, cleanliness, hard work, temperance, and sexual morality among African American men and women. My further studies and researches in the field resulted in publication of the biography of a major black nationalist, *Alexander Crummell: A Study of Civilization and Discontent* (1989). Crummell, who lived from 1819 to 1898, devoted the years 1853–72 to missionary and

educational work in Liberia and was the first African American
to get a degree from Cambridge University in England.

When in 1996 I published a collection of documents called
*Classical Black Nationalism: From the American Revolution to Marcus
Garvey,* one reviewer, aware of my interests over these many
years, attributed to me what he called a "commitment to a separatist mentality," and he went so far as to circulate that opinion
on the World Wide Web. The matter has caused me some discomfort, because I am definitely not a black separatist. I possess
nothing resembling a "commitment to a separatist mentality,"
and I am surprised that an academic reviewer can make the mistake of confusing scholarly interest with political advocacy. Not
everyone who writes a book about the Republican Party is a Republican, and not everyone who writes about African American separatism is a separatist. To acknowledge that a position
is interesting or understandable is not the same thing as
advocating it.

The narratives presented here, while colorful and interesting,
are relatively unknown, even to many specialists in African
American history. And although most general readers are aware
that there is a country in West Africa founded by former slaves,
they have little information on the history of that country. Most
history books about African Americans in the antebellum United
States focus on the problem of slavery. Until recently, historians
concerned with the "Free Colored People" have usually addressed the oppression and discrimination faced by that group,
rather than African American efforts to improve their condition. And even most historians who did focus on the Free Colored People's attempts at self-improvement have been occupied
with abolitionism to the neglect of the Back-to-Africa movement.

The documents presented here were once more widely available than they are today. Published in the 1850s, they were reprinted in the late 1960s and at that time readily available to
teachers, students, and lending libraries. For the past ten years,
however, they have been exceedingly difficult to access, having
become the protected treasures of rare-book rooms and remote

archives, and many of the reprint copies that were available in the 1960s have been lost or stolen from university libraries or have fallen victim to mindless vandalism. Thus, the typical college undergraduate of recent years has had little opportunity to become familiar with this important aspect of American history.

The Pennsylvania State University Press, and especially its acquisitions editor, Peter Potter, are to be commended for their cooperation in making these documents once again available to teachers, students, and the general public. Thanks are due to my copy editor, Peggy Hoover, for her diligence, her advice, and her encouragement. I also thank my wife, Maureen, who assisted with the deciphering of sometimes barely legible documents and carefully read my transcriptions against the originals. Her work with me on the index has been indispensable.

Introduction

The misty legend of "black Crispus Attucks," who died in the event that came to be called the Boston Massacre of March 5, 1770, tells us little about the thoughts and actions of black Bostonians in the Revolutionary period, although it has found its way into high school textbooks, poetry anthologies, and a speech by Martin Luther King Jr.[1] A less sentimental view of African American attitudes toward the Revolution is revealed in the action of four lesser-known black Bostonians on April 20, 1773. Their petition to the Massachusetts legislature three years after the death of Attucks casts a harsher but more revealing light on the thinking of African Americans in the Revolutionary period.

The petitioners—Peter Bestes, Sambo Freeman, Felix Holbrook, and Chester Joie—asked for the right to set aside a portion of the proceeds of their labors to purchase their freedom and return to Africa. "Even the Spaniards," they argued, "who have not those sublime ideas of freedom that English men have," allowed their slaves to work one day a week "to earn money to purchase the residue of their time." They assured the legislature that their attempts to gain freedom were "peaceful and lawful" and that they were "willing to submit to such regulations and laws, as may be made relative to us." Nonetheless, they expressed their unequivocal determination "to leave the prov-

1. "Black Crispus Attucks" is memorialized by poet Melvin B. Tolson in "Dark Symphony." A typical textbook presentation is in Carter Woodson and Charles Wesley, *The Story of the Negro Retold* (Washington, D.C.: Associated Publishers, 1959), 50. Another typical sentimental view of Attucks is in Lerone Bennett, *Pioneers in Protest* (New York: Penguin Books, 1969), 3–9. Martin Luther King Jr. celebrates Attucks in *The Trumpet of Conscience* (London: Hodder & Stoughton, 1968), 25. Problems having to do with Attucks's identity as a mulatto or half-Indian, and with his documentary status, are addressed in Sidney Kaplan and Emma Nogrady Kaplan, *The Black Presence in the Era of the American Revolution* (Amherst: University of Massachusetts Press, 1989), 6–11.

ince" as soon as their labors "should procure money to transport ourselves to some part of the Coast of Africa, where we
propose a settlement." [2]

When the Revolution was over, it was not the liberty-loving
Americans but the imperial British who effected the first major
repatriation of black Americans. This, ironically, was their reward for siding with the Empire against the colonies during the
American Revolution.[3] More than one historian has recounted
the story of Thomas Peters, who fought in the British Regiment
of Black Guides and Pioneers during the Revolutionary War,
and after the war was resettled, along with 3,000 other black loyalists, in Nova Scotia. Finally, in January 1792, some 1,200 African American loyalists, including Peters, were transported to
Sierra Leone, a West African territory the British had established
some years previously as a settlement for the so-called "Black
Poor," unwelcome residents of England.[4]

Many Americans shared the English impulse to ethnic purification and the desire to dispose of the black population by sending them back to Africa. In 1776, Thomas Jefferson headed a
Virginia Committee recommending gradual emancipation of
the slaves, which process was to be accompanied by African colonization. His *Notes on the State of Virginia,* completed in 1782,
shortly before the Peace of Paris, included a proposal for rid-
ding the United States of its African population that even one
of Jefferson's more idolatrous biographers called "draconian." [5]

2. Herbert Aptheker, *A Documentary History of the Negro* (New York: Citadel
Publishers, 1971), 7–8. See also Kaplan and Kaplan, *The Black Presence,* 11, 206.
3. Benjamin Quarles, "The Negro Response: Evacuation with the British," in Melvin Drimmer, ed., *Black History: A Reappraisal* (New York: Doubleday, 1968).
4. Ellen Gibson Wilson, *The Loyal Blacks* (New York: G. P. Putnam, 1976);
Kaplan and Kaplan, *The Black Presence,* 85–89; Gary Nash, "The Forgotten Experience: Indians, Blacks, and the American Revolution," in William M. Fowler Jr.
and Wallace Coyle, eds., *The American Revolution: Changing Perspectives* (Boston:
Northeastern University Press, 1979); Mavis Campbell, *Back to Africa: George Ross
and the Maroons, from Nova Scotia to Sierra Leone* (Trenton N.J.: Africa World
Press, 1993).
5. John Chester Miller, *The Wolf by the Ears: Thomas Jefferson and Slavery*
(New York: The Free Press, 1977), 17, 22, 271.

Jefferson believed that black and white populations could not live together on an equal basis in America: whites entertained "deep rooted prejudices" against the blacks and there were also the "ten thousand recollections, by the blacks, of the injuries they have sustained." [6]

Thus, despite his celebrated doctrine of small government, Jefferson advocated creating a massive governmental mechanism to carry out the work of deporting the Free African population. African children were to be separated from their parents at "a certain age, then be brought up, at the public expense to tillage, arts or sciences, according to their geniuses, till the females should be eighteen, and the males twenty-one years of age, when they should be colonized to such place as the circumstances of the time should render most proper." [7] Although Jefferson was inconsistent on numerous subjects, he never faltered in his commitment to ethnic cleansing. In a letter to James Monroe in 1802, he weighed the possibilities of colonization in Santo Domingo, or in some of the Spanish or Portuguese possessions in the New World. For more than forty years, he steadfastly maintained that emancipation of the enslaved Africans was unthinkable unless accompanied by colonization "beyond the reach of mixture." [8]

In the early days of the Republic, African American attitudes toward colonization and emigration were varied and complicated, fluctuating according to time and place. Prince Hall, a leader in the Free African community in Boston, supported African emigration in the years following the American Revolution. In fact, he represented a group of seventy-three "African Blacks" who in 1787 presented the General Court of Massachusetts with a plan for resettlement in Africa due to the "disagree-

6. Thomas Jefferson, *Notes on the State of Virginia*, in *Thomas Jefferson: Writings*, ed. Merrill D. Peterson (New York: Library of America, 1984), 264.

7. Ibid. Compare with Thomas Jefferson to Jared Sparks, February 4, 1824, in *Jefferson: Writings*, ed. Peterson, 1487.

8. Ibid. See also Jefferson to James Monroe, November 24, 1801, in *Jefferson: Writings*, 1098; Jefferson to Sparks, February 4, 1824, in ibid., 1484; and Jefferson to James Heaton, May 20, 1826, in ibid., 1516.

able and disadvantageous circumstances" that attended life in the United States:

> This and other considerations which we need not here particularly mention induce us to return to Africa, our native country, which warm climate is more natural and agreeable to us; and for which the God of nature has formed us; and where we shall live among our equals and be more comfortable and happy, than we can be in our present situation; and at the same time, may have a prospect of usefulness to our brethren there.[9]

The support of Prince Hall and others for African resettlement did not mean that they lacked commitment to the struggle for universal emancipation in America, or that they had abandoned hope that African Americans could eventually attain all the rights of citizenship. Hall was clearly not convinced by Jefferson's reasoning that antagonism between the races was inevitable. The first phase of the revolution in Haiti had inspired Hall to manifest a tragically premature and optimistic belief that slave societies could be transformed into peaceful communities where blacks and whites lived together in brotherhood and sisterhood. However, one cannot overlook the historically indisputable fact that Hall supported African emigration in the years immediately following the American Revolution. In this he was like several other black leaders, although some of them dramatically altered their positions in later years.

Prince Hall had been dead for nine years when the American Society for Colonizing the Free People of Color of the United States was organized on December 28, 1816. The organization, commonly called the American Colonization Society was of course for whites only and included such prominent people as Andrew Jackson, Henry Clay, James Madison, Francis Scott Key, and George Washington's nephew, Bushrod Washington. Jefferson was not among the founders, nor did he ever become

---

9. Kaplan and Kaplan, *The Black Presence*, 206–8.

a member.[10] The Society's mission was not to be confused with the plan for gradual emancipation that Jefferson had envisioned; its constitution made clear that it was not an abolitionist institution, and its official name was an indicator of its more sinister purpose: elimination of the "free colored" population. While not all the founders of the Colonization Society viewed slavery as a perpetual necessity in America, most of them believed that a Free African in the United States was an anomaly and were determined, in Clay's words, to "rid our country of a useless and pernicious, if not dangerous, portion of its population." As Henry Clay and John Randolph of Roanoke made clear, colonization was for the "free people of color," not for the slaves.[11]

From its origins, however, the colonization movement included a liberal wing, which had qualms about forced deportation and was dedicated to the more benevolent doctrine that the promise of systematic resettlement might be an inducement to gradual emancipation.[12] They believed that a successful colony in Africa would prove that Africans were capable of self-improvement and deserving of freedom. Eventually, an independent black republic might serve as a powerful magnet to draw the Free Africans out of North America. Nagging doubts persisted, however, as to the practicality of total repatriation, which even Jefferson came to admit was impossible.[13] Most thinking people eventually shared the skepticism of Alexis de Tocqueville, who observed that in the first twelve years of its existence the Colonization Society was responsible for the re-

10. Jefferson to Jared Sparks February 4, 1824, reveals the fixity of Jefferson's belief that emancipation must be accompanied by the colonization of freed African Americans "any place on the coast of Africa." See also Jefferson to James Heaton, May 20, 1826, in *Jefferson: Writings*, ed. Peterson.

11. Philip J. Staudenraus, *The African Colonization Movement, 1816–1865* (New York: Columbia University Press, 1961), 28.

12. John Hope Franklin offers a useful summary of the various "incongruous" motives of white colonizationists in his *From Slavery to Freedom* (New York: Vintage Books, 1969), 239–40, and does not deviate from this position in the McGraw-Hill 1994 edition co-authored with Alfred Moss.

13. Miller, *Wolf by the Ears*, 266.

moval of only 2,500 free Africans, while in that same period the black population of the South had increased by 700,000. "If the Union were to supply the society with annual subsidies, and to transport the Negroes to Africa in government vessels, it would still be unable to counterpoise the natural increase of population among the blacks." [14]

Nonetheless, there were always some African American advocates of voluntary migration. The best known of these was Captain Paul Cuffe, who in 1816 transported a small group of settlers to Africa in his own vessel, the *Traveller*. Cuffe, who was half Indian and married to a woman of the Pequot people, probably never believed in total "repatriation," but was instead committed to the idea that African Americans should participate in the economic and cultural development of Africa. His views were supported by James Forten, a sail manufacturer who, as a maritime entrepreneur, shared Cuffe's practical reasons for encouraging African American settlement and commercial ties with Africa. The question of whether the plans of Cuffe and Forten can be identified with the idea of black nationalism remains a matter of definition. One thing is certain: their understanding of capital accumulation and commercial development as essential ingredients of nationalism; without them the concept is absolutely unintelligent. [15]

Cuffe's death within a year of the Colonization Society's founding symbolized the demise of African resettlement as a respectable movement among African Americans. Some black leaders, notably James Forten, Daniel Coker, and Richard Allen, advocated voluntary migration, but Allen, and then Forten, became convinced that any cooperation with the Society was tantamount to renouncing all claims of American citizenship. Both

14. Alexis de Tocqueville, *Democracy in America* (New York: Everyman's Library, 1994), 1:377–78.
15. Some scholars have rightly been cautious about calling Cuffe a black nationalist; see, for example, John H. Bracey Jr., August Meier, and Elliot Rudwick, *Black Nationalism in America* (Indianapolis: Bobbs-Merrill, 1970), 38–39. Floyd Miller attributes "proto-nationalistic" tendencies to Cuffe in *The Search for a Black Nationality: Black Emigration and Colonization, 1787–1863* (Urbana: University of Illinois Press, 1975), 53.

men eventually shied away from the African emigration movement to become the bitterest opponents of the Colonization Society. Their associate Daniel Coker, a leader in the African Methodist Episcopal (AME) Church, never abandoned his belief in
African colonization. He was elected to but refused to accept
the AME bishopric in 1816, and he left for Africa in 1820 under
the auspices of the Maryland Colonization Society.[16] After Coker
declined to become a bishop of the African Methodist Episcopal
Church, Richard Allen accepted the office. Allen was not hostile
to Coker or to his missionary work, and he liked to claim, on
behalf of the AME Church, some responsibility for Coker's pre-
sumed successes in Africa. Furthermore, Allen was never totally
opposed to voluntary emigration on the part of individuals, especially when linked to legitimate missionary activity. It was the
American Colonization Society that he opposed, and his Bethel
Church in Philadelphia became the center of opposition to the
Society.[17]

In 1829, John Russwurm, co-founder of *Freedom's Journal*, the
first African American newspaper of record, migrated under the
Society's auspices. Historian Floyd Miller has noted that when
Russwurm announced his support of emigration he was subjected to what he described as "a violent persecution" by a seg-
ment of the black community.[18] His decision was, however, supported by Peter Williams Jr., a black Episcopal priest in New York
whose protégé Alexander Crummell later became an important
spokesman for black nationalism. Williams represented a minority of black leaders who attempted to remain loyal abolitionists while supporting colonization—until 1834, when, under
pressure from his superior, the white Bishop of New York, he
resigned from the American Anti-Slavery Society and endorsed
the American Colonization Society. Militant leaders saw this as

16. Betty Thomas, "Daniel Coker," in Rayford Logan and Michael Einston,
eds., *Dictionary of American Negro Biography* (New York: Norton, 1982), 119–20.
See also *Journal of Daniel Coker* (Baltimore: John D. Fay, 1820) and Ephraim
Bacon, *Abstract of a Journal*, 3rd ed. (Philadelphia: Clark & Raser, 1824).

17. Carol V. R. George, *Segregated Sabbaths: Richard Allen and the Emergence of
Independent Black Churches, 1760–1840* (New York: Oxford, 1973), 135–59.

18. Miller, *Search for a Black Nationality*, 84–89.

an illustration of the futility of trying to combine abolitionism with colonizationism.[19]

The most vocal black leaders in America were almost universally opposed to African emigration by the time of the first national convention of African American leaders, which met in Philadelphia in 1830 to establish the American Society of Free Persons of Color. They were not opposed to all forms of colonization, however, for the new organization was committed by its constitution to "the establishment of a settlement in the Province of Upper Canada." One must therefore question the assumption of historian Carol George that Richard Allen opposed the Colonization Society from a fear that its program would encourage the states to revoke the already limited citizenship rights of free black people in order to foster emigration. In his address to the Free People of Color, published with the minutes of the convention, Allen specifically and unequivocally endorsed Canadian emigration. It must be deduced that Allen and others were opposed not so much to migration in general as to African emigration.[20]

As noted above, many early supporters of colonization were conscientiously opposed to slavery. William Lloyd Garrison, a twenty-three-year-old white abolitionist, addressed the American Colonization Society meeting in Boston on July 4, 1829, and denounced slavery as a great "national sin." In the same address, he called on the American people "to sustain Congress in

19. For Peter Williams, see the analytic index to Wilson J. Moses, *Alexander Crummell: A Study of Civilization and Discontent* (New York: Oxford University Press, 1989). See Peter Williams's "Discourse Delivered in S. Philips Church for the Benefit of the Colored Community of Wilberforce in Upper Canada," in Dorothy Porter, *Early Negro Writing, 1769–1837* (Baltimore: Black Classics Press, 1995). Williams's resignation from the Anti-Slavery Society, dated July 14, 1834, is in Carter G. Woodson, ed., *The Mind of the Negro as Reflected in Letters Written During the Crisis, 1800–1860* (Washington, D.C.: Association for the Study of Negro History, 1926), 630–34.

20. George, *Segregated Sabbaths*, 119, 120; *Constitution of the American Society of Free Persons of Color, . . . also the Proceedings of the Convention . . . [1830]* (Philadelphia: J. W. Allen, 1831), also in *Minutes of the Proceedings of the National Negro Conventions, 1830–1864*, ed. Howard Holman Bell (New York: Arno Press and the New York Times, 1969).

any future efforts to colonize the colored population of the States."[21] He did not hold this position long, however. Black militants in Boston were increasingly vociferous in their opposition to the Colonization Society. Notable among them was David Walker, whose celebrated *Appeal to the Coloured Citizens . . . ,* published in September 28, 1829, contained an article titled "Our Wretchedness in Consequence of the Colonization Plan." Walker quoted at length from Richard Allen's letter denouncing the American Colonization Society, which had been published years earlier in *Freedom's Journal.* Early the following year, Garrison ceased to support colonization. On January 1, 1831, he founded *The Liberator,* and the next year he became a founder of the American Anti-Slavery Society, which was dedicated to the immediate overthrow of slavery. He demonstrated his total opposition to the Colonization Society with publication of his *Thoughts on Colonization* on June 2, 1832. That small volume included numerous statements against the Society, including one by a Philadelphia committee chaired by James Forten. Garrison himself described the "colonization scheme" as "inadequate in its design, injurious in its operation, and contrary to sound principle."[22]

Between 1820 and 1843 the Colonization Society resettled a little more than 4,000 African Americans in West Africa. The first settlers were transported to the British colony of Sierra Le-

21. William E. Cain, ed., *William Lloyd Garrison and the Fight Against Slavery: Selections from* The Liberator (Boston: Bedford Books, 1995), 69.

22. Letter in *Freedom's Journal* is cited by David Walker in article 4 of Walker's *Appeal in Four Articles, Together With a Preamble to the Colored Citizens of the World, but in Particular and Very Expressly To Those of the United States of America* (Boston, 1829). Walker published two subsequent editions of this document, and there have been numerous reprints, notably that of Henry Highland Garnet in 1848, but there is no analytical bibliography of the document. There is also no definitive scholarly "variorum edition," but among the more recent and reasonably available editions is that included in Sterling Stuckey, ed., *Ideological Origins of Black Nationalism* (Boston: Beacon, 1972), 94–95. See also the letter signed by Forten and others in William Lloyd Garrison, *Thoughts on Colonization* (Boston: Garrison & Knapp, 1832), reprinted with an introduction by William Loren Katz, ed. (New York: Arno, 1969), part 2, pp. 9–10. See also the quotation from Garrison in *Thoughts,* part 2, p. 2.

one, but in 1822 the Society's agents intimidated the king of the Bassa country into selling land at Cape Mesurado for its own West African colony, Liberia. Monrovia, the first permanent settlement and later the capital, was named in honor of the sitting American President, James Monroe, who strongly endorsed African colonization, referring to Free Africans as "a class of very dangerous people." [23] In 1834 the Maryland Colonization Society established its own colony of Maryland in Liberia, which merged with the older settlement in 1847 when Liberia declared itself an independent republic.

As a rule, African Americans were not convinced of the new nation's independence or of its viability. From their perspective, Liberia was under the control of proslavery white Americans and incapable of defending itself economically or militarily. They continued to heap contempt on the Society and all who collaborated with it, and in 1848 the Colored National Convention passed a resolution declaring: "That among the many oppressive schemes against the colored people in the United States, we view the American Colonization Society as the most deceptive and hypocritical—'clothed with the livery of heaven to serve the devil in,' with President Roberts of Liberia, a colored man, for its leader." [24]

Attitudes toward colonization began to shift again in 1850, however, with the passage of the Fugitive Slave Act, which challenged the free status of every free person of African descent living in the United States. [25] The Fugitive Slave Act eased the processes whereby any white person who claimed ownership of

23. Staudenraus, *American Colonization Movement,* 65 (on the king of the Bassas), 51 (Monroe quoted).

24. *Report of the Proceedings of the Colored National Convention, Held at Cleveland, Ohio, . . . September 6, 1848* (Rochester, N.Y.: John Dick, at North Star Office), 16.

25. Martin Delany's *Condition, Elevation, Emigration, and Destiny of the Colored People of the United States* (Philadelphia, 1852) represents a widespread reaction among Free Africans to the Fugitive Slave Act. For additional reactions by African Americans, see the documents by R. J. W. Loguen, Samuel Ringgold Ward, and others in Herbert Aptheker, ed., *A Documentary History of the Negro People in the United States,* vol. 1 (New York: Citadel, 1971), 299–309.

a black person in America could sue for possession of that person, but it denied black people the right to testify in their own defense. The enactment of this law caused a number of black leaders to reconsider plans for emigration to Africa, Canada, South America, or the West Indies. Others began to reflect discreetly on the idea of African emigration and to ponder the prospects of there ever being a truly independent center of "Negro Nationality" on the continent of Africa.

The years 1850–62 represented the first peak of black nationalism in the United States. During that period, almost every recognized spokesperson, from separatist Martin Delany to the usually assimilationist Frederick Douglass, threw some ideological ingredients into the seething cauldron of African American nationalism. The more devout African emigrationists frequently argued that before the African American people could be uplifted the redemption of Africa must be achieved. Hollis Read, a white clergyman, seemed convinced that if even one modern city could be developed in Africa the preachers of black inferiority would be confounded and the institution of slavery would be shaken to its roots.[26]

In order to revitalize what they began to call "The African Movement," the emigrationists of the 1850s had to reserve positions and dismiss arguments that they and their intellectual predecessors had vigorously championed for thirty-five years. They were hemmed in by the rhetoric of the 1810s and 1820s, for abolitionists had accurately stressed the attachment of the Colonization Society's founders to preachments of black inferiority and to the doctrine that Africans could never be Americans. In the past, the reconstructed emigrationists of the 1850s had often judged black colonizationists guilty—through their association with white supremacists—of racial treason and moral cowardice. They remembered the opprobrium heaped on John Russwurm, and they knew that the penalty for cooperation with the Colonization Society could be high. Thus, even the African

---

26. Miller, *Search for a Black Nationality,* 93; Wilson Moses, *The Golden Age of Black Nationalism,* 2nd ed. (New York: Oxford University Press, 1989), 6–7.

American nationalists who had come to support emigration
found it necessary to avoid any seeming connection with Liberia, and sometimes with Africa as a whole.[27]

A convention of African Americans meeting in Rochester,
New York, in 1853 issued a lengthy "Report on Colonization"
that included a traditional denunciation of Liberian colonization. But such manifestos could no longer be seen as represent-
ing the only legitimate opinion among African American abolitionists. Alexander Crummell, who had been studying at the
University of Cambridge in England, gave up on the United
States and decided to transport his family to Liberia in 1853 so
that he could bring up his children "under black men's institutions." He left directly for West Africa under the auspices of the
Episcopal Church Missionary Society and did not return to the
United States. Within the decade, Crummell was cooperating
with such moderate white colonizationists as Quaker wool merchant Benjamin Coates, a sometime member of the American
Colonization Society but also an abolitionist.[28]

Controversy abounds concerning the attitudes of the masses
of African Americans toward migration. Historians like Bell I.
Wiley and Randall Miller performed a great service by working
with and publishing collections of letters written by former slaves
who went to Liberia and sent back reports on their experiences.[29] Other letters can be found in correspondence files

27. Complexities of relationships between black emigrationists and the
American Colonization Society are discussed in Wilson J. Moses, *Classical Black
Nationalism* (New York: New York University Press, 1996), 27–28. See also
R. J. M. Blackett, *Beating Against the Barriers: Biographical Essays in Nineteenth-
Century Afro-American History* (Baton Rouge: Louisiana State University Press,
1986), 149, 151–55; Miller, *Search for a Black Nationality,* 170–231. There is also
material on the African Civilization Society in David Swift, *Black Prophets of
Justice: Activist Clergy Before the Civil War* (Baton Rouge: Louisiana State University
Press, 1989), 292–99. The Constitution of the African Civilization Society is in
Howard Brotz, ed., *Negro Social and Political Thought, 1850–1920* (New Bruns-
wick, N.J.: Transaction, 1992), 191–96.

28. Moses, *Alexander Crummell,* 122–23, 142–43.

29. See Bell I. Wiley, ed., *Slaves No More: Letters from Liberia, 1833–1869* (Lexington: University Press of Kentucky, 1980); and Randall M. Miller, ed., "Dear
Master," in *Letters of a Slave Family* (Ithaca: Cornell University Press, 1978).

of the American Colonization Society and its official journal, *African Repository*.[30] These letters of migrants are profoundly interesting, but John Hope Franklin represents the prevailing opinion that African Americans had little interest in resettlement. He based his position, reasonably enough, on the observation that the Colonization Society failed to transplant more than 12,000 individuals over a period of almost one hundred years.[31]

Miles Mark Fisher represented a dissenting view with his interpretation of "Negro Spirituals," including the famous "Swing Low, Sweet Chariot," as expressing the slaves' hope for reincarnation in Africa, or a more immediate repatriation in this life. Fisher spoke of the slaves' "colonization songs" and asserted that they "followed closely what the American Colonization Society was saying and doing. When they knew that Liberia had been established, the slaves burst forth in a spiritual about this African home."[32] Many historians, including the present author, have found Fisher's claims somewhat enthusiastic, if not extravagant; others, such as historian Ray Allan Billington, were seemingly convinced by Fisher's argument and agree that "the heab'n of the slave lay in Africa, not on some celestial shore. His all consuming ambition was to be sent to Liberia by the American Colonization Society."[33]

Historian Antonio McDaniel has seen a bitter irony in the "Swing Low, Sweet Chariot" refrain. To him it indicates the morbid conclusion of his study of death rates accompanying African resettlement. McDaniel found that crossing the Atlantic was, in far too many cases, almost the same as crossing over to the celes-

30. The Library of Congress Manuscript Division holds the records of the American Colonization Society, available on microfilm. *African Repository,* published from March 1825 to January 1892, is also available on microfilm. The *American Colonization Society Annual Report* (New York: Negro University Press, 1969) can also be consulted.

31. Franklin, *From Slavery to Freedom,* 169.

32. Miles Mark Fisher, *Negro Slave Songs in the United States* (1953; reprint, Secaucus, N.J.: Carol Publishing, 1981), 44, 130, 145.

33. In his foreword to the 1981 edition of Fisher's *Negro Slave Songs,* viii, Ray Allan Billington endorses Fisher's views.

tial shore. McDaniel notes sadly: "For Africans who returned to Africa from North America in the beginning of the nineteenth century, lives lost to disease—the 'mortality cost'—meant a death rate substantially higher than that of their brethren who stayed in the United States. . . . Liberian colonization, however, provides a natural experiment of the mortality cost to people who leave their childhood disease environment."[34]

That Liberian emigrants experienced a high mortality rate due to malaria or yellow fever, especially during the first year after their arrival in West Africa, has long been observed by historians of West Africa.[35] McDaniel provides technically sophisticated statistical analysis to support a well-established consensus that arose in the nineteenth century. He concludes that emigrants "experienced a great increase in morbidity and mortality as a result of their resettlement in Liberia [and that they] were not prepared by genetic advantages for the West African disease environment." As an appendix to his text, McDaniel includes the interesting May 1832 "Report on the Medical Statistics of the Colony by Dr. Henderson." Other contemporary documents shed light on the medical practices of the day, revealing a painfully tragic ignorance of the causes of tropical disease. There was even a tendency to blame the sufferers and to attribute their sufferings to moral weakness, as illustrated by the observations of Martin Delany, a black nineteenth-century physician who visited the coast in 1859:

> The density and rankness of the vegetable growth, the saturation of the air continually with fragrance and other *miasma,* and the *malaria* from the mangrove swamps, I assign as the cause of difference in the character of the same disease in different parts of the continent. The

34. Antonio McDaniel, *Swing Low, Sweet Chariot* (Chicago: University of Chicago Press, 1995), xvii–xviii, 125.

35. Tom Shick, *Behold the Promised Land: A History of Afro-American Settler Society in Nineteenth-Century Liberia* (Baltimore: Johns Hopkins University Press, 1980); Penelope Campbell, *Maryland in Africa: The Maryland State Colonization Society* (Urbana: University of Illinois Press, 1971); McDaniel, *Swing Low,* 126.

habits also of the settlers, have much to do with the character of the disease. A free indulgence in improper food and drink, which doubtless is the case in many instances, are exciting causes to take the malady, and aggravating when suffering under it.[36]

Admonitions by the same author were in the same vein and stated even more strongly:

Instead of going to Africa and quietly sitting down in utter idleness, in anticipation *waiting in anxious expectation for the fever to come*—in which cases the person becomes much more susceptible—did they go directly about some active employment, to keep both mind and body properly exercised, I am certain that there would not be one fourth of the mortality that there is even now, which is comparatively little.[37]

Problems of health and safety were among the several reasons that Martin Delany came to support emigration only by gradual degrees. He represented that group of nineteenth-century black nationalists who found it necessary to disassociate themselves from West African settlements, which he initially believed were doomed to failure. He strained the sometimes purely semantic distinction between emigrationism and colonization and was unrelenting in his attacks on Liberia, heaping abuse not only on the nation but also on its president, Joseph Jenkins Roberts. These attacks appeared in 1852 in a small book, *The Condition, Elevation, Emigration, and Destiny of the Colored People of the United*

36. Martin R. Delany, *Report of the Niger Valley Exploring Party* (New York, 1861), is reprinted in Howard H. Bell, ed., *Search for a Place* (Ann Arbor: University of Michigan Press, 1971). The quotation is from p. 65, but the reader should also see sections xi, ix, and xvii. "Dr. Henderson's Report on the Medical Statistics of the Colony" has been published in McDaniel, *Swing Low, Sweet Chariot*, pp. 153–57. See also J. W. Lugenbeel, *Sketches of Liberia: A Brief Account of the Geography, Climate, Productions, and Diseases of the Republic of Liberia* (Washington, D.C.: C. Alexander, 1850).

37. Delany, *Report*, 147.

States, where Delany argued the necessity of emigration and ana-
lyzed prospects in Canada, South America, and the western
United States, but considered Africa only as an afterthought.[38]
In an appendix to the treatise, he was willing to consider an expedition to East Africa, some 3,000 miles from the ancestral
homelands of African Americans, but Liberia was out of the
question.

In response to the attacks on Liberia by Delany and other
black abolitionists, the Reverend Daniel H. Peterson was sent
to West Africa in 1853 by the American Colonization Society
on a vessel named *Isla de Cuba.* He subsequently published *The
Looking-Glass: Being a True Report and Narrative of the Life, Travels,
and Labors of the Rev. Daniel H. Peterson* (1854), which is reprinted
in this volume. The early chapters of Peterson's work have little
to do with emigration, but they do provide unusual insights into
the mind of a man who passed up few chances to deride African
Americans or to praise paternalistic whites. His commitment
to Liberian resettlement appears to have been superficial and
fleeting, for he did not remain long in Liberia, and after publication of *The Looking-Glass,* his colonization commitments are
obscure.

These facts make it tempting to believe that Peterson was
little more than a creature of the American Colonization Society. He does not appear to have been prominent in abolitionist
circles, although, to his credit, his book does offer an unequivocal denunciation of "the great evil of slavery." Peterson crypti-
cally asserted, at one point, that African Americans should adopt
"a national point of view," but he was not prominent among
black nationalists of the period. On the other hand, Peterson
was not an imposter; he gave ample evidence that he was well
known in both the black and the white communities of Baltimore, Philadelphia, and New York. He gave the names of his

38. Delany, *Condition . . . of the Colored People,* 209–15; Victor Ullman,
Martin R. Delany: The Beginnings of Black Nationalism (Boston: Beacon Press,
1971); Dorothy Sterling, *The Making of an Afro-American: Martin Robison Delany,
1812–1885* (Garden City, N.Y.: Doubleday, 1971).

past employers, alluded to his contacts in the AME Church, referred to the family of his wife, and mentioned the various well-known white colonizationists with whom he was associated.[39]

An entirely different but no more convincing view was offered by another voyager on the *Isla de Cuba,* William Nesbit, whose blistering attack on colonization, published in 1855 and reprinted in this volume, was entitled *Four Months in Liberia; or, African Colonization Exposed.* Little is known about Nesbit; he did not leave a conspicuous trail through the contemporary antislavery movement. As were the majority of the passengers on this voyage of the *Isla de Cuba,* Nesbit was a Northerner. Nesbit gives us no information on how long he pondered before reaching the decision to visit Liberia, but his disillusionment was immediate, for he tells us: "On stepping ashore, I found that we had been completely gulled and done for. . . . The whole country presents the most woe begone and hopeless aspect, . . . a region of darkness and desolation, for which there is no hope."[40] This was grist for the mill of Martin R. Delany, who as a resident of Pittsburgh was well acquainted with and much opposed to the Colonization Society's activities in Pennsylvania. He wrote an introduction to Nesbit's volume reflecting his well-known hostility to Liberia, to the Colonization Society, and to West Africa in general.

Samuel Williams's *Four Years in Liberia: A Sketch of the Life of the Rev. Samuel Williams, With Remarks on the Missions, Manners and Customs of the Natives of Western Africa, Together with an Answer to Nesbit's Book,* represented a balanced view of the colony and an excellent example of the origins of modern anthropological writing in nineteenth-century missionary activity. Williams made two trips to Liberia in 1853, the first being an exploratory visit that lasted about as long as Nesbit's, before bringing his wife and family over. Williams represented the group of African Ameri-

39. Peterson provides the names of numerous references, both black and white, throughout his autobiographical narrative. See esp. *The Looking-Glass,* 17–19, 45–47 (10–12, 22–23 in this edition).

40. William Nesbit, *Four Months in Liberia* (reprinted in this volume), end of chap. I.

cans who took seriously the idea of Christianizing the continent and who actually devoted time and energy to attempting to
learn something about the indigenous people. His observations
on the traditional culture of the natives were, on the whole, respectful, although his mission was to convert them to European
"Christianity, Commerce, and Civilization." [41]

The Augustus Washington letters reprinted here provide
more information on Washington than has previously been
available for students of the "African Movement" of the nineteenth century. Unlike the other narrators represented in this
volume, Augustus Washington was active and well known in the
abolitionist movements during the 1840s. Martin Delany described him as an "unmixed representative of the colored race,"
such a matter being of much importance to Delany. After studying for two years at Dartmouth College, Washington set up shop
as a daguerreotypist in Hartford, Connecticut, and in November
1853 he migrated with his family to Liberia. Washington, also an
amateur violinist, taught Greek and Latin at the Alexander High
School in Monrovia for fifteen months while continuing to ply
his trade as a daguerreotypist. He soon became convinced that
"the true interest of Liberia consisted in the development of her
agricultural and mineral resources," and he established himself
in the settlement of Careysburg as a sugarcane farmer and river
merchant.

Washington also engaged in commerce with the British West
African colonies of Gambia and Sierra Leone. He was elected to
the Liberian national legislature during the 1850s and was eventually appointed to a judgeship.[42] Unlike Peterson, Augustus
Washington was his own man, rather than a colonizationist tool,
and he was therefore demonstrably more capable of question-
ing colonization motives and methods than Peterson. Washington was an outspoken and enterprising man whose success both

<hr />

41. The report of Williams's first visit is included in Williams's *Four Years in
Liberia* under the heading "Notes on Liberia."

42. Sources for the life of Augustus Washington are *The Black Abolitionist
Papers* (New York: Microfilming Corporation of America, 1981–83); and Delany, *Condition . . . of the Colored People* (1852).

in business and in politics, as well as in his activities as an abolitionist, gives him far more credibility as a nationalist than Peterson, for example.

The first of Augustus Washington's public letters defending colonization was written in 1851 before his departure; many others followed during the years after his arrival in Liberia.[43] The first of his narratives is a unique document that offers not a "recapitulation" but a *critique* of the colonizationist position. In fact, Washington presents us with an unusually balanced pro-and-con treatment of *both* the abolitionist position *and* the colonizationist position. I cannot think of another document in which arguments concerning the merits of emigration are set forth as systematically and reasonably as they are in Washington's. The unique feature of Washington's argument is that he writes from the perspective of an educated man. Many of the published documents in favor of colonization were written by people who had considerably less education and lacked Washington's command of English prose style.

Why Peterson objected to Augustus Washington is not clear, for Washington seems to have been a man of substantial ability, in the realm of arts and letters as well as business. Washington's letters will be of considerable interest to those who desire a complete portrait of this man who was the object of Peterson's mean-spirited attack. Furthermore, the letters provide us with detailed information on what a Liberian immigrant was likely to find on arriving at the "Receptacle" for new immigrants in the early 1850s. Additional information along these lines will be found in the writings of Thomas Chester Morris, the African American emigrant in charge of the Receptacle whose life and writings have been the subject of recent publication by historian R. J. M. Blackett.[44]

In 1854 Martin Delany called a National Emigration Convention in Cleveland, Ohio, and in 1858 Henry Highland Garnet

43. See *African Repository*, 27:259–65.
44. R. J. M. Blackett, ed., *Thomas Morris Chester, Black Civil War Correspondent: His Dispatches from the Virginia Front* (Baton Rouge: Louisiana State University Press, 1989).

organized the African Civilization Society. These associations, although suffering from severe financial restraints, advocated settlement in the portion of West Africa that is now Nigeria. In
1859, under the nominal auspices of the Emigration Convention and Civilization Society, Martin Delany and Robert Campbell undertook an expedition to West Africa and published separate narratives of their adventures. The present volume does
not include these documents, but only makes more readily available a small number of publications related to the voyage of the
Isla de Cuba in late 1853. While it is not intended as a defense
of the logic of African colonization, of black nationalism, or of
racial separatism in any form, it does reveal the complexities
of African American thought in the mid-nineteenth century. It
also illustrates the overlap of institutions and ideologies between colonizationists and emigrationists. White colonizationist Benjamin Coates agreed with black abolitionist Frederick
Douglass that the only difference between black emigrationist
organizations and the Colonization Society was that the former
were avowedly antislavery.[45]

Students of the Back-to-Africa movement may legitimately
inquire about the nature of African American dealings with
the indigenous peoples. Specifically, did the Americo-Liberians
make the same mistake other settler states made, and did they
see themselves as entitled to appropriate native lands by force?
Was it their policy to dominate the peoples of West Africa or
push them into the interior, or to exterminate them? Human
nature being what it is, we are not surprised at reports that some
Americo-Liberians secretly advocated such policies, but it is difficult to document such attitudes because people who held such
opinions were ashamed of them. On the other hand, it is relatively easy to document the ideas of people like Alexander
Crummell and Edward Wilmot Blyden, who believed in "civilizing" the indigenous peoples, intermarrying with them, and

---

45. Coates is quoted in Ulmann, *Martin R. Delany,* 214. See also Frederick
Douglass, "African Civilization Society," *Douglass Monthly,* February 1859.

bringing them into the body politic of Liberian republican government.[46]

Controversies concerning the emigration movement from the United States to Africa, and indictments of Northern free-born and literate black Americans who cooperated with the Colonization Society, persisted well into the twentieth century. Movements for voluntary emigration to Africa flourished between 1910 and 1925, with at least the nominal support of white supremacist organizations, heirs to the American Colonization Society. Black intellectuals of the sort who wrote history books, especially in the years following World War II, were rightly concerned with the struggle for civil rights and understandably preoccupied with demonstrating the loyalty, patriotism, and fitness for citizenship of African Americans. They did not believe their task was to write a history emphasizing black alienation or separatist militancy. Not until the early 1970s did we witness a black history that, stimulated by the black power movement of the previous decade, began to focus on black nationalism as a topic of scholarly research.

Some present-day historians cling to the opinion, dominant in the 1950s, the era of civil rights militancy and cold war patriotism, that emigration under the American Colonization Society's auspices amounted to nothing more than a capitulation to white supremacy.[47] The idea is not entirely insupportable, but many close students of the period have found it in their hearts to abstain from making so harsh a judgment. After passage of the Fugitive Slave Act in 1850, life was hard for African Americans, and there was a variety of heroism in the decision of a few adventurous souls to brave the dangers of an ocean voyage, the ravages of malaria, and the hardships of a frontier society to seek

46. Moses, *Alexander Crummell;* Edward W. Blyden, *Black Spokesman: Selected Published Writings of Edward Wilmot Blyden,* ed. Hollis Lynch (New York: Humanities Press, 1971); Hollis R. Lynch, *Edward Wilmot Blyden: Pan-Negro Patriot, 1832–1912* (New York: Oxford University Press, 1964); Edward Wilmot Blyden, *Selected Letters,* ed. Hollis R. Lynch (New York: KTO Press, 1978).

47. Franklin, *From Slavery to Freedom,* 239–40.

their fortunes in Liberia. The African colonization movement, despite its unrealistic goals and sometimes cynical motives, held out the possibility that people of African descent could achieve independence and self-respect in a country of their own. For this reason, Liberian emigrants made their truce with white colonizationists and nurtured their hopes of eventually giving substance to Henry Highland Garnet's dream, albeit expressed in another context, of "a grand center of Negro Nationality." [48]

48. Quoted in Earl Ofari, *"Let Your Motto Be Resistance": The Life and Thought of Henry Highland Garnet* (Boston: Beacon Press, 1972), 86, 210 n. 30 (reference to the *Weekly Anglo-African,* September 10, 1859).

THE

LOOKING-GLASS:

BEING

A TRUE REPORT AND NARRATIVE OF THE LIFE, TRAVELS, AND LABORS

OF THE

REV. DANIEL H. PETERSON,

A COLORED CLERGYMAN;

Embracing a period of time from the year 1812 to 1854,

AND INCLUDING

HIS VISIT TO WESTERN AFRICA.

1854

PREFACE

The author of this work has for a long time, been greatly concerned for this land and nation, and for the human family in general; but, more particularly, for the unfortunate African, both in this and every other part of the world which he has seen or read of. The Author desires, and his prayer is, that tranquillity, peace, and happiness may cover the earth, as the waters cover the great deep.

Forasmuch as there has been a great deal of confusion in relation to my afflicted nation, and different parties holding opposite opinions have come forward with a design to alleviate their condition, which good intentions have all failed, therefore I have made it a matter of prayer, if peradventure I might be enlightened with respect to the best plan for the relief of the colored people. I now feel that I am able to answer this great question in full.

First, It is necessary to become Christians, to love and fear God, and keep his commandments, to have patience, and faith in our Lord and Saviour Jesus Christ: then we shall be delivered in due time. Secondly, the reader is referred to the pages of this work. Please read it impartially and carefully. You will see plainly that the Author's sole aim is to promote the happiness of the human family here and hereafter. Therefore, I pray that

[EDITOR'S NOTE: Publication data carried on the original title page of Peterson's *The Looking-Glass* reads: "New-York: Wright, Printer, 146 Fulton Street. 1854."]

those who will read this book may be forever blessed in this world, and receive endless happiness in the world to come.

D. H. PETERSON.

New-York, May, 1854.

CONTENTS.

tentions of Capt. Miller. Warm weather on the Coast of Africa.
Unsuccessful attempts to take a turtle. Serious accident to the
mate, Mr. Hatch. They catch a shark, and cook him for dinner.
Description of Cape Mount. A beautiful fish. Visit from a little
bird. Visits from the natives on the Coast. Arrival at Monrovia.
Mr. Cauldwell goes on shore.

CHAPTER V.

The Author goes on shore. Kind reception. Visits the President,
Judge, and other distinguished persons. Beauty of the country. Description of the town, the soil, and the inhabitants. Good opportunities in Liberia for emigrants. Mechanics, farmers and schoolmasters wanted in Liberia. Those who lay the foundations of this
great nation should be moral, industrious, economical, and religious persons. With the aid of friends in the United States, the
cause of colored emigration to Liberia cannot fail to prosper.

CHAPTER VI.

The Author visits several places in the vicinity of Monrovia. He
speaks a number of times in the Churches. He sails for Sierra Leone. On the passage Mr. Caldwell is very sick, and the Steward
tries to get possession of his property. The Author opposes this
nefarious attempt. They arrive in Sierra Leone. The Author finishes his business and sails for Gambia. Arrival in Gambia. Mahometans; Idolators; treatment of criminals under the British
rule. The Author prefers the United States Government. He sails
in the Isla de Cuba for the United States. Storms at sea. The Author trusts in the Lord. Two men concealed on board. The Gulf
Stream. Arrival at New-York.

CHAPTER VII.

The Author relates part of a conversation with an English officer.
Some description of Gambia and its inhabitants. Necessity of cultivation. The minds of the natives must be cultivated as well as
the land. Fine opportunities in Africa for steamboats, and enterprising men generally. Cape Mount. No newspaper in Liberia.
An excellent opening for Frederick Douglass. Address to the rulers of Liberia. The necessity of treating the natives well and respecting their rights. Duties of parents and teachers. The young
should be instructed. Mr. Horne in Monrovia. Mrs. Ann Wilkins.
Mr. Phillips, a colored teacher. The Rev. Samuel Williams and
family, formerly of Pennsylvania.

CONCLUDING REMARKS.

Certificates, including one by His Excellency J. J. Roberts, President of Liberia, Western Africa. Notice of the Return of the barque Isla de Cuba. Resolutions adopted by the Passengers highly complimentary to Capt. Miller, on approaching the Coast of Africa.

Church Collections—On the mode of making them.

THE LOOKING-GLASS.

CHAPTER I.

The Author purchases his Mother's freedom. An excellent young lady. He goes to Baltimore. Early religious impressions. He goes to Philadelphia and becomes united to the Church. Is Steward on the Delaware. Remarkable vision. His ministry.

MY parents were slaves. The place of my nativity was in the State of Maryland, near Baltimore, in the respectable family of a Mr. Tyler, near connexion of the Hon. John Tyler, late President of the United States.

In the year of our Lord 1812, my mother was too aged to be emancipated, and was left in slavery. She, however, desired her liberty, but knew not how to obtain it. The Author, although but a small boy, readily agreed to enter an apprenticeship for the redemption of his mother. Children can never remunerate faithful parents for the care that has been extended to them in their tender years, and for the trouble and anxiety of which they have been the cause. Therefore it is in obedience to the dictates of wisdom, that children and youth obey and honor their parents. If they do this, they will be blessed for ever. I realized this blessing from that time forth: and my dear aged mother died a free woman in the year 1844.

I fulfilled my obligations faithfully in all things, and was treated as one of the family. Among those with whom I lived, was a young lady, Miss S. T., highly accomplished and benevolent, with fine Christian feelings, and very kind to the poor. Through the blessing of the Lord, she took the oversight of me, and from that source I received instruction and other great benefits. I parted from this family at length, not without regret and sorrow on both sides, for I esteemed them for their kind treatment of me, while they respected me for my obedience and the faithful service which I had rendered them. But I desired to acquire attainments by which I might become useful to my fellow-men. I remembered the impressions that had been made upon me, when a child, at the prayer meetings that had been held in the house of my parents. Those religious impressions were the first that I had experienced, and they never left me. They preserved me from vice, and influenced my conduct in all times and places. They were like grain that is sown, and continues to grow until it has arrived at full perfection. Therefore, prayer is always good, and to be recommended to all persons under all circumstances. The aforesaid family is certainly a great and noble family, and have done much for me, in the way both of example and of instruction, but the time came for us to part, as I had a greater work to do.

I then took up my residence in Baltimore, with respectable and eminent families. I was treated well and allowed money, and excellent privileges, which I endeavored to improve both by moral and religious exercises. I avoided all bad company, and was full of zeal for the Church, and of love for all mankind. I continued to look ahead, and pressed forward to the mark of a higher calling, which I believed it was possible for me to obtain. I lived a considerable time with Mr. Hopkinson, by whom I was well treated: also, with Messrs. Cook, Gilmore, Hollins, McBlair, and Commodore Ridgely, who were good men: also, with William Hollins, Jr., Esq., and Col. P. Workman. These were all gentlemen of the highest standing, merchants, &c. I also lived with many others, among whom were Messrs. Oliver and Thompson, all of whom moved in the highest circles of that city; they supplied me with whatever was necessary to my comfort and convenience. When I wanted clothing, I had only to call upon the tailor and get a supply, these gentlemen freely paying all my bills.

Many colored persons entertain the opinion that all white people are their enemies. That is not true, for I declare that, from a child unto this day, I have found all my best friends among the white people. Therefore, the prejudice which I have mentioned is the child of ignorance, resulting from the want of a clear conception of facts, and sometimes from impropriety of conduct. A great many men bring trouble upon themselves, by their own mismanagement.

While living with the gentlemen whom I have named, I applied myself to the study of the Word of the Lord, with prayer and meditation. I found it good so to do. I perceived that the spirit of the Lord was with me, and felt an impression that I must labor in the vineyard of the Most High.

In the year 1815, I left Baltimore and went to Philadelphia, in the State of Pennsylvania. There I united with the Church and became a member, under the influence of the gospel preached by Rev. Mr. Fox, an old minister from Frenchtown. His text was Matthew xiii. v. 48. "They gathered the good into vessels, but cast the bad away." It was under the power of these words, that the spirit came home to me. I rejoiced in the blessed Lord and his great mercies, for he redeemed me from sin and death. I was still impressed with the idea that there was a greater work for me to do than to remain an ordinary member of the Church. I made it the subject of prayer, and besought the Lord to instruct me in regard to his will. In that condition I remained for a season, awaiting an answer. During this time I was engaged in domestic life, having good employment in the best families. I was sent for, to come to Burlington, N.J., and act as steward in the house of John Griffith, Esq., at Green Bank, the building occupied by the British Governor while the country was subject to the English crown. I went to Green Bank and lived with the family awhile. I was much pleased with them, and they were well satisfied with me. They wished me to remain with them, but I was sent for by those honorable gentlemen, the Captains of the steamboats on the Delaware river, in connection with the establishment of Robert L. Stevens, Esq., and Brothers of New-York, the first engineers in the country. I engaged in the employment of those favorite Captains A. and M. Jenkins, and remained with them a number of years as chief steward, having full charge of the Bar and Table, and control over all the cabins, &c. Those excellent men will never be blotted from my remembrance.

Notwithstanding my good situation, ample wages, and kind

treatment, I found it my duty to leave all. I was impressed with the conviction that the Lord had other work for me to do. I said to the Captain—"Sir, I shall be obliged to leave you. I have no fault to find with my place, but I am impressed with a belief that I am called elsewhere by the Spirit." Our accounts were then settled in an honorable manner, and having put another man in my place, I took my departure. I then travelled with James Mc-Clanaghan, Esq., to New-York, who went from Baltimore to the former city with his family, soon after losing his wife. He was connected with the great house of John B. Murray and Son. I remained awhile with Mr. McClanaghan, and was treated well by him.

At the time appointed, I left him and went to Philadelphia. There I settled and began to look out for a bosom friend, one to whom I could confide my secret thoughts, and whose advice would always be of service to me. After a time I became ac-quainted with one of the most respectable colored families in the city of Philadelphia, that of Mr. Jonathan Trusty, residing in Locust street. I married his eldest daughter, Mary Trusty. At that time Mr. Trusty was a man of property and a trustee of the Church, over which he exercised much influence. I then settled down and went into business for myself for a few years. During that time I applied for a license to preach. I had difficulty in obtaining it but succeeded after a while. I labored in the city and county extensively for several years. The Lord blessed my labors, I had a good wife very kind on all occasions, and I continued awhile in Philadelphia with my agreeable family. But the blessed Lord showed me that this could not always be. "Not so," said He—"thou art a chosen vessel, and I will send thee far away. Thou shalt bear testimony for my name's sake in distant lands, even among those who know me not, and have not heard the glad tidings of the gospel."

The Lord showed me in the visions of the night, upon my bed, the dreadful state of mankind throughout the world, living in sin and wickedness. "Oh! wretched man!" said I—"who shall deliver me from this body of sin and death! There is none can do this but our Lord and Saviour Jesus Christ, and He only, for

Christ has become a sacrifice for us. Therefore let us keep the feast with love and unity which is well pleasing in the sight of the Lord." In the vision of the night, I saw come to the door of my dwelling, a coach and four white horses, with a good driver. I was taken into the carriage, and it was driven off. We travelled far away in a South-Western direction, until we arrived at a large village. There I alighted from the coach and saw it no more. But the people of the town were in a state of intense excitement, and for some cause unknown to me, they were filled with fear and horror. I then saw a garden in which there was no grass, but a number of young vegetables had sprung up and were in a flourishing condition. I passed through the garden with a saw in my hand. I looked, and beheld a number of people gazing from their windows, both above and below; and then I saw a cloud rising in the West. There was thunder and lightning, and the people were much alarmed. I passed out of the garden with the saw in my hand, and was fearful that it would attract the lightning. As I left the garden, the cloud became more dark and terrific. I saw ships tossed to and fro upon the cloud; and after that, I saw two persons of very solemn appearance ascend from behind, and stand upon the top of the cloud. Above these two beings, the sky was perfectly clear, and their feet rested on the very summit of the cloud. One of these men held in his hand a sword, and the other was armed with a spear.

These two men appeared to be very angry with the world of mankind. They turned swiftly around and brandished their weapons in a threatening manner, and soon afterwards they disappeared again behind the cloud, the one following the other in his descent. As soon as the two men were gone, fire came from the cloud. The earth itself was ignited by this fire, and the flames ascended to the skies. The conflagration extended so swiftly along the earth, that neither beast nor bird could escape its fury.

After witnessing this vision, I came to the determination to leave all and enter fully into the vineyard of the Lord. "Every one that hath forsaken houses, or brethren, or sisters, or father, or mother, or wife, or children, or lands, for my name's sake, shall receive an hundred fold, and shall inherit everlasting life."—Matt. xix. 29 v.

The reader will please observe, that the family with which I was connected was that of Mr. Jonathan Trusty and his wife Esther, a religious family, in which there were only three children—Mary, the eldest, whom I married, Hannah, who became the wife of Mr. Wm. Tucker, of Lexington, Ky., and Esther, who remains single and resides in my family at the present time. The worthy gentleman referred to on another page, M. Jenkins, Esq., has retired from business, and now resides in Trenton, N.J., surrounded by his worthy family—a perfect gentleman and sincere Christian.

It must be borne in mind, that in my vision I beheld the great evil of slavery in this gigantic Republic, as well as the magnitude of other sins. I prayed that the iniquities of the nations might all be removed, so that this great earth might become a perfect Paradise, a place of happiness and joy, instead of sickness, sorrow, pain, and death.

I consulted my wife in regard to the new views that had been opened to my mind, to which she replied, "If you must leave us, the will of the blessed Son be done. I will, with the help of the Lord, do the best that I can in all things; but you will remember me and all others in your prayers, at all times and places, and we will remember you in our weak way." I next waited upon several of the clergymen in the city. I told them that my intention was to embark upon the great Gospel ocean, and endeavor to turn men from darkness to light. They gave me the right hand of fellowship, and said, "Brother, go on, and may the Blessed One be with you for ever." They then presented me with letters of recommendation to all people among whom my lot might be cast. So I entered fully into this work, in the year of our Lord 1848.

CHAPTER II.

The Cholera in Philadelphia. The Author is concerned for the poor and afflicted; he visits them. Good fruits of Gospel labor.

Pride and vanity in the Bethel Church. Desecration of the old
Church. Pulling down the old building. Fatal accident. Miscon-
duct of the Church authorities. An Epistle from D. H. Peterson,
warning the Church to take heed of their ways, and admonishing
all men to lead a just and holy life on the earth, that they may
partake of a heavenly reward hereafter. The Author enters the
great Gospel field; leaves Philadelphia, and travels in the Ministry.

It is now necessary for me to go back a little, and give some
account of the condition of the Church in Philadelphia, at the
time that I officiated there.

At the time of the Cholera in Philadelphia, I was there. The
disease was very violent and contagious, but I was in the midst of
it. I went into the sick house which was provided by the Corporation for the poor and friendless sufferers. This place was vocal
with the groans of the sick and dying. I prayed and sang with
these afflicted persons, and administered to their several wants.
I also went out upon the Commons, where the poor were en-
camped to prevent the spread of the disorder, and received no
harm from my attentions to the sick. I was not afraid of the Cholera, for I knew that the Lord was all-sufficient everywhere, and
under all circumstances.

The good effect of laboring with these people at such a time
was soon apparent; for by this means a Church sprang up for
the gathering in of the lost sheep of the house of Israel. As a
result of those labors, there still remain many members in good
standing. Some of them became preachers. But the time came
when I must leave them all. Before I left Philadelphia, I warned
the Churches, particularly Bethel Church. The members of this
Church first commenced their worship in a blacksmith's shop.
At that time, they were humble and pious. After a while, they
built a good, plain, brick church; but afterwards they began to
grow proud, and wanted a more fine and showy edifice in which
to worship the Most High. A public meeting was called to consult upon the subject. I attended this meeting, and as they had
not the money for building, and the church they had would last
yet a long time, I recommended to them that they should post-
pone the work for the present, and not commence it until they

were better prepared. They would not listen to me, but went on in their own way.

They finally declared their intention of holding a Fair in the old church, and then pulling it down to make way for the new one, which they would build on the same site with the money that had been raised by the Fair. So they went on with the Fair in the church for many days, during which time there was much strife and contention among them. As soon as the Fair was over, they commenced pulling down the old church. With sorrow, I add, that a part of it gave way and fell upon several innocent persons, who were killed. One misfortune after another followed. Among other things, the gas pipes burst; and then came a great law-suit, which cost more money and time, and occasioned more idleness, than ten Fairs were worth. Finally, it ended in the division of the Church. Many of the old members, who had toiled many years and spent all their living to build up the society, were cast out, and in this way divided from their parents, children, and friends. Something more may be said of this hereafter, but I will here observe, that sinful acts like those will be decided upon in the great day of final account.

I left them all, and took the Lord for my portion, and him only. Before I departed from Philadelphia, I addressed the following circular to the Church.

CIRCULAR.

"To the true Ministers of the Gospel of Christ, to the Clergymen of every denomination, and to all those who undertake to govern and rule the Church of God: to all Itinerant Ministers, and more particularly such as belong to the Bethel connection: knowing that these last are not so mature as some others, and for that cause are more liable to be led astray, and taken captive by the gods of this world, becoming worshippers of idols. By such means, the Church grows barren and unfruitful, and the members become lukewarm and contentious, causing the true members to mourn, while the Church, instead of being a blessing and a comfort, brings forth wrath and malice, and the fruits of bitterness.

But if the members of the Church would keep the commandments, and live according to the Gospel, the world would not be in such a dark and wretched state as it is at this time; for the blessed Saviour said, 'Ye are the light of the world; ye are a city set upon a hill.' Therefore, you ought to attend only to spiritual things, and not to suffer anything to approach the holy place of worship like sin, or anything that would cause contention amongst the members, except the board and body fully consent to their introduction among you. But to force such things upon the members, whether or not, is unlawful, and cannot be approved either by saint or by sinner.

About eighteen months since, the ministers, trustees, and members proposed to take down and rebuild Bethel Church, at which period the society was free from debt, and owned property worth from $25,000 to $50,000; they having begun from nothing between forty and fifty years since, under the direction of Rev. Richard Allen. At that time, they trusted in the promises of a merciful God, and the good feelings of the humane citizens who aided them with means, and granted them a charter and a discipline that we might do justice to each other and all mankind, at the same time that we honored and worshipped the God of glory in spirit and in truth, under our own vine and fig-tree, with none to make us afraid: for the wholesome law of the land would protect us while we acted the part of Christians. Now, we must have a new church, which is very right; but let us have it in peace and harmony, and let us not leave the good old way. But I am sorry to say that we have left that path, and have gone rather astray. It is a shame that, in this day of light, we should have given occasion for any to say that we are going after the gods of this world. In so doing, we have even trampled upon the wholesome laws of the land granted by the honorable Legislature of the State of Pennsylvania.

Herein, you will understand that a charge is made against all those among us who are entrusted with authority, whether temporal or spiritual, because they have neither considered nor cared for the feelings of their brethren and sisters, fellow-members of the Church; and have been scarcely careful enough of their own word, for they promised one thing and did another.

For their unlawful acts, there was a charge entered against these men who hold authority over the Church; and it was placed in the hands of Bishop Brown, by E. Mann and J. W. Stokes. After the Bishop had held the charge a few days, he reported to the Board that he would call in three itinerant ministers and try the case. Instead of doing as he had reported, he called the Board together and exonerated them from the charge, without examining witnesses on the strength of the Church. So they voted themselves innocent of the charge, and went on as before, judging and condemning others. Therefore, I ask you, God-fearing men, and those belonging to the Itinerancy, whether these things are right—whether they are according to discipline and to the charter which is granted unto us. I think *not*. Therefore, according to discipline, I entered a charge against several persons, which remains still untried, and those persons are continued in their several stations as before. It was published in the Church that Quarterly Conference would take place on July 6th, 1841. Accordingly the members met, and instead of doing the business of the Conference, they spent the whole evening in striving to exonerate the Elders, Rev. Richard Williams, and the Trustees. This they did by mob and gag law; and so they proceeded till the time for adjournment. The above meeting was entirely illegal, and contrary to good order: because the same men who committed the offences which caused disorder, sat as judges to try the case.

I ask you if this can be right. If this is according to rule, there is a great deal wanted to put the Church in order—a new Church, a new government, new hearts, and new rules. Therefore, let old things be done away, and all things become new.

The principal cause of this trouble in the Church is, that the Trustees and Elders suffered a fair to be held on that consecrated and sacred ground, in a place where the first bud and branch of spiritual liberty sprang forth and produced fruit that was healthy and sweet to the taste of the poor, despised race, and to all the human family—a place of deposite for the dust of our ancestors. On that holy spot are the remains of the Right. Rev. RICHARD ALLEN, the founder and promoter of that sacred institution, and the father of her faithful members.

Many of the members of the Church were very much opposed to the scheme of holding a fair upon that spot, and the Trustees and Elders promised that it should not be held there. But, a few days afterward, Rev. Walter Proctor announced from the pulpit that a fair would be held in Bethel; and it was again proclaimed by D. Ware, shortly after its first promulgation. Notwithstanding these proceedings, a great number of the members were still opposed to holding the fair in the church: but it was held, after Sabbath evening preaching, between 5 and 12 o'clock. The Bishop, the Elders, and Trustees, all state that they knew nothing about it, and lay the whole blame upon the carpenter, while he says that they asked him to let those women have the church for a fair.

As the first evening meeting on Sixth street was a breach in every point of view, and as one had existed for many months, a legal charge was made by D. H. Peterson at that time, against the following persons, and others since deceased, and placed at the tabernacle in Wagner's Alley:

Rev. W. Proctor,	A. Brown,
V. Neal,	A. Crippen,
T. Gibbs,	A. Till,
J. Lesby,	J. Eddey,
B. Johnson,	H. Dickenson,
M. Young.	

We trust that all persons who say they love and fear the Lord, and endeavor to keep his commandments, will not suffer anything like this fair to be carried into their holy places of worship, though they may gain ten thousand dollars by it; for what is the whole world to them, if they lose their own souls? The great evil of the thing is, that we show more love for this world than we have for the Lord, and thus we lose the power which the Lord confers upon us to rule his people, remaining in ignorance and darkness, by reason of our disobedience.

While they were endeavoring to settle the aforementioned cases, the Rev. Bishop stated that he had a charge in his pocket, handed him by a respectable member named Benjamin Wilson, against the Trustees, for misdemeanor and violation of the Constitution.

If matters cannot be conducted better than they are at present, we had better call a General Convention, and see if there cannot be some improvements made in the spiritual government of the Church: for, while three or four thousand souls are looking for instruction, there is only confusion and strife among us by reason of bad management. The old and sorrowing members must not be forgotten. They should be aided and preferred in all things, because they have borne the heat and burthen of the day; and let the man of God attend to godly things and have no fellowship with the unfruitful works of darkness.

Therefore, I do sincerely trust and hope that those matters will be taken up in a proper time, either before or at the General Conference, and sifted to the bottom, so that holy things shall be no more trampled under unhallowed feet, and that the blessing of God may flow through the whole world, and his grace may be received by all men.

In the year of our Lord 1842, a circumstance somewhat similar to that which has been mentioned occurred in New-Jersey, in which Butler and the Author were involved. The case was given to the Bishop, who called three official men to his side and settled it without trouble. Liberty of conscience was granted, and worship was allowed to be performed at any convenient time and place. It was signed as follows:

> Rev. W. Proctor,
> Rev. D. Ware,
> Rev. Jeremiah Durham,
>> Right Rev. MORRIS BROWN.

This is the third GENERAL EPISTLE OF PETERSON, in defence of the Church of God, written with good feeling towards his brethren, without respect of persons, in his official capacity, in full standing, and in the performance of all his duties (as is well known), both spiritual and temporal.

I am truly, your friend and brother in the Lord,

D. H. PETERSON.

In the year of our Lord 1841, August 28th.

P.S.—A reformation in our spiritual government is very loudly called for, and must be effected ere long. At the time of our ignorance God winked. At the commencement of this religious establishment, there was but little learning, poor judgment, and few people. It was nearly half a century ago, when money had to be obtained, though there was much darkness in the land, and enemies were numerous: though, even then, the Church had some friends. They concluded to elect nine trustees, and to unite them with the Bishop or Elders in charge, the trustees to be subject to the Bishop or Elders, particularly in spiritual matters. That was well enough at that time: but now see how different things are. We want fine churches, and have them we must, at all hazards; also large congregations and a plenty of learning.

Now, I ask you, if those nine trustees are elected for nine years to do justice to the people in all things, and they often do wrong, and if, when a charge is entered, he that is placed at their head will not proceed against them, but the discipline, the constitution, itinerant principles, and the resolutions of the Conference are all forgotten, and those nine men and their head will do as they please with the means, and manage the affairs of two thousand people without regard to justice or right, and there is no remedy for all this—if, I say, such be the condition of things among us, must there not be something done in order to insure the prosperity of the Church?

Again, the Scriptures say, "Wherever the Spirit of the Lord is, there is liberty": but there is no liberty here; for, if a man expresses his opinion freely, they take away his liberty, whether he speaks rightly or wrongly. The ministers are not permitted to preach at times and places, according to their own sense of duty and propriety. If their liberties must be taken away in this manner, I pray that the Lord will, in his mercy, use some means to enlighten the human family so that they may be able to discern good from bad, and may be led to choose that good part which cannot be taken from them.

To one of the nine Trustees the opportunity has been afforded of becoming a joint-heir with the Church, the greater part of an estate having been willed to him, and but a small part of it to the Church. It is said that the testator was insane at the time he disposed of his property in that manner. It will be but right and honorable in the Church to disclaim all right or title to the property, as the owner of it left a widow and several helpless children without any support. It is the duty of the Church to make known, through the medium of the public press, that they have neither part nor lot in this unreasonable matter.

Again—the man who is appointed to stand at the head of the Church government should possess a strong mind, a sound judgment, a good knowledge and understanding of the Scriptures of Truth, and the Gospel of Christ: he should also love and adhere to the discipline, and the Lord would then direct his way and preserve him in the right path through life: and if we walk by the rule of the Gospel, he will save us in the eternal world.

Old age is honorable, and should be respected at all times and upon all occasions: but there is a fitness to be observed in the administration of public affairs; and when a man is far advanced in life, he is generally incompetent to govern a great body of men. Therefore, there is a change required in this respect. Then it will be made known to us all, that nothing of a temporal nature should be suffered to be introduced among the followers of the blessed Lord and Saviour, Jesus Christ, without first consulting the oracles of God, and getting the consent of the Board and body. Even after obtaining their consent, there may be sin in doing such things. It is, therefore, good for us all to confess our faults, for we have been unguarded in this matter, and repent and pray that the Lord will pardon and forgive us our folly, and repair the breach that this evil has made in the wall, and bring us all into the bonds of love, and keep us forever, through Jesus Christ our Lord and Saviour.—Amen. I may write again, God willing. I will endeavor to show those who have turned their coats in this matter, and how unstable some men are in all their ways. There are many other important points which I shall endeavor to lay before you for the good of the rising generation and mankind at large.　　　　D. H. P."

Being now clear of the Church in Philadelphia, I prepared to go forth into the great vineyard, and labor in the bonds of the everlasting Gospel. The following certificates were given me by my clerical brethren, that I might be known to those whom I visited:

"Philadelphia, Jan. 2, 1849.
"This certifies that the bearer, Rev. Daniel H. Peterson, is an acceptable member of the A. F. M. E. Church, a member of Conference, and a preacher of the Gospel.

JOHN CORNISH,
Pastor, &c., Bethel Church."

"Philadelphia, Jan. 24, 1849.
"This will certify that we have known Rev. D. H. Peterson a number of years. We have ever found him to be an honest man, whose word is to be depended upon. He is a full member of the Christian Church, of good standing, &c. He is an official man; therefore, we recommend him to all, and sincerely trust that the Christian community and good citizens will receive him, and give him the right hand of fellowship, and in his mission, aid him with such things as he may stand in need of. Such is the duty of Christians in all cases. Therefore he has our sincere prayers and good wishes, that he may be useful in all sects and denominations. Such is his desire: to promote the Kingdom of the Most High God, and to benefit the world of mankind.

"We subscribe our names most respectfully:

Rev. JOHN CORNISH,
Pastor of Bethel Church.
Rev. STEPHEN GLOUCESTER,
Pastor Presbyterian Church.
Rev. GEORGE GALBRAITH,
Pastor Wesleyan Church.
Rev. DANIEL SCOTT,
Baptist Church."

With these certificates I went forth, and since that time I have endeavored to proclaim liberty and free salvation in the Gospel of our Lord and Saviour Jesus Christ, to a dying people throughout a great part of the United States of America, this great Republic, the garden-spot of the world, which is lighted up with the Gospel of our Lord and Saviour Jesus Christ. I, therefore, do trust and pray that through this great light, all the evil, and sins and oppressions, may be plainly seen and purged away, that she and her inhabitants may be blessed for evermore.

CHAPTER III.

The Author addresses his brethren in bondage. A door is open for the relief of the people of color. Bethel Church of Philadelphia is reproved for her folly and pride. A great blunder at the Conference in Buffalo. Oppression and persecution. Church in Sixth street, Philadelphia, and her minister. No facilities in the United States for educated colored men. Slavery of the Africans was permitted on account of their rebellion and idolatry. Brilliant prospects for the colored man in Liberia. The Author exhorts his colored brethren to reflect seriously, and choose that good part which will not be taken from them.

I WOULD commence this chapter with some remarks about my colored brethren who are under the yoke of bondage. Let me address you one word of consolation. At the time that your ancestors were brought from Africa, the rights of man were but little understood; while Africa itself was a land of darkness, where the people made merchandise of each other, and entirely neglected the true worship of the Almighty God. You were brought hither by a nation who are now said to be your best friends, but they left you here in bondage. The land from whence you came is still in darkness, while here you are daily gaining light and religion; and although you may have suffered, and may suffer still more, yet it will all redound to the glory and honor of the Lord; and, in the fulness of time, we may be the instruments in the hand of the Lord for redeeming that very land, from the darkness of ignorance and superstition, and planting the banner of the Cross in that wilderness of thorns from which our forefathers were taken.

The great evils which we have suffered came upon us, our forefathers, and our nation, on account of our disobedience, rebellion, and neglect of God. Dear brethren, the remedy for these evils is righteousness and truth. Be willing and obedient, and you shall eat the fat of the land. Wait patiently upon the Lord, and he will bring about all things in the fulness of time; and when we are qualified, we shall return to that country out of which our fathers came, and light it up with the pure flame of the Gospel, so that all our afflicted people may be restored to their liberty, land, and nation, and the Lord's name be praised and glorified for ever.

It is said that the number of colored people who are bound is three millions, while the free are about one-third of that amount. In this you can plainly discern the wonderful agency of the Lord, for at one time they were all bound. Since then, many have been released from bondage, and are now nominally free: but there is not an actually free colored person in the United States, for they are not citizens. Every intelligent person knows this to be a fact. It is for this cause that there are now so many wise and good men, wealthy men also, together with a great number of honorable and benevolent ladies, standing up in our behalf and pleading our humble cause. They have even opened for us a door of deliverance, so that we may enjoy all the rights and privileges of men, both religious and civil—so that we may serve and worship the Lord under our own vine and fig-tree, where none can make us afraid. It is wonderful to see what pains and care those kind people have taken for our comfort and happiness. Observe the great provision that is made for us both on land and sea. No steamer or vessel of any kind could have treated their passengers better than those were treated who sailed in the barque Isla de Cuba, A. Miller, master, and Mr. Hatch, chief mate. There was every attention paid to all the passengers, and nothing which could be necessary to their comfort and convenience was denied them, that I can assure you.

I will now address a few words to that portion of the colored population which is called free, to the colored Churches at large, &c.

My dear brethren, I have zeal and love for all mankind, but particularly for you, my afflicted brethren, bone of my bone, and flesh of my flesh. I am sorry to say, that I know many of us are misled by wrong instruction, by not taking the counsel which

the Saviour gave his disciples—that is, to come and see for yourselves. But, brethren, you see what your condition is in the
United States of America: you know that you cannot obtain your
citizenship. You are greatly in the minority: the best of you are
deprived of their rights and privileges, and so you must continue
to be, as long as slavery continues; for we are all bound, in part,
by the same cord, the laws and customs of the country recogniz-
ing us as an inferior people.

It becomes us, then, as rational beings, to examine these
things. I feel myself bound, and I trust that every intelligent
man and woman is bound, to leave no stone unturned for the
bettering of the condition of the colored population at large,
in a peaceable, quiet, and religious manner, to the glory and
honor of the Lord, and the peace of all mankind. Remember,
that the people of God suffered four hundred years in Egypt,
and in the fulness of time the Lord sent them Moses as a deliv-
erer; but that work was not accomplished in one day. It required
a long time and much labor to accomplish it. The sufferings of
the Israelites in Egypt, were much greater than ours in this country. Their children were put to death by oppression, and they
lost the covenant of their forefathers which they made with the
Lord. But Moses was an instrument in the hands of the Lord, in
leading the people out of bondage. Those people were among
the heathens, but we are in the midst of Christians: their task-
masters made no provision for improving the condition of the
sufferers, but there is good provision made for us by the true
friends of the colored race, comprising many comforts and conveniences. You are now invited to come and embrace the offer,
lest the time may arrive when this great door shall be shut, so
that you cannot enter in and enjoy the blessings which are now
held out for your acceptance. Therefore, come, now or never.

There is another advantage which you have over the Hebrews. The rulers of Egypt did not aid them in their religious
worship by providing churches or any other conveniences: but
the Christian community of these United States has ever been,
and still is, very kind and benevolent towards us in all cases. They
have ever aided us very kindly in obtaining places of worship for

the religious instruction of our unfortunate people. New-York, New-Jersey, and Pennsylvania, have ever been willing and ready to aid us in obtaining places of worship and all other good institutions. So you see that we are greatly blessed in those important particulars. We have now Churches and Free Schools in every county and city, village and neighborhood.

It is therefore manifest, that there is no lack on the part of the religious community, though there is no inconsiderable neglect upon ours. We are greatly indebted to all the States East of New-York for their kind treatment, and for the aid which they have so cheerfully extended to us in all our humble enterprises. They have done much for us in a great variety of ways.

But what is the state of those Churches of ours that have been so much favored? How do they prosper *now?* They are all fast asleep. They are sheep scattered in the wilderness without a shepherd, or like men upon a raft drifting about on the sea without captain, pilot, chart, or compass. They are carried every way but the right way. They have suffered shipwreck by reason of sin and self-interest on the part of their spiritual rulers. Ministers of my colored brethren, it is needful that all of you should wake up: otherwise, your captains and shepherds, crews, cargoes, and passengers, will all be swallowed up in the great maelstrom of perdition.

Therefore we call your serious attention to a great work. Thou that sleepest, awake, for the night is far spent, and the day is at hand. Watch and be sober, as we have never yet been free men and women in this country. Now the time has come when we all have an opportunity to embrace our freedom, both moral and religious, military and civil—houses and lands all free! What more can we ask, or what more can be done for us at this time? It is now high time for us to go to work in the right way and help ourselves, and then we shall find help in the time of need. Now let us make this contract—if you awake first, please wake me to a sense of my duties, and I will arise and go to work; but if I awake first, I will wake you up, and you must go to work for yourself, and for your Church and people—in fact, for all the human family. This is the duty of all ministers of the Gospel.

Brethren, what have we been doing, and where are the fruits of
our labor? I fear they are but very few. What is the cause of this?
We have departed from the first principles of the Gospel. Then,
let us stop short, retrace our steps, and do our first works, and
the Lord will bless us: he will bless you and yours for ever.

I am now speaking more particularly to my Presbyterian
and Baptist brethren. With both denominations I am well acquainted, with you and your Churches, both white and colored.
You are all kind and friendly, and do give all Christians the right
hand of fellowship. I have ever found Christian fellowship with
you; indeed, more so than with many others who make much
louder professions. Therefore, I say unto you, be faithful, and
consider the good of all mankind. I have found the ministers
and members of the Protestant Episcopal Church kind and benevolent in almost all cases: also, the Universalist ministers and
societies are kind and benevolent people: also, the Friends—
their kindness is seasoned with humanity and friendliness.

But, I am now about to speak to my colored brethren of the
Methodist order. I want you to hear me. Wake up, Zion, from
your slumbers, shake the dust from your souls, put on the beautiful garment of salvation, and shine in the brightness of re-
newed hope, for the light is come and the glory of the Lord is
risen. Let all darkness flee away like the shades of night at the
rising of the sun. We have been too long in obscurity already; we
have stumbled one over another; we have stood in our own light.
We are carelessly drifting down with the tide of prejudice which
has set against our best friends: we have wrongly and ignorantly
advised our people to continue in the same course; and what is
the result of all these things? Bad—bad—bad enough! In the
first place, it has introduced enmity into your Churches, and old
members have been disregarded and cast out, until at length the
Church is divided. "A house divided against itself, it cannot
stand." It must fall, and become desolate.

Had we been deeply engaged in sending the Gospel to the
heathen and to our afflicted brethren in Africa and elsewhere,
you would not have had all those confusions and troubles which
now disgrace your Churches. While these evils remain in your

Churches, religion and the Son of God are gone out of them, and all your labors and offerings are vanity and vexation of spirit. Therefore, look well to those things, and consider your own salvation and that of all those under your charge.

Let us not rest in idly persuading people to that course which we know nothing about; but let us instruct them to love and serve the Lord. But let them be their own judges in other matters, for they know what is best for themselves. As ministers, let us faithfully do that which is appointed for us to do in the Gospel, and it will go well with us in time as well as in eternity.

I now speak to your backsliding sister and her ministers, namely, Bethel and all her branches. Her acts have been like those of Zion, but rather worse in many cases, which I shall endeavor to show hereafter, with the blessing of the Lord. I thought once that you were true-hearted and faithful followers of the meek and lowly Lamb, and good Christians. I therefore joined in faith with you: I travelled a long time with you: I was well pleased with the Church government at the time. They were poor and humble: I believe that the blessing of the Lord was with them: I held prayer-meeting with them: I led their classes and exhorted them: I preached for them, and remained with them a number of years, until the second administration ended. After that they grew fat, like the heifer at grass, kicked up their heels and bellowed, waxed proud and self-willed. I therefore left them. With credit, I was there a long time. But I thank the Lord that there was never a charge brought against me. Yet I was envied and deprived of my legal rights. I saw their backsliding and ignominy, and fully I told them thereof to their faces.

What I foretold them came to pass. I, therefore, cleared my skirts of their blood. I now speak more plainly to them than before. Dear brethren and sisters of the Bethel M. E. Church in Philadelphia, the mother of all the branches, your Church commenced under the superintendence of Rev. RICHARD ALLEN. Since 1816, it had increased very considerably, and they did well until after the election of Rev. Paul Quin of New-York, but formerly of Pennsylvania.

After his installation, there was great dissatisfaction with respect to the neglect of the discipline and other rules of the Church. It ended in a heavy law-suit and a split in the Church— a malicious division. The Church has never since been settled, and yet they wanted to extend their borders and their power. They petitioned for two more Bishops, and the petition was granted. Therefore they appointed a Mr. Willis Nazua, formerly from Virginia, and Daniel A. Payne, from Charleston, S.C. Thus they have three bishops: the two last were elected in 1853. Now they have their desire; but there is a great deal to do. Those three bishops must be supported, their board, lodging, and travelling expenses paid by their poor societies and classes.

The question may arise, Why do they want three bishops? I answer, Why does the ape attempt to imitate the human family? It is because he lacks understanding, and does not perceive that Nature has never bestowed upon him the proper faculties for doing the works or performing the part of a human being. They aspire to stand on a level with the white brethren of the Methodist Episcopal Church, and will have three bishops because the white Methodists are ruled by three bishops. If they had reflected a moment, they would have seen the absurdity of the proceeding. There is as much difference between the two societies, as there is between the Hudson River and the great Atlantic Ocean. The wealth of the other Church and her members, the intelligence and literary talent of her ministers, their extensive fields of labor among all nations, and the mighty influence which they wield, have opened a passage to all the benefits and blessings of the world, while the power of the Gospel which they preach has opened Heaven and all its glories to thousands whom they have persuaded to live righteously and godly in this present world. But our backsliding and rebellious sister, Bethel Church of Philadelphia, the mother of all the branches, has revolted twice already; then was guilty of oppression, and violated the discipline of the Church and rules of government from motives of malice and revenge; and even, with three bishops at her head, made a most stupid mistake and blunder in Conference at Buffalo, N.Y., in the year 1853, of which I may speak hereafter.

I thank the Lord that I left you, with my own skirts untarnished by your blood. Nothing could induce me to be a bishop among you. I thank the Lord that I am a free man in our Lord and Saviour Jesus Christ, and I am an humble Elder in the Church of God, on board of the barque Isla de Cuba, with a two-fold mission for Monrovia, Liberia, Western Africa; firstly, to bear the Gospel to my brethren and see how they do, and secondly, to see and hold an interview with the head of that Government, touching the condition of those who are there, and the prospect for those who are about to go to that quarter of the globe. I go also to see what good results from cultivating the minds, as well as the lands, of the heathen. I believe that great treasures are embedded in those lands, and that only understanding and enterprise are wanting to bring them to light. It remains for us to go forth, sons and daughters of Ethiopia, embrace our privileges, obtain the lands, dwell thereon, and become a great nation. Then the heathen will be turned from their idols, and join the true worship: then Ethiopia will stretch her hands unto God, and the islands shall be filled with his glory. Thus shall we be a blessing to all people, and all people will be a blessing to us, and the Lord will prosper us in all things.

To return to our backsliding sister and her rulers: Dear brethren, I hope that you will examine yourselves well in the Gospel glass, and see if you are what you ought to be, if you are doing what you ought to do, that is, to preach the Gospel faithfully to all, walk humbly, do unto others as you would have them do unto you, not spending your time in giving unwholesome advice to the people and to the members of your Church, but suffering the people to judge for themselves in temporal matters. I have said that those three bishops of yours must be supported. It is true that they should be, if they were the right kind of men. But they spend too much of their time in giving bad advice to the people, and raising evil reports against a humane, benevolent, and Christian institution, making them believe that good is evil, and that light is darkness. Such teachings are abominable. Look in the glass and see yourselves, all in the dark as you are. It is better for you to retract—to cease to do evil, and learn to do well. The question comes up—why do you give the people such advice? It is easy to give the answer—it is because you must keep them together that they may maintain you and the ordinary ministers. You would keep them up like sheep, that you may catch them easily, and shear off their fleece for your own benefit. You will not let them go to Africa, or anywhere else, lest you lose the support which you derive from them while they remain with you. What is the condition, and what are the circumstances of those from whom these Bishops receive their support? They are, generally, very poor people, with little employment, and paying heavy rents, with large families to maintain, which is enough to sink them to the earth, without the super-added weight of three bishops, two of whom are of no more necessity to that little society than a pair of double spectacles to a blind man.

How do the old and sickly members fare? Badly enough! After having served the Church, aided in paying the ministers for some fifteen or twenty years, and having labored thus for the support of the Gospel all through their best days, they have found no help in their old age from either ministers or lay members. It is a shame to tell these infirm and faithful brethren that they must go to the Poor-House, at the very time that they ought to be taken care of by the Church. But they are cast off when they should be provided for, and are permitted to pine away and die among those who are called "sinners" and "the ungodly." It is a shame that this should be the case in any Christian Church; and therefore it would be well for those gentlemen who have charge of institutions for the poor, to look well to the matter when they are applied to for the purpose of giving admission to an individual, and discover whether he belongs to a Church or not.

Dear brethren, and rulers of the backsliding sister and her branches, let us pray for this Church; for the Lord will hear prayer. Oh! backsliding sister! why will you die? Return, repent, and do thy first works, and the Lord will have mercy and abundantly pardon you and receive you, "and you shall be my sons and daughters, and I will be father unto you," saith the Lord of Hosts. Dear brethren, we will go back to Buffalo for a few moments, for in wise counsel there is safety, but in ignorance, there is great danger.

You remember that in Conference, in New-York a year since, there was an application made for an individual to receive orders and join the travelling connection; but Messrs. R. R., J. P., L. E. C. and others, rose and said "we don't know you," &c. At that time Bishop Quin was in the chair, and was weak enough to give way to those unreasonable men. He was silent upon that important occasion, and thus the matter ended. So the applicant went about his business, and thought no more of the affair; but, at their Conference in Buffalo, they wickedly called this man in question, although he had no seat there, nor voice, nor business. Neither was there any charge against him, nor any notice given him. He knew nothing of the matter; yet they took up the case and acted upon it. After that, they published him to the world, through their minutes, as an offender. The innocent man knew nothing of the case for some time, until passing through Bordentown, N.J., he met with one of their ministers (a Mr. Catto), who informed him that he had been tried at the Buffalo Conference, and that he could not admit him to his pulpit, because Bishop Nazua had charged him not to allow the man any privilege in his Church, as he was an offender. But Mr. Catto advised the man to see to the matter, and if his persecutors had acted as related above, to bring them to an account for their unlawful dealings; for they were contrary to the Church discipline, and the laws of this country.

I next call your attention to the Sabbath schools. At the Conference, they came to a resolve that no white person should teach in the schools: they would have none but colored teachers. The other proceeding which I have related, shows how well qualified *they* are to teach their pupils. Mr. Robertson stated that the great blunder in the Buffalo Conference was caused by the advice given by the Bishop, the Rev. Wm. P. Quin: but I think him a man of better judgment than to advise such proceedings.

There were several ladies and gentlemen—very kind friends of the colored people—who had been laboring a number of years to impart instruction to colored children. They had become much attached to the children, and the children had also become much attached to them. When it was told them that Conference had decided to reject white teachers, they withdrew from the schools. The consequence was, that both parents and children became very much dissatisfied, and left the Church; for nothing reigned there but tumult and confusion, instead of peace and harmony.

These calamities arise from putting men at the head of the Church who are no more fitted for the station than is a child three years old to act as captain of a ship in a storm upon a lee shore.

Among others who assisted the colored people, were Dr. R. F. Hibbard and ladies, Dr. Worrel and ladies, and that benevolent lady, Mrs. Few, of Ninth street. She came in person, and aided the Church, and gave good advice in relation to the management of the school in Sixth street. It is by ignorance and oppression, that the Church in Second street became divided. It is a branch of Bethel, the backsliding sister.

The Church in Sixth street bids fair to become a very useful and beneficial institution. It contributes greatly towards the moral and religious improvement of the colored population. Their minister, Rev. L. Telmon, the founder and pastor of that Church, is an active, capable man. That Church is established on better principles than any colored Church in the States—on free, republican principles. Her pastor has done, and is doing, all that he can for the improvement of the rising generation; and if he continues to be faithful, he will be a blessing to the people, and a blessing to himself. If he fail, it will be otherwise. I therefore recommend humiliation, faith, and fervent prayer to himself and congregation, and to all others, that it may be well with them in time and in eternity.

I believe that the Rev. L. Telmon is a man of too much sound judgment to teach the people folly, and to prejudice them against their best friends. He will permit the people to act for themselves in temporal matters, and to go where they please. If any of them wish to go to Canada, let them go; if any want to go to Hayti, let them go. They should be at liberty to go where they please; but there is no *better* place than Liberia for the sons and daughters of Ethiopia. Therefore, I say, let us embrace the opportunity while we can, and pray that the blessing of the Lord may go with us and keep us for ever.

What I have done and am still doing, is, and has been, without fee or reward, and solely for the welfare of my afflicted nation: for I have now seen for myself, and am bound to make a true report in all things. I say, let no men speak evil of things that they know nothing about. If they do, it is the blind leading the blind.

The person that was so badly treated by the Conference at Buffalo without having committed any offence, was the man whom they knew to be engaged in looking into these matters. He was concerned for the welfare of his brethren in Africa, in America, and elsewhere. Therefore they conspired together to kill and destroy his influence. They are wicked men: they are such men as those who opposed Moses in Egypt; they shall proceed so far and no farther, for the Lord is over all, blessed for evermore.

Dear brethren, I now propose to consider a moment the school instruction of our people in the United States—their Infant Schools, Sabbath-Schools, Free and Pay Schools, Seminaries, Academies, and Colleges. Some of our afflicted people have been assisted in all those places, and have been admitted to all the advantages thereof. Now, what have they gained by all these advantages? Very little, indeed. But why is this? It is because the laws, customs, and usages are such as to impede their improvement. The United States are a wise, wealthy, and proud nation, and will not be coerced into anything which does not suit their pleasure. Notwithstanding this, if we take them right, there are no better people in the world. They are kind, humane, and benevolent to all those whom they deem worthy of their attention. But, dear brethren, I want you to consider at this time, that this nation was not the cause of our forefathers being plunged into bondage. It was the British nation, who, in an age of darkness, made slaves of the colored people; and although we are multiplied to millions and have grown up under the laws and customs

of this country, yet three-fourths of us are in bondage; and are
we so very weak as to imagine that a wise nation like this will take
those who are free and place them upon an equality with themselves, while so great a majority of our afflicted people are in
bondage under them?

Dear brethren, know ye not that every colored person, of
whatever shade, so that he have African blood in his veins, is
ruled and governed under the same law and viewed in the same
light? Therefore we need not look to the right or to the left—
neither to brother John, uncle Tom, nor to sister Nancy, for our
deliverance; but let us look to the blessed Lord, and be faithful
in all things, take the good advice of our best friends, be willing
and obedient, and we shall enjoy the good of the land.

Dear brethren, I want you to examine yourselves well in the
glass, and consider all things well, and thus you will discover
what is good for you in time and in eternity. Let us think of Africa for a few moments. Know you not that, in the beginning,
the blessed Lord gave this great quarter of the earth to our nation, and bade us keep the Law and live? But our progenitors
were rebellious and disobedient, and refused to serve the true
and living God. They worshipped other gods, and wasted their
substance upon idols. Therefore they were left to follow the desire of their own wicked hearts; and finally, they were suffered to
be carried away captive, like the rebellious Israelites, barefoot,
naked, and in fetters. They were borne to a strange land, and
left among a people whom they knew not. But what is the result?
Solomon says, "There is a time to all things." In the fulness of
time, the Lord will bring everything to bear in its right place. It
is of no use for man to hurry and push things of this weighty
nature. We can do nothing without help from the Lord.

The reason that our brethren who have had the advantages
of the high schools do not arrive at eminence, has already been
given. Although they may have received all the knowledge required for preferment, they have no facilities for bringing their
accomplishments into exercise in real life. They go forth looking for employment; they wander through many places seeking
for business and finding none. They knock at many doors for

admittance—the porter looks out, sees the complexion of the applicant, and bids him go farther and fare worse. He wanders away dejected and forlorn, and perhaps plunges into vice, and, lamenting the time which he has squandered in procuring an education which seems to be so useless to him for all practical purposes, he joins with the ignorant and profane in some low pursuit which his superior education has rendered unsuitable for him.

But he hears a white citizen knock at those doors. They fly open as of themselves, and a cheerful voice says, "Walk in, brother, and view the beauties of the place, the wealth, honor, peace, and happiness that bloom perennially in the field before you. Partake with us of those blessings, from which the colored applicant is shut out."

You know that these are facts. Also, many of the hotels will not admit you. The street conveyances close the door against you. We labor under many disadvantages: and do you not, dear brethren, see plainly, that the hand of the Lord is in this great matter? In by-gone times, we were carried away naked from the father-land, but are now going back with the arts and sciences, with the Bible in our hands, to plant religion and civilization.

The blessed Lord has raised up great and good men who have opened this door, more effectually than any other door which can be opened in this country, or in any other part of the world. For there is no part of the known world to which you can go, in which you will not be subjected to disadvantages, with the sole exception of Liberia, in Africa. There the laws are liberal, and all men fare alike under the flag of that young republic, and encouraged by that great nation, the United States of America. This greatest republic in the known world is bound to protect and raise up that young nation to a level with herself, if we, as a people, will take counsel and seek the right way. By obedience to the truth, we shall then eat the good of the land. In that country is a field large enough for the employment of all your talents in every way and shape, either moral, religious, civil or military. There no doors will be shut against you, but all is as free as the air of heaven.

Therefore, go forth without delay, and claim your rights as freemen and freewomen, and you will have great cause to rejoice. But nothing like vice should be carried into that country. Violins and other trifling kinds of music should be left behind—they only gender idleness and folly: but let us keep the fear of the Lord before us, and in a few years we shall be a great nation, respected by the rest of mankind. The fruits and productions of Africa will be carried throughout the world; her ships will visit all nations, and her flag will wave in every sea.

CHAPTER IV.

Good treatment on board the Isla de Cuba. Departure for Liberia. Worship on board every Sabbath. Much sea-sickness. Kind attentions of Capt. Miller. Warm weather on the Coast of Africa. Unsuccessful attempts to take a turtle. Serious accident to the mate, Mr. Hatch. They catch a shark, and cook him for dinner. Description of Cape Mount. A beautiful fish. Visit from a little bird. Visits from the natives on the Coast. Arrival at Monrovia. Mr. Cauldwell goes on shore.

ON board of the Isla de Cuba we had passengers of all ages, from infancy to the most advanced stages of life. Some were eighty and even ninety years of age. They were all well treated by Capt. Miller, Mr. Hatch, the mate, and the crew. You can see that all things are made easy and convenient for us. It is only for us to be ready and willing.

By aid and good counsel of ministers of the Gospel, and all good men who possess sound minds, and desire the welfare of the colored people, more good can be done in one year than has ever been done by them before, in pointing out the right way for our relief. There is great power vested in the administration of the Gospel; and if the ministers were all of one mind, they could carry every thing before them. They have been too much divided, but I pray that the time may arrive when they will all see eye to eye.

I will now observe that I was very agreeably disappointed with regard to the treatment of the emigrants on board the Isla de

Cuba. When I went on board of the barque, I saw the passengers coming from all quarters, from the North, the South, the East, and the West. Some came without any clothing except what they had on, and also without bedding. The ship was about to sail, when the Rev. J. B. Penny came on board to see the state of the passengers. He found some in a very uncomfortable condition, owing to the fact that they had neglected to bring their goods with them. There was a Mr. Jacklin, from Franklin County, N.Y., with his wife and two sons, who were destitute of any comforts at all. The ship lay a mile in the stream, but Mr. Penny returned to the city, and although the wind was very high and the water rough, he came off to the barque again, and brought with him new beds and clothing for the destitute emigrants, amounting in price to nearly one hundred dollars. He came off to us in a small boat, at the risk of his life. He made sure that every one was comfortable, then gave them the right hand of friendship, and bade them adieu.

We sailed the next day with prosperous gales, Nov. 10th, 1853. Capt. Miller, Mr. Hatch, and all the crew, were very kind to us. We wanted nothing, and we all fared alike. It was the beginning of better days. The steerage passengers had more than an abundance of everything. I am fully persuaded that there was no deception about the matter. The truth has come out at last, and if the truth shall make you free, then will you be free indeed.

Capt. Miller is a first rate officer on board ship, a perfect gentleman, and a Christian. He spares no pains to insure the safety of the ship and the comfort of his passengers and crew, attending faithfully to the cleanliness of his vessel, above and below. Mr. Hatch is also a first rate man, and both of them from the State of Maine. I never heard the Captain speak a harsh word from the time that we left the dock at New-York till we arrived at our port of destination. All things were conducted as peacefully as they could have been managed in any family. Therefore, I feel very thankful for the blessing of the Lord, which has preserved me from childhood up to the present time.

I will say in this place, that those who go to Liberia should be careful to take with them such medicines as are calculated to keep the bowels free. That will add much to their health when they reach port, and as going to sea produces costiveness, this caution should be remembered. Some were quite sea-sick, and I aided Capt. Miller in his attendance upon them. They all recovered and became fully restored to health, and we went on our way rejoicing.

I thank the Lord that I was able to fulfil all my duties while on board the barque, that is, to preach once on the Sabbath, hold prayers every morning and evening, and say grace at every meal.

I kept the following account of the passage:—

Nov. 7th, 1853. I went on board the barque Isla de Cuba, Capt. Miller, bound to Monrovia, Liberia, Africa, and lying at New-York.

8th. A steamboat came alongside, and towed us down the river, where we came to an anchor. The Captain went ashore for the ship's papers.

9th. The Captain returned to the ship at 10 o'clock A.M. Rev. Mr. Penny, the agent, soon after came on board with bedding and clothing for the poor strangers who had come from afar, and were bound to Liberia. Mr. Penny paid great respect to all the passengers, both male and female, and bade us all goodbye in a very friendly manner. He then went ashore. Capt. Miller weighed anchor at 4 P.M. and we went down the Bay. We had on board fifty-six passengers—first mate, Mr. Hatch, second mate, Mr. James Magill, with steward, cook, and ship's company. For all, there were good accommodations. We came to an anchor on the same evening at 6 o'clock, near the light-house which stands on the Highlands, Sandy Hook. Some of the steerage passengers were quite sea-sick.

10th. In the morning, we left the anchorage and went to sea, with a fair wind and bright sunshine. All in good spirits upon leaving the High lands of New-Jersey upon the starboard, and that of New-York on the larboard quarter. Same morning we met a pilot boat, No. 1, going to New-York.

11th. At 10 o'clock, we made the Gulf Stream. Rough sea, and passengers very sick. Ship is getting on very well.

12th. Very rough. All sick. Some glass broken by the motion of the vessel.

13th. Sabbath. Strong gales from the South-East. All sick.

14th. The same. Steward sick, with a pain in his side and head. Ship driven by contrary winds in the Gulf Stream for three days. Capt. Miller and chief mate are quiet and skilful men. They do all they can for the good of the ship's crew and passengers. The Captain stated that he had not experienced worse weather for fifteen years.

15th. We caught a fair breeze and steady. Made good headway. The passengers are getting better, but the steward continues sick with a pain in his side and head. The captain paid every medical attention to him, and to all others.

16th. Steward a little better, but still very sick. A pleasant day. In the evening the wind rose. Heavy sea. Weather over-cast. We sprung a leak, but pumped out dry. Mr. Cauldwell was sitting near me conversing, when there came a heavy sea which threw him against the vessel's side and hurt his head very much. Rough sea, and all sick. I have eaten no meat for nine days.

17th. Very rough. They have removed a sick woman up in the cabin with Mrs. Gibbons. There were some spars carried away during the night. I thank the Lord that I was comfortable and without fear. I endeavored to put my trust in the Lord.

18th. Very stormy. Many sick. Cook very sick. We passed three vessels—a ship, a brig, and a barque. I thank the Lord that we have had singing, and praying, and grace before meat, all the passage, the same as we have on shore.

19th. A ship passed us in the morning early, probably bound to New-York. We passed a large school of porpoises and flying-fish. It has been blowing a gale all day. The steward is better.

20th. Sabbath. A beautiful day. Prayer morning and evening. I preached in the afternoon from Jonah, chap. ii., verse 11. We were then about one thousand miles from New-York. We saw a ship bound to America. I have seen on board what I have prayed for, the worship of the blessed Lord at sea as well as on dry land.

21st. A fine morning. A perfect calm, and the sea as smooth as the river Delaware. All well.

22nd. A fine day. Very pleasant; neither too warm nor too cold. Light breezes, favorable. The blessings and glory of the Lord seemed to be with the ship, officers, crew, and passengers.

Behold the rising sun, the clear sky, the flying clouds over our
heads, and we riding on the bosom of the great ocean. There
behold the wisdom and the wonderful works of Almighty God.
Passengers young and old came on deck to get the fresh air, and
to dry their clothing and bedding, all in high spirits. With respect to the fare on board the Isla de Cuba, we had at all three
meals, the best beef and pork, fatted fowls, desserts, cheese, butter, pickles, hard biscuits, fresh baker's bread, and hot rolls, with
other good and palatable food. There was no respect of persons,
the captain and his mate treating all persons according to their
behaviour without regard to wealth or station. Captain Miller is
a noble officer, and so is his mate, Mr. Hatch. The cabin passengers are Mrs. Gibbons, from Camden, N.J., Mr. Caldwell, of New-
York, Mr. Augustus Washington, wife, and two small children,
from Hartford, Mr. Truman, from Western Pennsylvania, and
myself. Rev. Mr. Williams, with his wife, family, and his company
of 30 or 40, occupied the steerage, and performed their religious duties in the most orderly manner. Six o'clock P.M., fair
wind and all well.

23d. A very fine day; clear and calm; wind at South-East, not
fair; but, thank the Lord, we are all tolerably well at this time.

24th. We have been at sea 16 days. Fine weather. Thank the
Lord, we are all well. A flying-fish was found on board this morning. The Captain requested that good order should be preserved in the cabin, that the men might get their regular rest;
for there were some that wanted to play the fiddle, with other
vain amusements. I am very glad that the captain spoke against
such proceedings. There were two fiddles. Augustus Washington
from Hartford had one, and a man named Kelly, from the West,
had the other. It was not well to take them on board.

25th. A fair wind and very stormy. Many were sea-sick. We saw
a ship ahead early this morning. Some of our forward rigging
was carried away during the night. Very rough.

26th. Stormy and rough. Thank the Lord we are all well. It is
very singular that among all our passengers there are not more
than four or five dark persons.

27th. Sabbath. The blessed Lord has thus far preserved us all in safety, and I pray that he will keep us all forever. The colored people in general seek too much after the world for their own good. If they had as much zeal for the Gospel as they have for the world, they would become a great people in Africa, but if they carry vice and a love of trifling amusements with them, it will be a curse both to themselves and the natives. I trust that all will take heed to these things, for I saw the evil effect of such folly on board the ship, as well as in that country. We held meeting to-day in the cabin, with the full consent of Capt. Miller. Rev. Samuel Williams preached, and I closed with a few remarks. A brisk, fair wind all day: 6 o'clock, P.M. I thank the Lord we are well. John, chap. iii., v. 2.

28th. We have been 20 days at sea. The steward has fully recovered his health. The captain paid great attention to him, and had him bled. Thank the Lord we are now all well. We are more than two thousand miles from New-York, getting on very well. We are more than half way to Africa. The Lord has helped us. This is a fine morning, and the wind is fair. We have seen two rainbows at sea. We saw a school of porpoises this afternoon. I said that we might look out for a squall. In 48 hours it came, and lasted two hours. Then all was calm again. Thank the Lord.

29th. Fair wind. We saw a ship under way. Thank the Lord we are all well.

30th. All well, the Lord be praised forever. Since seven, A.M., the wind has been fresh through the day and evening.

December 1st. The wind is very high, but it is fair. A fine day. The sea is rough. Mr. Augustus Washington, from Hartford, broke his looking-glass in his state-room last night.

2d. We are 24 days at sea. Fine weather and wind fair. Thank the Lord, we are all very well at this time, and going forward at a good rate. We have been much favored on this voyage. We saw the new moon at sea, this evening, for the first time. It appeared to be about three nights old, and it showed three moons distinctly, as though you looked through a silk handkerchief. We rejoiced to see it.

3d. Fine weather and fair wind. We saw a ship in the forenoon. I thank the Lord, we are all well at this time.

4th. Sabbath. Fine weather and a fair wind. I preached on board at 2 o'clock P.M., on the after-deck, the captain, crew, and all the officers present. I spoke from Paul's Epistle to the Hebrews, chap. xi., v. 24. "By faith, Moses, when he was come to years, refused to be called the son of Pharaoh's daughter." We had a good time; all was peace and unity, and everything was done in order like a family singing and praising the Lord all through the Sabbath.

5th. Fair wind, but light. Fine summer weather. Thank the Lord we are all well and peaceable.

6th. Fine weather, all well. Very light wind and slow sailing. It was reported that the land was seen this afternoon, the Cape de Verd Islands.

7th. We are 29 days out. Fine weather and fair wind, but very light. I thank the Lord we are all well. The mate was very angry with one of the crew this evening.

8th. Fine weather and fair wind. We are within a few days' sail of the coast of Africa.

9th. Fine weather. The wind is fair, but light.

10th. Fair wind, but light. We are getting along very well. We are on the coast of Africa. The sea is very calm.

11th. Sabbath. Very warm weather. The sea is perfectly calm. Porpoises and other fish are playing around us and showing themselves like the flocks and herds of the field, or the cattle upon a thousand hills, as though they knew this day was the Sabbath. We saw a very beautiful fish indeed. I never saw anything greener in my life. Its fins and tail appeared to be tipped with gold. The whole ship's company ran to see it. It continued with the ship some time, and then vanished from our sight. As we arrive on the coast of Africa, more than thousand miles from Liberia, the sea is as smooth and calm as the Delaware or the Hudson River, very suitable for steamboats and light craft of every description. We had preaching this afternoon. Rev. Samuel Williams spoke from John. We had a prayer-meeting in the evening, singing altogether on deck. It was a good time.

12th. At four in the morning, we were visited by a violent storm, and the ship was in great danger. Both captain and mate were on the look-out. The ship was under full sail when the gale came suddenly upon her. All hands were called, steward, cooks, and all, and it was as much as they could do to stow the light sails and get the top-sails under reef before the worst came. Some of the sails were torn from the yards and carried away, the captain, mate, and crew doing all they could to save the ship. Knowing that the Lord possesses all power, and that we are in his hand, we made it a matter of prayer, and implored the Divine Throne of Grace that He would save us from the stormy winds and raging seas, and from all other dangers, and save us forever both in time and in eternity. This storm was attended with thunder and lightning, and many of the passengers were much alarmed. I thank the Lord I was perfectly calm and without fear. The Lord is all in all. The storm continued till noon. The wind changed, and we had it fair all the afternoon. A little bird came on board and alighted on the rigging. They caught it. Thank the Lord we are all here, and are doing well.

13th. We are 35 days at sea. It is a fine morning and very warm and calm. We let the little bird go at liberty this morning. We saw some sharks, and also a sea-turtle. We lowered a boat and went after the turtle, but could not find it. Afterwards we saw a shark. The captain harpooned him in the head, and we took him on board. He was skinned and dressed, and we had him for dinner. He made dry meat.

14th. Fine weather. A perfect calm and very warm. We are near Liberia, but we have no wind. We threw the lead, and found that we had sixty fathoms water. We caught two or three small fish; but they were of a kind that I never saw before. The little bird that we caught and set at liberty, continues with the ship. It has come on board and died. Before it died, a drab-colored bird came and sat on the rigging, and after awhile it went away. Mr. Augustus Washington kept the little one in his basket at night, and let it out in the morning.

15th. The weather is very warm. A perfect calm in the African sea. This morning an accident happened: Mr. Hatch fell from the quarter deck, a distance of nearly fourteen feet. He was very much hurt. It aroused all the passengers. The second mate thought that his leg was broken; but the Captain found upon examination that such was not the case. He was taken into the Captain's apartment and made as comfortable as possible. He was bled, rubbed, &c.

16th. Very warm and calm. Scarcely any wind. Thank the Lord, the mate is much better. We saw another sea-turtle. The Captain went after it in a boat, but it sank beneath the water on his approach. The Captain went a third time to take a turtle, but it escaped him. One day's fair wind would bring us to land. We caught some small fish that they call the sea eel.

17th. We are thirty-nine days out. Very warm and calm. We are in sight of land at this time. We called a public meeting this afternoon to return thanks to the Captain and Crew for their kind treatment of us during the passage, and also to express our gratitude towards our friends in America. We had a good time together, the Captain being present.

18th. Sabbath. We arrived off Cape Mount, forty miles from Liberia. A beautiful scene indeed, A small boat came off to the ship from the shore, containing two natives who were perfectly naked. We spoke with them as they came alongside. One of them spoke the French language. Both of them were fine-looking men. They were the first human beings that we had seen or spoken with, except those on board, for the space of forty days. Cape Mount stands right on the sea-board, is covered with trees and abounding with fruit, grass, and other vegetation. Belno is a beautiful sandy beach. It was a lovely Sabbath morning indeed, and long to be remembered. The chief mate, Mr. Hatch, who has been unwell, came to the breakfast table this morning for the first time. A boat load of natives came off to us. They were all naked, but quite a sensible people. I thank the Lord that we came to an anchor at half past nine o'clock P.M. after forty days passage, all safe and sound. Mr. Caldwell went on shore the same evening.

19th. On board of the Isla de Cuba, Capt. Miller, mates Messrs. Hatch and Magill, now lying in the harbor of Monrovia, Liberia, Africa. I thank the Lord that we are all well. This morning I intend going on shore early in the day.

CHAPTER V.

The Author goes on shore. Kind reception. Visits the President, Judge, and other distinguished persons. Beauty of the country. Description of the town, the soil, and the inhabitants. Good opportunities in Liberia for emigrants. Mechanics, farmers and schoolmasters wanted in Liberia. Those who lay the foundations of this great nation should be moral, industrious, economical, and religious persons. With the aid of friends in the United States, the cause of colored emigration to Liberia cannot fail to prosper.

DURING the morning we went on shore at the port, and were received with much joy, and in a very friendly manner, by all the people.

I called upon his excellency the President, both at his office and at his dwelling. I found him very competent and much of a gentleman. He has a good library. I was offered a home at many respectable houses, but I preferred a more private residence, as I had much writing to do. I put up at the house of Rev. Henry Teague, an aid to the President. He has a very fine family. I called upon the Judge and Dr. Roberts; also upon Mr. James Magill, and a number of merchants and others.

The President's lady is a very fine looking woman, and so is Mrs. Dr. Roberts. There is no better society to be found in any part of the world. I am very much pleased with it, and with the appearance of things here. The President and his lady are strict members of the Church.

The whole view from this spot is beautiful; and upon summing up, and taking into consideration the country, sea-board, rivers, mountains, vales and plains, I must say that I never saw a more attractive place. Monrovia is perfectly healthy, and contains, at this time, three large stone Churches, an Academy, and High School, and all other conveniences required by a large town. There are four ministers.

The people all look well, and have fine cattle, pigs, and goats. In fact, this place looks more like the Garden of Eden, than any place that I have ever seen or read about.

There are a number of vessels in the harbor, American, English, and Spanish, both war vessels and merchantmen, with captains and officers of all kinds. I am now writing in a very pleasant room with six windows, airy, cool, and well carpeted, with a handsome mirror, and other furniture of the best description. The people are all very kind and respectable.

The port is on elevated ground, commanding a full view of the sea, the three rivers, Montserrado, Junk, and St. Paul's.

I am very sorry to say that many false things have been said about this place, and the people who inhabit it: and even in the colored Churches of the United States, currency has been given to slanderous falsehoods of the most glaring description. Thus they talk of things about which they know nothing, instead of preaching the pure Gospel of Christ. I can assure the reader, that the people in Liberia look as respectable as the best of the colored people in the United States, while they enjoy five times as much liberty, as ladies and gentlemen in the possession of all the comforts of life, and this in a nation of their own.

The Legislative body is now in session. Respectable citizens from every county are doing the business of Government; and it is delightful to behold. Ladies and gentlemen from the United States men-of-war came to see those colored men making laws for their young republic, and it is truly wonderful to see how well they get on.

There are several wealthy merchants here. Messrs. Payne and Yeats, J. B. and Uriah Magill, D. B. Warren, and Mr. A. Johns, J. M. Roberts, and Mr. Roy.

If a number of our enterprising citizens of the United States were to turn their attention to this country for a few years, with their modern arts and sciences, and means, they would make a fortune in a few years from minerals and the natural productions of the earth. Not only that, but they would, also, so improve the country that it would be the beauty and desire of the whole world. We want silversmiths and mechanics of all kinds. They would find a great deal to do here. The people of the Eastern and Western States are known to be a peaceful and thriving people, of great enterprise and intelligence. Those are the people that we want here to light up this great quarter of the world with religion, the arts and sciences. Agriculture would also thrive well here, and is much needed. The water, both in the wells and springs, is good. It is very pure and sweet. I find the weather no warmer here than in the United States during the summer.

Money seems to be plenty, but provisions are scarce. We want more men on the land, so that the earth may bring forth of its abundance.

Judge Benedick, who is a very worthy man, is quite wealthy, and has a beautiful coffee plantation, with numerous flocks and herds. There is here room for plenty of blacksmiths, shoemakers, tailors, carpenters, cabinet-makers and bakers, who could make a noble living in this country. A butcher would do well, as he could get his cattle of the natives extremely low, and supply the shipping. That business would pay well.

A man came out from Indiana, in the last ship, to get land for the free colored people of that State. He is a minister, Rev. Mr. McKay. He preached on Sabbath morning, Christmas day. A great many are coming out at this time, and the most of them are well pleased with the country. The most of those who came out some three or four years since have become wealthy. Among these is Rev. Dr. John Moore, from Baltimore, a worthy man, who is not only useful in the Church, but also as a physician. He has two stores, and is also a farmer. A man named Murray, who came here a short time since with $16, is now worth $1,600. He trades with the natives.

Two men went from Charleston, S.C., with the intention of going to Liberia, but the people of the Northern States advised them not to go. That was a great error. If Mr. Payne and Mr. Catto had gone forth according to their covenant, they would have been doubly useful in the Church, and would, by this time, have been men of wealth and eminence. But they are just as they were, and no better, like many others who would rather remain half free and half slave, in a country that they cannot travel without being stopped and examined as though they were thieves and robbers.

I have visited Liberia without fee or reward, or any salary, or any promise of remuneration, trusting only in the promises of my blessed Lord, for the benefit of my beloved and afflicted brethren, and the promotion of the Gospel. I thank the Lord that I was obedient unto the heavenly calling, for it is of great value to me, and a blessing to my fellow-men. I have seen the wonderful works of the Lord both by land and sea, and I can say of a truth unto all mankind, serve the Lord, and it will go well with you forever. If half the time and money that has been spent to oppose this noble enterprise, had been expended to favor and to aid it, one half of Africa might have been civilized by this time, the Gospel preached in the midst thereof, and missions and Sabbath-schools dotting its hills and valleys. The great amount of time spent in contention on the floor of Congress and elsewhere, in relation to this subject, is a clear loss. There is no other way than this by which the colored people can obtain their deliverance and return to their own land—no other way by which they can arrive at self-government.

Since I have visited Africa, I can say of a truth that that noble institution is the most important and beneficial philanthropic movement in the United States of America. It has done, and is still doing, more for the benefit of the colored people than anything else which has been attempted for that object.

It does not appear to me to be anything like wisdom for men to condemn matters they know nothing about. Let them first see and examine, and they may then be able to judge in part; but the judgment of ignorant men is worse than nothing. But it is too late now to oppose this good and noble work. It is going forward. I believe that the Lord is in it, and it will go on, and I trust that the blessed Son will prosper it in all cases. Monrovia stands upon a hill—upon rocks, and a vast bed of iron ore.

There is another thing which would be of great benefit to this settlement. Let men of science, both white and colored, go out to Liberia to instruct the youths of both sexes—to make them acquainted with all useful knowledge, which has been denied to us in by-gone days, by reason of prejudice and slavery. But, thanks be to the Lord, these evils exist not in this country.

We want no drunkards in our land, nor fiddlers, nor dancers, nor gamblers, nor idlers of any kind. But we want good men and good women; upright, honest, sober, industrious, moral and religious persons, economical in their habits and setting good examples to those who come after. These are the kind of people that we want for laying the foundation of a great nation, like unto that which is now about to be laid in Western Africa. By the blessing of the Lord, and the aid of our good friends in the United States of America, we bid fair to become one of the greatest nations upon the earth.

I say that we want farmers, which are the bone and sinew of a country, and mark out the only path which leads to prosperity, wealth and plenty. The earth is pregnant with all kinds of mineral and vegetable productions. All we need is the ways and means, and proper instruction, to enable us to come at them. We are looking to our good friends in America to aid and assist us in all those important enterprises. If they aid us, we shall do well.

CHAPTER VI.

The Author visits several places in the vicinity of Monrovia. He speaks a number of times in the Churches. He sails for Sierra Leone. On the passage Mr. Caldwell is very sick, and the Steward tries to get possession of his property. The Author opposes this nefarious attempt. They arrive in Sierra Leone. The Author finishes his business and sails for Gambia. Arrival in Gambia. Mahometans; Idolators; treatment of criminals under the British rule. The Author prefers the United States Government. He sails in the Isla de Cuba for the United States. Storms at sea. The Author trusts in the Lord. Two men concealed on board. The Gulf Stream. Arrival at New-York.

On Thursday evening, Dec. 22, 1853, I preached in Monrovia, from the 133d Psalm, "Behold, how good and how pleasant it is for brethren to dwell together in unity." The meeting was well attended. The President is a member of the Methodist Church; and all the distinguished men are members of some Church. I have an appointment again on Sabbath evening, the Lord be pleased.

Liberia would never have been the home of the immigrants,

had it not been for a woman. When the first settlers were preparing themselves resting-places, the natives came upon them
with hostile intent. One woman only remained in her house, the
other inhabitants having fled. She fired upon the natives until
she had succeeded in killing quite a number of them. The survivors fled. The name of the woman was Mrs. Newport; and she
secured a *new port* for the colored people. The natives never
returned.

On Sabbath, Christmas-day, a man from Indiana spoke in the
Church, from Isaiah, 53d chapter. I spoke in the afternoon to a
very full house. All the first families were present, the President
and his family, the Vice-President, Secretaries, Merchants, &c.
I spoke from Matt., chap. ii., v. 10.

On Thursday, 29th, I spoke at Millsburg. I went from Monrovia with a number of men to examine the land. We went up
St. Paul's river. We travelled through the woods, thickets, and
brambles. We spent the most of the day in this great wood. We
did not see so much as a frog or any other animal. In the evening, we returned to Caldwell, and spent a very agreeable evening with Mr. Richardson. We finished our business, and on Sat-
urday came back to Monrovia. I stopped with Squire Moore, as
Mrs. Teague was sick and her house shut up.

Rev. Mr. McKay spoke on Sabbath afternoon, and I spoke in
the evening. Rev. Mr. Burns spoke in the morning.

On January 2d, 1854, President Roberts and Vice-President
Benson were both installed in office. The utmost decorum was
observed. The hall was crowded; all the first people of the place
were present, officers of the Navy, ladies, &c.

On the 6th, Mr. Caldwell and myself took a walk to the Government Farm, a very thriving spot, and extremely pleasant.

I closed the meeting on Sabbath forenoon, and spent the day
very agreeably with brethren and sisters. But I do not say that
everybody is good in Liberia, for there are some disorderly persons here as well as in other countries.

President Roberts and family attend meeting every Sabbath,
and sit directly in front of the altar. Both himself and lady

are very mild and pleasant people, hospitable and attentive to strangers.

On Friday, 10th January, we all dined with Judge Benson, now Vice-President. On the 13th, all the ministers went to Conference, down to Sino, and the Senators all went home. On the 14th, we had a severe thunderstorm, and another on the 16th of the month. On Sabbath, I spoke at the Baptist Church at 3 P.M. There was a full house, and we had a very good time. I closed meeting in the evening, at the Mission M.E. Church.

David Moore, Esq., at whose house I put up, is a judge, and stands high in the community. He is also quite wealthy. He owns much land, which is well cultivated, also flocks and herds, such as cattle, sheep, goats, and hogs. They come every evening and lie down before his door in a grove of orange and coffee trees, which are breaking down under their burden of ripe fruit. This man was once a slave, but is now a government officer in this young and growing Republic. Mr. Moore is a tanner, a shoe-maker, a soap-maker, a farmer, and a justice of the peace. He is quite dark in his complexion.

On the 18th of January, I went on board the English steamer Hope, from Plymouth, bound to Sierra Leone. She is a mail boat. The company have four boats on the line. One is called Faith, another Hope, and another Charity. When I first went on board, I did not know that the time of sailing would be delayed till nine o'clock at night. After enjoying a good supper, with the company and a number of passengers, all very respectable persons, we set sail for Sierra Leone. It is about 240 miles from Monrovia. From Sierra Leone to Gambia is about 412 miles.

We had a very pleasant passage. The sea was as smooth as the Hudson River. The fare on board was excellent. I never found a better table on board of any boat; all fared alike, without distinction. During the passage Mr. Caldwell was very sick, and Dr. Paterson placed him under the charge of the steward of the forward cabin. A spoonful of brandy was ordered to be given him every quarter of an hour, which was done for twenty-four hours or more, so that the poor man was permitted to rest in quiet but a little while at a time; I spoke against such proceedings, and they were very angry with me, and said that I had no business to interfere, as the doctor gave the patient up to the steward's charge. The steward's aim was to get the man's effects into his possession. He had a good watch and clothing; and therefore, the steward made the sick man believe that he was his best friend. He would not leave him for a moment; he hugged him and kissed him, and declared that although he was a white man and Mr. Caldwell was a colored man, yet he would never leave him or forsake him. He drew up writings for Mr. Caldwell to sign, in which all the effects of the patient were made over to him. He urged Mr. Caldwell to sign these writings, while in his weak and dying state.

I opposed all this strongly, but I had no power, for it was a British vessel and British officers, bound to one of their own ports. As I was only one, and they were many, I left the whole matter in the hands of the blessed Lord. He pleaded my cause, and fought my battles, and overthrew all their wicked designs. He kept the man alive until we got into port.

While we were at sea, I told them that if they took any improper steps, I would report them to the American Consul. They did not care much for that; but the blessed Lord is high over all, and blessed for evermore. Therefore, I recommend to all mankind that they serve Him in spirit and in truth.

After I had settled my affairs in Sierra Leone, I went on board the steamer Hope, bound to Gambia, on the coast of Africa. We had a pleasant passage, no distinction was made in the treatment of passengers.

When we arrived at Gambia, I visited the Churches, schools, markets, and public buildings, and took note of the manners and habits of the people. Many of the inhabitants are Mahometans. Others wore charms about their persons and are loaded with idols. They may be seen sitting or lying in the sand, in large gangs, worshipping their false gods. They wear long robes and sandals, but are half naked. There are more than a hundred tongues or languages among them, so that the one part do not understand the rest.

Criminals are put in prison, and formed into chain gangs. These are chained two together, and on the back of their jackets is the word CONVICT. They wear red caps. They are made to work in the streets, and every three months they are flogged on the back. Such is the rule under the English Government: but in Liberia there is no such barbarity practised.

Jan'y. 31st. The United States ship-of-war Constellation, Com. Mayo, arrived at this port and fired a salute, which was answered by the fort at Gambia.

The barque Isla de Cuba, now lying in this port, will sail in a few days for New-York, United States. Capt. Forsyth is going passenger in the Isla de Cuba, Capt. Miller.

I remained in the town of Gambia nine days, and spent three days on board the ship.

3d. All hands on board. Mr. Forsyth and lady came on board at 12 o'clock. On the evening of Thursday, Mr. Forsyth spent the time very agreeably with some of his friends over champagne. They then bade adieu and parted. The pilot came on board at half past three on Friday morning. His name is Pompey Gay. He makes about £260 a year, and out of that he receives £60 for his own use. He is a colored man. The colored people do all the out-of-door work here, but the *sixty pounds for himself!* Such is the boast of English freedom. Give me the Government of the United States forever, in preference to such liberty. Take away slavery, and nothing like the U.S. Government was ever known. I have learned that by travelling abroad, and making use of my eyes and ears.

The author conceives that, at this rate, those who are called *free* in England give to their employers a much larger portion of the proceeds of their toil, than the American planter receives from those colored men in his service who are called *slaves*. And the gains of this colored pilot are in about the same ratio as those of other "free" colored men who are subjects of the Crown.

Feb. 4th. At sea. All well. We left the Capes on the forenoon of 3d inst. In a short time, we caught a favorable breeze, stiff and strong, and we made good headway.

5th. Sabbath. We have been at sea three days. Fine weather and fair wind. All well.

6th. Thank the Lord we are well. The wind is fair, with occasional calm.

7th. Thank the Lord we are tolerable. Good weather; light wind, but fair.

8th. Fine weather and fair wind. Thank the Lord, we are all tolerably well.

9th. Fine weather and fair wind. All well.

10th. All well. Fine weather and fair wind.

11th. Fair wind and weather. All well at this time.

12th. Ten days out. This day is the Sabbath. Fine weather. Thank the Lord, we are all well.

13th. Fine weather; all well. We saw a ship to-day, to leeward. The seamen are all busily engaged in cleaning and painting the ship. Capt. Miller is a very particular man.

14th. All well. A little breeze.

15th. All well. Light breeze. In the afternoon a good breeze sprung up and we got on finely.

16th. All well. We had a fine rain shower this morning. In the afternoon we had quite a gale; but we are in the hands of the Lord. He is our only help in the time of trouble. When we left Gambia, Africa, there were two Frenchmen stowed away in the hold of the ship, and after we got to sea, they came up and showed themselves to the captain. When the captain heard their story, he put them in charge of the mate, to work their passage to the United States.

17th. All well. A fair breeze. We are getting on very well, thank the Lord.

18th. Fine weather and a good breeze. The mate found a live scorpion on board. They killed it. We saw several whales; they were quite large ones.

19th. Sabbath. It is a little stormy, but we are getting on very well.

20th. Light, fair breeze; getting on very well.

21st. Fair wind, but light; getting on very well. We are thankful that we are all well.

22d. Fair wind, but light. All well.

23d. Fair, but light breeze.

24th. We have a fair wind from the East, with rain. In the afternoon it blew a perfect gale, and rained very hard. All hands were called, cook and steward. At about 4 P.M. the storm ceased. The clouds broke away, and the sun shone again, thanks be to the Lord. Before the gale came on, we were in that part of the sea where the winds are variable, between the coast of Africa and the West Indies. There was a calm for some days; the wind shifting all around the compass in a few hours. The gale carried us swiftly over that part of the ocean; until we caught the American breeze, which is sweet and cool. There is a great deal of grass afloat in the sea for thousands of miles. It looks pretty, and is called the gulf weed. It grows in or near the Gulf Stream. We see many birds flying on this coast, of different kinds.

25th. A severe gale from the East for more than 24 hours. We are thankful that the wind is favorable. We have seen three ships since we left Gambia.

26th. Sabbath. We are 24 days out. The wind is high and the sea rough. We are near the Bahama Islands, getting on very well.

27th. We have a good fair wind, and are getting on very well. We are near the Gulf Stream.

28th. The wind is high and not fair. The sea is rough, and the weather getting cold. We saw one schooner to-day, the fourth vessel we have seen since we left Gambia, Africa.

March 1st. We are in the Gulf Stream. It is quiet and calm. We saw two ships to-day going out. This evening, we saw the new moon.

2d. We are getting on slowly. Quite calm. Saw this morning a fore-top-sail schooner, supposed to be bound to New-York. She kept company with us all day. We came to the Gulf in the night. It was very rough indeed.

3d. The sea is very rough. Wind high: we are thankful it is favorable. We have shipped several very heavy seas this morning. It is said that we are about 400 miles from New-York. The blessed Lord has ever been, and still is, our only defence and help in the time of need; therefore, we will do the best we can, and trust

Him in all cases. I thank the Lord, we have got through the Gulf. This afternoon it is four weeks since we left Africa. We are now on the coast of America.

4th. It is said that the Gulf Stream is 70 miles in width. It is very boisterous and rough indeed. We had to take in and reef sails. We crossed near Norfolk, Va., and are now steering up the coasts of Maryland, Delaware and Jersey. The wind is not fair. A steamer going South, passed us last evening.

5th. Sabbath. Very windy, stormy and cold. We saw the Jersey shore. All well.

CHAPTER VII.

The Author relates part of a conversation with an English officer. Some description of Gambia and its inhabitants. Necessity of cultivation. The minds of the natives must be cultivated as well as the land. Fine opportunities in Africa for steamboats, and enterprising men generally. Cape Mount. No newspaper in Liberia. An excellent opening for Frederick Douglass. Address to the rulers of Liberia. The necessity of treating the natives well and respecting their rights. Duties of parents and teachers. The young should be instructed. Mr. Horne in Monrovia. Mrs. Ann Wilkins. Mr. Phillips, a colored teacher.

IN the last chapter, I gave an account of my passage from Gambia to New-York. I thought myself fortunate in finding the barque Isla de Cuba, Capt. Miller, at Gambia, and also in securing the same state-room and berth that I had occupied in the outward passage.

While on my passage in the British Mail Steamer Hope, I conversed freely with one of the chief officers, who informed me that their company were fitting out a strong line of steamers in England, for the coasts of Africa and America, and also to explore the river Niger. They intend to leave no stone unturned in their African researches. He said that Africa would be the land of a great nation. He spoke in favor of Liberia. I told him that her Government was better than any that I had seen, except that of the United States.

The town of Gambia looks well as you approach it in front from the sea, but the most of the people seem to be wild and uncultivated. The greater part are the blackest persons that I ever saw. Among them are some Portuguese, but they are all under the English Government. But all are free in the Republic of Liberia. That seems to be the most desirable part of Africa. It was very cold in Gambia in the morning; I walked through the markets and saw the people lying about in the sand like pigs, half naked, both heathen and Mahometans, loaded down with charms and idols, going about shaving each other's heads, and cutting up a hundred pranks which you never saw nor heard of. We see many new things in this country, but the power of the Lord is here as well as elsewhere.

It is very interesting, and also very solemnizing, to visit the Protestant Episcopal Church in Gambia; to see the various nations, with their varied manners, dress, features, and complexion. This last is of every shade, from the white to the most intensely black. Some of the congregation are dressed in the most fashionable style of the day—many of them with turbans as high as a sugar-loaf, and of the same form, composed of handkerchiefs of different colors; while the greater part are barefooted and half-naked. But they are all seeking the same thing, and in this they understand each other. They seem to be all in unity; they all come to Church to hear the Gospel preached, and to hear of the wonderful works of the Lord.

I visited the Wesleyan Methodist Church in Gambia, Rev. Mr. Meddows, pastor. He preached from the 33d Psalm. I saw a great many natives there, dressed in all forms and fashions, nearly all of them barefooted. There were six or eight very respectable looking white persons present. There were more than three hundred school children present, who performed the singing. They practise every day under their worthy teacher, Mr. Boaza, a colored gentleman of high standing in that community. The organ and the player are just behind the children, who are instructed in all the arts of civilization. They are put to all kinds of trades, learning of ship-carpenters, smiths, tailors, &c.

I attended a meeting in which I heard a colored man preach

and pray in the native tongue. He is one of the natives, and having experienced religion, and learned to read the Bible, was considered capable of explaining it to the natives in their own language.

I trust that all good people of all nations will be roused up to the great work of civilizing the human family, and spreading the Gospel throughout the whole world, so that peace and tranquillity may prevail in every part of the earth, and the triumphant songs of redeemed spirits be heard in every green valley and upon every hill-top. Then will the nations learn war no more, and all tears will be wiped from the eyes of the mourners in Zion.

The only way to redeem Africa is to settle it as soon as possible. Take hold of the land, cultivate it, and in employing the natives, cultivate their minds at the same time that the land is rendered fruitful. Set good examples before them, and treat them well. In that way, we should soon gain both themselves and the land, and should all become one people in manners, habits, and religion. Then we should all become full citizens, and enjoy all the privileges of other nations.

The minds of the natives and the land are just alike while uncultivated. The lands want ploughing up and sowing down with grain, and the different kinds of herd grass, and it is necessary to cross the breed of their flocks and herds.

The minds of the natives must be broken up with the ploughshare of the Gospel, and the seeds of grace, love, and unity must be planted in their minds, and they will bring forth much fruit to the glory of God, and be a blessing to the human family. I see that the Law and Gospel must work together in unity for the improvement of this country; and when brought to bear upon it, they will carry everything before them. Darkness and heathen principles will flee away, and wisdom and light must follow. Therefore, we have nothing to fear if we live according to the Gospel of our Lord and Saviour Jesus Christ; for it will then go well with us in time and in eternity. If the Lord is for us, he is more than all that are against us: therefore will I ever trust Him in all things.

I saw that a number of the natives had joined the Church in Monrovia, and had become good members; and still more of them are coming in. They are very much pleased with our people, and always ready to serve them. Therefore we ought to treat them well in all things, for the lands were in their possession until those days when a more enlightened people came among them. They want more ministers in Liberia, for the harvest is great and the laborers are few. Therefore pray that more laborers may be sent forth into the vineyard.

I am about to join the mission, myself, if the Lord be pleased, and permit me so to do; for I always endeavor to obey the dictates of the Good Spirit, knowing that in doing so, I am sure to do right.

When I went up Saint Paul's River, I spent about eight days at the Mission House, with Mrs. Wilkins, a white lady, in the town of Millsburgh. I preached there in the evening. Saint Paul's is a fine river for steamboating; and if some of the New-York go-ahead citizens were to put a steamboat upon its waters, they would soon become rich men. If a steamboat ran between New-York and Africa, there would be an immense trade carried on of great value to the two nations. Besides, there are about two thousand miles of distance on the African coast where the sea is as calm as the Hudson or Delaware river, so that a good steamer could run along the coast without the least danger.

The flag of this young republic is *one star and eleven stripes*. We trust that many stars will be added, until all this quarter of the globe will be brought fully under the Law and the Gospel. If so, this will be the garden spot of the world. In Liberia, three parts of the day are very pleasant, a fresh breeze blowing in from the sea. The nights and days are always equal, twelve hours each. The fruit and coffee trees are bending with their luscious burdens, which, with many other valuable articles ready for market, are held at disadvantage for want of more speedy means of conveyance.

There are a great many very respectable colored people in Liberia. If I must speak the truth, they seem to be better informed than those who are in the United States. The Church and the Sabbath-School are conducted as orderly as among us, and I think are doing more good, in every respect, than ours.

I hope that the good citizens of the United States will put steamboats between New-York and Africa very soon, and upon the waters along the coast, wherever emigrants may be settled from any part of the world. The boats would all pay well: therefore, gentlemen, you have nothing to fear. Go a-head, and you will be successful, and will do much towards building up this young Republic.

I say of a truth, that if the colored people neglect to embrace or refuse this noble opportunity now offered to them, and let it fall and come to nothing, they will never rise above their present condition. They will be doomed to slavery forever. But I have a better opinion of my colored brethren in the United States. I trust that all of them will see and know that it is upon this noble enterprise of settling Liberia, that the salvation of the whole colored population depends. It depends upon our own actions and efforts to do our duty, and to secure our rights and liberties in Monrovia, Liberia—a land that has been kept and preserved for us for thousands of years: and now the time is fulfilled, and the friends of the colored race have opened a door for us that we might enter in and enjoy our rights and privileges without money and without price. In a few years, the independence of Liberia will be acknowledged by all nations.

I think that Cape Mount is a rich and beautiful part of Africa, and when cultivated and the inhabitants civilized, will be a very desirable place of residence. A great deal of wealth is yet to be obtained from that elevated portion of Africa. In fact, it is a pleasant country throughout; all things are plenty, the leaves are all green, the sufferings of slavery are nowhere to be seen, all men enjoying their rights and liberties under their own vine and fig-tree, with none to make them afraid.

All those who are not friends to the settlement of Liberia, are no friends to the African race, nor to themselves or their country. A great many people are prejudiced by stupid reports founded upon ignorance and idle conjecture. But the colored man who is wise, will do like the Queen of Sheba; he will go and judge for himself, and then he will say that this work is of the Lord. He has prospered our labors thus far, and with his help, we are bound to go on in this noble enterprise, for the benefit of the African nation, who are as precious in the eyes of the Lord as any other nation upon the face of the earth. What a blessing it is that the people of the United States have laid a foundation for us sure and steadfast! We trust, therefore, that every wise man will see eye to eye on this subject, and lay aside all opposition. Let every one join in this noble work, and all the sons of Africa will soon be free, and religion and civilization will spread over that great quarter of the earth, to the glory and honor of the blessed Son, and the happiness of the human family, and to the praise and prosperity of the United States, which the Lord has made the instrument for bringing about this great deliverance for the sons and daughters of Africa. It may be the means of civilizing the whole world of mankind, and also fulfilling the Scriptures of Truth, which say that the Gospel of the Kingdom shall be preached unto all the world for a witness, and then shall the end come. Oh! that this great republic may be the agent in fully accomplishing this great and glorious work, so that an everlasting blessing of peace and happiness may rest upon this land and nation!

There is no newspaper published in any of the places which I visited on the coast of Africa. I think that if such men as Mr. Frederick Douglass would give their time, attention, and talent to Liberia, they would do more good in one year, than they can in a whole life-time in the United States. They would make five times as much money, and impart instruction and civilization to our heathen brethren. There we may do a great deal of good without opposition or confusion; for many things which we are endeavoring to do in the United States, are like pouring water upon a goose's back; it has but little or no effect. Therefore such labors are of no value at all. We hope that all persons who wish the colored man well, will give their aid and attention to this noble work, so that light and the Gospel may soon spread over that dark and benighted land of our forefathers in Africa.

I must confess, that at one time I was blinded, like many of you, to these important matters which regard the welfare of the colored population: but I now see plainly what must and will be done, for their general good and elevation; and I thank the Lord that the work is commenced, and, with his blessing, will go on.

Now let me make a few remarks to the humane rulers of this new Republic: Gentlemen, I have had the pleasure and honor of visiting your well-founded government, with which I am very much pleased indeed, and I am under a thousand obligations both to the chief officers of State and Church, for their Christian fellowship, and kind, gentlemanly treatment while I was among you. I had never before seen freedom and liberty existing among our people, until I saw it in Monrovia, Liberia, Africa, under the administration of his excellency President J. J. Roberts, and his wise counsel, in the year of our Lord 1854. There is nothing to be compared with this on the face of the earth for the colored nation, nor ever has been since the days of Noah. If we neglect this great opportunity, we shall be undone forever, in a temporal point of view. Now, to the rulers of this republic: forasmuch as the Lord has blessed you, and has lifted you up above your fellow-men, and has set you up on high—whether in Church or State—it is for you to take heed to yourselves. In all your doings, remember the commandments of the Lord. Do not oppress the poor, the fatherless, the widow, nor the stranger. Do unto all men as you would like to have them do unto you. Consider well the natives of that great quarter of the earth. It has been theirs for nearly four thousand years. They, truly, were the sole proprietors: but we see that sin and idolatry have brought them to their present, low, degraded position. Now, all they want is good government, good rulers, good instructions, and good treatment. If they have these, they will all be brought in, and we will become a great nation, for the good of all mankind, and to the glory and honor of our blessed Lord and Saviour Jesus Christ.

Therefore, let us be very careful how we deal with those natives, lest we bring upon ourselves a reproach and incur the displeasure of the blessed Lord, and be finally driven out of that land in a more degraded condition than the present natives are at this time. And now, as the Lord has placed wise and good men at the head of the government in Liberia, we pray that there may be always good men to fill the important offices of State. If not, let the same remain in office who have been faithful in the fulfilment of their duties from the commencement of the Republic up to the present time. Bad men make bad governments: good men make good governments.

In conclusion, I must say that it is the duty of all persons to seek the peace and happiness of their families, neighbors, Churches, States and nations. The way to obtain these blessings is to commence early: the heads of every family to give early instruction to their children; teach them to love and fear the Lord; teach them to love and obey their parents; teach them to love themselves and respect their neighbors; teach them to conduct kindly towards all mankind; teach them to love the ministers of the Gospel and the Church of Christ; teach them to respect and obey magistrates, principal men, and those who are in power; teach them to love their books, and the use and benefit of learning.

If you, as fathers and mothers, will carry out these duties, I can assure you that you will have happy families, good neighbors, Christian Churches, peaceable nations; and the blessing of the Lord will rest upon you and yours forever.

If you desire that your children should be respectable, give them trades, and all the learning that you possibly can. Let them understand reading and writing well. Give them a full knowledge of arithmetic, grammar, geography, navigation, and mensuration; and let them learn every other useful science and art that they possibly can. It will do them good, and be a blessing to themselves and others.

I pray that the rulers of nations, ministers of Churches, heads of families, and all those who have charge of the rising generation, will please consider these important matters well; and if they are fully carried out, in a few years you will have a heaven upon the earth; and what a noble blessing it will be to that young and flourishing Republic, Liberia, in Western Africa, and to the colored population throughout the world!

There is the Rev. Mr. Horne, in Monrovia, a real Christian and gentleman, who has done, and is doing all the good he can, by preaching to colored people in Liberia. He is chief teacher in the academy also. He is a white brother, faithful and worthy. I hope that the good people of the States will not let him suffer. There is Mrs. Ann Wilkins also, who, as well as Mr. Horne, has been there a long time, and both have done a great deal of good. They must be cared for. Mrs. Wilkins intends shortly to return home; and Mr. C. A. Pitman and Miss Sarah M. Reynolds, both colored persons, will remain as teachers. Mr. Phillips, a colored brother, teaches on the lower floor, and is a worthy man also.

> Let every soul in every station
>   Join their assistance, who can tell
> But God may turn and bless this nation—
>   Let no contention among them dwell.

May the blessed Lord ever bless the labors of his faithful servants in all places.

Before concluding, the Author would draw the attention of the reader to the case of the Rev. Samuel Williams, of whom mention is made at page 85,* as being one worthy of notice.

The Rev. Samuel Williams, an Elder, and one of the most respectable inhabitants of Johnstown, in Western Pennsylvania, some time since, visited Liberia with his son, 16 years of age, who was very sick; and after remaining there a year, returned to the United States with his son, entirely recovered, in good health, and greatly improved in growth and appearance. His mother was so rejoiced on seeing her child fully restored to health, he

---

*[EDITOR'S NOTE: The reference to "page 85" is to page 85 of the original. In this edition, the Rev. Mr. Williams is mentioned on pages 42–44.]

having been sickly from infancy, that she determined at once to remove to Liberia, Western Africa, and there to dwell, with the blessing of the Lord. The Rev. Mr. Williams took all his family with him, young and old, including his respectable and venerable mother, nearly ninety years of age, and was accompanied by more than thirty of the most respectable colored persons in the State of Pennsylvania. They embarked in the good bark Isla de Cuba, at the same time as the Author of this work, and arrived there safe, and in good health. The Author visited them previous to his departure, and found them very comfortable and pleasantly situated, and well pleased with the country—the old lady sitting on the porch apparently as happy as the Queen of Shebah. They testified to their preference for that young and flourishing Republic of the Single Star and eleven stripes. May the Lord prosper it forever!

The Hon. J. J. ROBERTS, at present President of the Republic of Liberia, Africa, stands higher, in a national point of view, than any colored person in the United States, or in any other portion of the known civilized world.

CONCLUDING REMARKS.

I THANK the Lord that he has raised up many kind friends to the colored people, who are willing to aid them in obtaining a resting place, so that they shall no more be driven about the earth, without a home and without a country, mere hewers of wood and drawers of water for those who are more favored by the laws and customs of those countries in which they live.

There are many such good friends to us in the United States, and particularly in New-York and New-Jersey, ladies and gentlemen of high standing, of wealth and intelligence, and of most exemplary lives and the most exalted piety, who have devoted their time and their talents to our benefit, in order that they may provide a home and a country for my afflicted nation. Among these are the following names, which I give in this place, in order that my colored brethren and sisters may know upon whom they may depend:

Hon. Anson G. Phelps, the distinguished Christian and Philanthropist.

A. G. Phelps, Jr. Esq., the Rising Star of the Empire City.

Hon. J. A. Westervelt, Mayor of New-York.

E. Canning, Esq.

Robert Lewis, Esq., No. 209 Fulton street.

O. B. Porter, Esq.

E. Harrison, Esq., who promises to aid the Author.

R. Bowler, Esq.

Rev. J. B. Wakely, Forsyth street.

Rev. J. B. Pinney, Bible House.

Rev. Mr. Jessop, Second street.

Robert P. Cune, Esq.

P. S. Peet, Esq.

Mr. Kelso.

Mrs. Few.

Rev. Dr. Cox, Brooklyn.

Rev. E. Johnson.

Rev. Mr. Whitaker, M. E. Church.

W. C. Barker, Esq.

David S. Holmes, Esq.

Mrs. Pierrepont.

T. Price, Esq.

J. Beebe, Esq.

H. L. Williams.

D. Galliway, Esq., Grand street.

Messrs Phillips & Hadley.

Mrs. Eliza Doughty.

Mr. Marven, Water street.

Joseph Hegerman, Esq.

S. Knowlton, Esq.

Mr. Ward, Greene street.

Rev. Dr. Bond, Greenwich street.

Dr. W. W. Hall, Ewen Place.

Rev. Mr. Benning, East Twenty-Eighth street.

Rev. M. Bell, Brooklyn.

E. Spencer, Esq.

John B. Wilson, Esq.

Hon. D. S. Manners, Mayor of Jersey City.

B. B. Grinnell, Esq.

G. W. Cassidy, Esq.

J. J. H. Beck, Esq.

A. G. Mason, Esq.

Joseph Kissam, Esq.

Henry Demarest, Esq.

John D. Jones, Esq.

S. Davidson, Esq.

M. Daniels, Esq.

David Taylor, Esq.

A. A. Dean, Esq.

George Peters, Esq.

W. E. Whiting, Esq.

Dr. S. P. Townsend.
Stephen Willets.
J. W. Knapp, Esq.
Dr. N. A. G———
Dr. D. E. C———
Wm. Janeway, Esq.
R. Minturn, Esq.
J. Chandler, Esq.
R. H. Hopkins, Esq.
H. M. Schieffelin, Esq.
Mrs. A. G. Phelps.

AT ROME AND UTICA.

Hon. Seth Roberts, Judge.
Hon. E. Huntington and Brother.
C. Comstock, Esq., Editor.
Messrs. A. S. Sanford & Co., Editors.
P. Ainsworth, Esq.
Hon. Judge P. Gridley.
N. H. Dering, Esq.
O. B. Mattison, Esq.
H. Green, Esq.
Dr. G. W. Pope.
S. W. Moody.
H. Rogers.
Mrs. Blanchard, 61 State street, Brooklyn.
Mrs. Jacobs, 77 Henry street.
Dr. Jackson, Albany.
Mrs. Delavan.
Mrs. Bosely.
Mrs. Bradford (of the Boudinot Family), Burlington, N.J.
With many other kind, liberal, and humane friends whom we
shall mention in a second edition.

The Author is fully satisfied that nothing can elevate the colored population to an equality with the rest of mankind, but the
full and free enjoyment, in a national point of view, of civil and
religious rights, in addition to a system of universal education.

The benevolent ladies of the United States are the main-spring, movers, and sustainers of the Christian Churches, and all humane and benevolent institutions.

Although I am happy to see there are many kind noble-hearted and liberal citizens in the city of New-York, both gentle-men and ladies, there is a large number said to be our best friends, who are somewhat left-handed and very close, only aid-ing one way, let the distress of others be as it will. This is not according to the Gospel of our Lord and Saviour Jesus Christ.

I do truly and sincerely thank those benevolent ladies and gentlemen of New-York and New-Jersey, to whom we are so much indebted, and pray that all the blessings of this life and that which is to come, may forever surround them—in this world, health, prosperity and happiness, and in the next, life everlasting.

Owing to the want of time, and the desire of the people to see this report of my visit to Liberia, the Author has made but little mention of his labors in this country, subsequently to leaving Bethel Church of Philadelphia. In a second edition, he will en-deavor to be more full on that point. It may not be amiss, how-ever, to append a few certificates delivered me by friends in Rome, State of New-York:

(CERTIFICATES.)

"Rev. D. H. Peterson has faithfully finished his services in behalf of the colored Church at Rome, Oneida County, New-York, which Church is now free from all embarrassments. He has for a long time been laboring to instruct and improve his breth-ren spiritually and temporally, but he is led fully to believe that their prospects here are not very encouraging. Therefore, many of his best friends, both white and colored, have advised him to go to Liberia in Africa, and see if the prospects are not better in that young Republic, where his brethren can become full citizens at once, and freeholders, and enjoy all the comforts and privileges of the country both in Church and State—where all may become a happy and religious people, and, if faithful among themselves, may eventually be the instruments in the hands of the Lord to restore that dark and great quarter of the Earth to civilization, together with the light of the Gospel and its pure teachings, that will bring an everlasting blessing upon all who are now, and have been, instrumental in carrying out this great and noble work. He is now ready to comply with the advice of his friends and brethren, as soon as practicable. We, therefore, cheerfully recommend him, and sincerely hope he will meet with favor and aid from all, more especially the Christian community at large."

"To all whom this may concern:

We, colored citizens of Rome, State of New-York, do hereby certify, that the Rev. D. H. Peterson has, for the last three years, been employed in erecting a Church at Rome, which he has fully accomplished. We now have a comfortable, neat house of worship, all paid for, and balance over. We found him faithful, and perfectly honest in his undertaking. We, therefore, cheerfully recommend him to all.

THOMAS JOHNSON,
SAMUEL DEBOIS,
WM. JOHNSON,
STEPHEN THOMPSON,
GEORGE GILBERT,
HIRAM GILBERT,
MARGARET GILBERT.

Rome, Nov. 30th, 1852."

"The bearer, Rev. Daniel H. Peterson, has been an agent in the ministry for the colored people, in Western New-York, two or three years past, in collecting funds to build Churches. He has been a faithful agent, and I believe him to be a worthy man and a Christian. Anything you can do for him will be thankfully received, and bestowed upon a deserving person.

JAMES ERWIN,
Pastor M. E. Church, Fulton, Oswego Co., N.Y."

"I am acquainted with the Rev. DANIEL H. PETERSON, and fully concur with the above recommendation and statement of the Rev. James Erwin, in relation to the bearer.

SETH B. ROBERTS,
Justice of the Peace.

Rome, Nov. 22, 1852."

The following is a true copy of a letter received by the Rev. D. H. PETERSON, from His Excellency J. J. ROBERTS, President of the Republic of Liberia, in Western Africa, written in Monrovia, the Capital of Liberia. The author has preserved the original.

"*Government House,
Monrovia, Jan'y 14th, 1854.*

This is to certify that the Rev. D. H. Peterson, from the city of New-York, United States of North America, has visited Liberia for the purpose of making observations respecting the condition, &c. of this country, for the information of his colored friends in the United States. During his visit, though short, the Rev. Gentleman, I believe, has been indefatigable in his efforts to obtain correct information on all subjects of interest connected with this Government. And I am happy to find that he is well pleased, and expressed himself highly gratified with the country, and the prospects of the people.

J. J. ROBERTS."

"January 17th, 1854.

I have had the pleasure of an introduction to the Rev. D. H. Peterson, from New-York, in the U.S. of North America. He is now on a visit to this country. I have met him in company, at different times and places. I have had the pleasure of hearing him speak in the Churches in public, and on private occasions. He came to this country on a mission to the Government and Churches. I am happy to say, that he appears to be highly pleased with the country, Government and Church, and whatever came under his observation in Liberia and the adjacent settlements, and will, no doubt, give a correct and satisfactory report upon his return to the United States of America. Our prayers are for his protection on land and by sea, and his safe return to his family, and the people, and the nation from whom he came, and that the blessings of the Almighty may attend his mission and all those who are interested in the welfare of those people.

Rev. JAMES W. HORNE.
Principal of the Academy, Monrovia,
Capital of the Republic of Liberia."

EXTRACT FROM THE JERSEY CITY SENTINEL AND ADVERTISER, OF MARCH 11, 1854.

MISSIONARY INTELLIGENCE FROM AFRICA.—The barque Isla de Cuba, Capt. A. Miller, 29 days from Gambia, West Coast of Africa, has just arrived at New-York. Among the passengers we notice the following: Rev. Mr. and Mrs. Lacy, missionaries at Lagos; Mr. and Mrs. A. Forsyth, of Gambia; and Rev. D. H. Peterson, a very intelligent and useful colored clergyman.

It will be recollected that Mr. Peterson (who publishes a card in another column) visited this city last fall, to solicit aid in a very laudable undertaking. He left New-York in November last, for Liberia, aided by gentlemen and ladies here, and in other parts of the country, interested in the welfare of the African population in the United States, to examine and report upon the condition and prospects of the new Republic. Mr. Peterson arrived at Monrovia the last of November, and spent upwards of two months in the country. The Legislature of the Republic was in session at the time, and Mr. Peterson was consequently enabled to gather from Representatives of the more remote districts, ample information pertaining to the condition of their constituents. In Monrovia he was treated with great hospitality, having been entertained by the chief functionaries of the Government, and by the principal citizens. He enjoyed uninterrupted health, and reported that to have been common to the inhabitants generally at the period of his visit.

The capital and country presented every indication of prosperity. A general sentiment of contentment pervaded the population. Industry was everywhere pursued, and thrift and comfort followed in its train. Mr. Peterson preferred the aspect of the Republic, in those respects, to that of the British settlements. Liberty, equality, and self-government, exhibit in Liberia their benignant influence.

Mr. Peterson went from Monrovia in the English mail steamer Hope, to Gambia, touching at Sierra Leone. Among his fellow-passengers was Mr. Abm. Caldwell, of New-York, who visited Liberia as an agent of a New-York Agricultural Association, part of whom have already emigrated to the Republic. Mr. C. was unwell on leaving Monrovia, and in the progress of the voyage his illness increased so as to endanger his life. An attempt on the part of one of the stewards of the ship to induce the dying man to bequeath to him his effects was foiled by the interference of Mr. Peterson, who rebuked the mercenary spirit of the interloper, and succeeded in preserving for the wife and children of the emigrant, his watch and clothing. Mr. Caldwell survived till the steamer reached Sierra Leone; he was landed about 3 P.M. and died at about eight the same evening, while under the care of a competent physician and nurse. His remains were interred the next afternoon in the Queen's burying-yard, with every appropriate demonstration of respect. Mr. Jones, the Episcopal clergyman of the place, reading the funeral service.

Mr. P. having expended all the money contributed to pay the cost of his tour, solicits contributions for his support, while engaged in completing the object of his mission.

TESTIMONIAL OF THE PASSENGERS ON BOARD THE ISLA DE CUBA.

BARQUE ISLA DE CUBA,
Approaching the Port of Monrovia, W.A.
December 17, 1853.

At a meeting of the passengers held to express their feelings in regard to the excellent qualities and conveniences of the barque, and their high appreciation of her officers, the Rev. D. H. Peterson was called to the chair, and A. Washington and William Nesbitt appointed Secretaries. After prayer, by Rev. Samuel Williams, and thanksgiving to God for his mercy and kind protection in guiding us safely over the boisterous seas and through violent storms, and permitting us to gaze over the sunny hills and verdant vales of our long-desired and adopted land, a brief, eloquent, and appropriate address was delivered by Mr. Alfred Truman. After this, the Committee reported the following resolutions, which were unanimously adopted:

Resolved, That we hereby return our thanks to Capt. Austin Miller, master of the barque Isla de Cuba, and Messrs. H. K. Hatch and McGill, first and second mates, whose kind attention and gentlemanly conduct towards us during our passage, both in sickness and in health, have secured for them a grateful place in our memory, and whose prompt attention and skill in guiding their barque safely through perilous storms, have convinced us that they are able and efficient officers.

Resolved, That duty and justice to ourselves and our friends in America, compel us to express our thanks to the American philanthropists, and record the fact that, so far as we have yet seen, they have freely done all for us that they have promised, and that we see nothing that tends to deprive us, in the least, of our free agency, and they, in this, as well as in former cases, have spared no pains in assisting the emigrants in their preparation, and in fitting out this expedition with an abundance of the best provisions that the markets afford, and in many acts of kindness, at their own expense and labor.

Resolved, That we recommend to our friends in the North who may wish at any time to emigrate to Africa, to secure their passage from the port of New-York, both for convenience and comfort, and the greater facilities for obtaining everything necessary for the passage and for trade.

Resolved, That the Committee present copies of these resolutions to the Captain of the Isla de Cuba, and to the Editors of those papers which are friendly to the emancipation of the colored population.

Rev. D. H. PETERSON,
Chairman.

A. WASHINGTON,
WM. NESBITT,
    Secretaries.
        ABRAM CALDWELL.
        JNO. H. M. HARRIS.
        JOSEPH P. BROOKS.
        THOMAS LILLASON.
        EDMUND BROWN.
        A. JOHN.
        DARIUS JACKLIN.
        SYLVANUS JACKLIN.
        Rev. SAMUEL WILLIAMS.

CHURCH COLLECTIONS.

On Sabbath-days the Collections made in many of the Churches in the United States are very badly managed. Much better plans might be adopted than are now in use in many of the Churches, both in cities and villages. Preaching three times a day, a call is made at the end of each sermon for money, &c., which destroys the good effect of the instruction just received by the congregation. Arrangements should be made with the members, and others who favor Church governments, to appoint one day in the week or month, and then pay in whatever amount they may be able for the support of the Church, &c., and thereby let the Sabbath be wholly set apart for Spiritual services.

The Author, in making the suggestion, earnestly prays that the above principles may be adopted in all Christian Churches.

––––––––––––

☞ Any communications for the Author may be left with Dr. R. F. Hibbard, No. 93 John street; or with Mrs. Hardy, at No. 35 Wall street (Mr. Furniss' office, No. 27, in the rear).*

*[EDITOR's NOTE: This statement from the original edition is obviously no longer operative. It is preserved in the present edition for reasons of historical interest.]

FOUR MONTHS IN LIBERIA:

OR

AFRICAN COLONIZATION
EXPOSED,

BY

WILLIAM NESBIT,

OF HOLLIDAYSBURG.

WITH AN INTRODUCTION

BY

DR. MARTIN R. DELANY

1855

INTRODUCTION.
By Dr. Martin R. Delany

MR. NESBIT: Having been favored, in company with other gentlemen, with hearing your MSS. read previous to going to press, and requested to give an opinion of its merits, permit me to say, Sir, that there is nothing which I could express, would add any additional interest to your graphic portrayal of the infamy of that most pernicious and impudent of all schemes for the perpetuity of the degradation of our race, the AMERICAN COLONIZATION SOCIETY. I say *most* pernicious, because it was originated in the South, by slave-holders, propagated by their aiders and abettors, North and South, and still continues to be carried on under the garb of philanthropy and Christianity, through the medium of the basest deception and hypocrisy.

Your words convey with them, their *own* introduction; and although several pamphlets, purporting to be exposures, and many letters have been written from, and concerning Liberia, yet, I venture to assert, that your description of the real state of affairs in that most unfortunate locality, by far exceeds all others which have, as yet, ever been given to the public. The subject is handled in a manner which does credit both to the head and heart of the writer; and I am much mistaken, if your little book does not meet with its deserved success. Mr. Washington's letters, written from Liberia, come nearest in inter-

[EDITOR'S NOTE: Publication data carried on the original title page of Nesbit's *Four Months in Liberia: or African Colonization Exposed* reads: "Pittsburgh, Printed by J. T. Shryock, No. 84 Fifth Street. 1855."]

est to your meritorious production, though falling far short of the *general* information contained in your work.

There are several points of interest contained in your pamphlet, which are nowhere to be found, as I remember, in any other place, and, therefore, deserve particular attention.

In the first place, it is not known by the people of this and other countries, that the *whole country* of Liberia is *daily* overflooded—the face of the earth completely *covered* by the *tide-water* from the ocean—the people being, consequently, compelled to confine themselves to the few hill-points which border the sea-coast. This is a natural hindrance to the *health* and *growth* of Liberia as it is, which the art of man, nor the laws of science, can never obviate. As well might be attempted a purification of the waters of the Dead Sea, or a successful habitation of the territory which is daily or periodically washed and overflooded by the fearful tide of the Bay of Fundy, as to attempt to remedy the diseases, and settle Liberia. They are simply a moral impossibility. That which is not in the power of man to do, and, consequently, contrary to the laws of nature.

In the second place, *slavery* in Liberia claims the attention of your readers; and on this point, I beg leave, and take the liberty of calling the particular attention of *Benjamin Cotes, Esq.* of Philadelphia, a gentleman much devoted to the cause of African civilization, giving much means thereto, but, at the same time, desirous of seeing the elevation of colored Americans at home, towards which object he also contributes very freely. I do not regard him in the light of a Colonizationist—certainly not after the manner of the Cressen and Pinney school.

This slave-holding in Liberia, may, in this country, be regarded as a libel on the people of western Africa, treating the matter with marked indifference, and unworthy of respectful consideration. Mr. Cotes is among those; but I am satisfied that a perusal of your pamphlet will fully disabuse his mind in regard to the true state of things in that miserable hovel of emancipated and superannuated slaves, and deceived colored freemen, controlled by the intrigues of a conclave of upstart colored hirelings of the slave power in the United States.

Doubtless, when the truth comes to be known, as given in your book, that advantage will be attempted to be taken of it, by proving the depravity and inferiority of our race, from this very circumstance. Our argument against this will be, that these people, the true Liberians, have mainly been themselves the servants and slaves of the whites, and, consequently, have acquired all of the folly and vices of their former wicked and unprincipled masters, considering themselves their equals, the more nearly they ape after them.

But, aside from this, they are not worse than the Circassians, the model type of the *pure white* race, inhabiting Circassia and North Georgia, in Asia; the women of whom stand continually in the public places and bazaars, offering their *daughters* as *slaves* to the passers-by; exhibiting their charms as the greater inducement to the purchaser. This, for ages, has been, and continues to the *present day,* to be the custom of the *pure white* Circassian race—the race from whom the proud Anglo-Saxon boasts of having descended. Certainly there is no custom in Africa, among the blacks, can excel, if equal, the self-degradation of this self-styled "superior" white race. But this will not palliate the villainy of Roberts, and others who servilely minister at his bidding in Liberia. The just "execration" of an injured and outraged people, must fall upon the heads of all colored men, who knowingly, are instrumental in entrapping their brethren in the trammels of this hell-originated scheme.

Concerning the Missionaries, I have always been suspicious and fearful of this class of men, along the western coast of Africa, ever believing that their presence generally among the natives, had an injurious effect,

in more ways than one. But your exposure of their pernicious and wicked traffic in *rum,* their systematic and
established rule of *cheating* the natives, and justifying
themselves therein, and probably dealing in slaves, I am
certain, however little surprised I am to hear it—and I
am *not*—will startle the true Christians of both hemi-
spheres. The conduct of these American hypocrites, is
in character with that church and religion, which can
condemn the amusement of dancing as a great sin, but
acknowledge *slave-holding* as a *Bible* institution!

Your statements but confirm a long-maintained opinion of mine, that white men generally, and *American*
white men in particular, are wholly inadequate to the
important undertaking of the establishment of colonies,
and the spread of the Gospel as missionaries among the
colored races. For the simple reason, that they are not
the proper representatives of the people for whom they
profess to act; and, therefore, cannot be proper instru-
mentalities, because of the absence of due interest and
regard for their welfare.

Had half of the money been spent in the proper education and preparation of young colored youths of both
sexes, to carry the gospel to the foreign heathen, that is
spent in support of pompous white men as missionaries;
men who have neither interest, regard, nor respect for
those races; the Gospel of Jesus Christ would have long
since been spread throughout every heathen land beneath the sun. Of this fact I have not a shadow of doubt.

Another, and the most objectionable feature of this
white missionary policy is, that their continual advent
and presence among those races, create the impression
that all great and good things are inherent in the whites,
and, therefore, must necessarily emanate from them;
thus irresistibly fixing in their minds, the assumptious
dogma of the *superiority* of the *white* race. Such are the
effects of this policy, that the people of those countries
invariably prefer the whites as teachers and rulers, to

those of people of their own race; as the course pursued in the Missionary scheme, plainly implies incapacity and insusceptibility on the part of the colored races, to occupy and fill such positions. These facts have fully developed themselves in all parts of this country, where a similar course of policy has been pursued toward the colored people, by the domineering Directors and Superintendents of the Common Schools. So servile have they become, in consequence of this, that a community in any State or County, can scarcely be found, where a *preference* is not given, as a teacher, professional or business man, or mechanic of any kind, to a *white*, by the colored people generally, rather than to one of their own color! To this there are individually exceptions always; but very few.

These Missionary operations go farther; they afford an opportunity, and induce those "men of God" to select the best portions of those foreign countries, which are quickly followed by a much more potent and effective— a *military* operation, resulting in the total overthrow and loss of such countries. Such have been the effects of their operations in Asia, different parts of Africa, the greatest islands of Oceanica, and such is likely to be the case, as the legitimate fruits of their operations in the Sandwich Islands. As in all other cases, there are a few exceptions among them. Some men and women, I believe, go out with pure and holy motives; but these are very few.

But one effect, must certainly and assuredly follow your exposure of American Colonization and Liberian infamies: a re-action among the colored people of this and other countries (as Canada and the West Indies), which shall so effectually recoil upon their heads, as to prove their successful overthrow.

The wretches who selected the tide-swamp of the coast of Guinea, instead of a healthful location in Africa, as a colony for the colored people of America, knowingly and designedly established a national Potter's Field, into which the carcass of every emigrant who ventured there, would most assuredly moulder in death.

I simply conclude by saying, that every individual in America and the world, should read or hear read, your truthful exposure of Liberia and the American Colonization Society.

Your Friend and Brother,
M. R. DELANY.

PITTSBURG, June 1st, 1855.

CHAPTER I.

False Representations of Colonization Agents. Reasons which induced me to Emigrate. Arrival There. Kindly Received. Realized the Deception.

Being a colored man, and having keenly felt the persecutions and annoyances to which my race is subject in this country, the result of the base pandering of the dough-faces to the inhuman spirit of Slavery, which has bred up the American Colonization Society, which, on all occasions, becoming and unbecoming, seeks to impress us with the doctrine that, although natives of the soil, this is not our home; that our presence here is not agreeable to the whites, nor is our condition advantageous to ourselves; that we are morally, mentally and physically, inferior; an idle, worthless, vicious population; nuisances, &c.; that there is no part of the American Continent on which we can live, and thrive, and grow; that the genius of progress has reserved the Western Hemisphere exclusively for the possession and development of the Anglo-Saxon race; that all our efforts to better our condition must prove abortive, so long as we remain occupants of the same soil, a distinct and antagonistic race. Learned divines, statesmen and logicians, assert this. They say that the God of nature designed that it should be so; that the spirit of the age and the history of American Institutions, prove that the two races cannot exist on equal terms here. And through their wiles they have succeeded in verifying these dogmas. For a colored man, let him possess ever so large a share of intelligence, refinement, wealth or enterprise—though by every principle of right and justice entitled to all the privileges and immunities of every other citizen—is basely discarded by the land of his birth, and told that if he wishes to enjoy his God-given rights, to escape the vortex they have opened for him, he must emigrate to Liberia, in Africa, which they represent as a flourishing republic, possessing the elements of greatness and usefulness; in short, being the only panacea for our wounds. This institution is a scheme of the most consummate villainy ever enacted, and though supported and applauded by some of the greatest and best of the land, by

different men, from different motives, has enlisted in its cause
as agents, some of the most unscrupulous men, white and colored, to be found anywhere; men who for the love of gold, create and circulate the most egregious falsehoods for the purpose
of fleecing the public out of their money, and living on and vic-
timizing the unsuspecting colored man. From reading and hearing on this subject, I became fired with anxiety, and determined
to test its realities; but after a brief residence there, having ocu-
lar demonstration of the iniquitous swindle, I left that, in disgust, thinking myself amongst the happiest of men to escape
that infernal snare, and believing it to be my duty to spread
these facts before the people, that they may read, reflect and
understand.

Our expedition, which consisted of fifty-three persons, all
from the Northern States, and principally from Pennsylvania,
sailed from New York on the 10th of November, 1853, under the
auspices of the American Colonization Society, on the barque
Isla de Cuba, Capt. Austin Miller; and after a passage of thirty-
eight days, having experienced probably every variety of weather
incident to a voyage at sea, we anchored off Monrovia, the Capital of Liberia, on the 18th December. Having coasted from
northward of Sierra Leone, about three hundred miles, we were
enabled to form a pretty correct idea of the coast, which is universally low, only interrupted by the high promontory of Cape
Mount.

We were kindly received by the citizens of Monrovia; indeed
I will do them the justice to say, that in their intercourse with
strangers, they are kind and hospitable, and very anxious to encourage emigration. On stepping ashore, I found that we had
been completely gulled and done for. The statements generally
circulated in this country by the Colonization agents, respecting the thrift and prosperity of that country, are most egregious
falsehoods. Everything is exaggerated. The whole country presents the most woe begone and hopeless aspect which it is possible for a man to conceive of, and having lived in this country
and seen and enjoyed the blessings of civilization, he readily conceives that he has been taken out of himself, metamorphosed

into something else, and cast away into a region of darkness and desolation, for which there is no hope.

CHAPTER II.

Describes all the Settlements in Montserrado County. No Manufactories. Trade. Titled Gentry. Slavery, &c. Treatment at Receptacle. M.E. Mission. Attempts at Farming. Cape Mount. Marshall. Population.

Monrovia, which is eligibly situated on high land on Cape Montserrado, contains about eighteen hundred of a population, colonist, and native, and presents an ancient and dilapidated appearance. The streets are broad and straight, but are so grown up with bramble bushes as to leave but a narrow path for the pedestrian. I know places in the streets of Monrovia, in which elephants might hide in perfect safety. The public buildings are three churches, Methodist, Baptist and Presbyterian, an academy, and a high school. A wooden building called the Government House, used as the head-quarters of the President, Secretaries and Post Master; also, as a printing office. A small stone building, on the first floor of which, the Courts are held, while the upper story is used as the Senate Chamber. Another small stone building in which the lower House of Representatives meets, and a rickety old jail. There are seven brick houses here, a few comfortable frame houses, but by far the largest number are very indifferent dilapidated frame and bamboo huts, certainly not worth ten dollars a piece. On all these buildings the climate has such a blighting effect, that they wear a withering and ruinous appearance; indeed, the meanest village that I know in the United States, far transcends Monrovia in the beauty of its buildings, and the appearance of its thrift. As there are no horses, cattle or beasts of burthen of any kind, all the labor has to be performed by the naked natives. The only attempt at manufacturing at all worthy of the name, is the boasted building concern of Mr. Warner—even that is on a very small scale. A great many are in the employ of the Missionary and Colonization Societies, but all, including the Missionaries themselves, are traders. Some few are wealthy and keep tolerable establishments; mostly, however, they are small affairs, low doggeries that deal out to the poor ignorant natives, rum, tobacco, cotton cloth, trinkets, &c., &c., at enormous prices—in exchange for which they get Palm Oil, Camwood, &c., trading off these articles again to merchant vessels that frequently visit the coast. Thus they get their living, entirely neglecting agriculture and everything else that would tend to develop the resources of the country. Among all those miserably poor people, there is scarcely one too poor to have some kind of a handle affixed to his name.—They have all high sounding titles; nearly every man you meet is a General, Colonel, Major, Captain, Judge, and at the very least an esquire. They have only to make friends with the President, and ever afterwards are classed among the titled gentry, and, as may be imagined, they constitute a sort of cod-fish aristocracy, amusing to look at. Every colonist keeps native slaves (or as they term them servants) about him, varying in number from one to fifteen, according to the circumstances of the master. These poor souls they beat unmercifully, and more than half starve them, and all the labor that is done at all, is done by these poor wretches. They (the colonists) assume to be very pious, and indeed make a great deal of outward show of religion, but if half that is said of them be true, the best among them are but whited sepulchres, and there is certainly no people anywhere more fond of fine dress and vain show.

Eight miles above Monrovia, on the St. Paul river, and near its junction with Stocton creek, is the receptacle or long-house, used as the residence of new emigrants, during the first six months, which is supposed to be the most critical time in the acclimating. This is a long low brick building, divided off into little stalls or rooms, just large enough to admit a bed, table, and a few chairs. Into each of these stalls which open into a common hall passing through the centre, just like those in a large barn or stable, they usually huddle together a family (if they happen to be poor, and without influence), paying no regard to their comfort, delicacy or health, or to the number confined in each of them, and the stalls being badly ventilated, and the poor emigrants uncared for, of course a very large disproportionate number of these deluded victims of the cupidity of Colonization agents, after a brief incarceration in that miserable place, breathing that stifled air, fall unwept, unhonored and unsung, far away from the land of their birth, and from every pleasing recollection of life; their corpses hurried out of sight only to give place to others following in their wake. These things are known to the Colonization agents in this country, and they certainly deserve, as they will ultimately receive, the execrations of all the friends of outraged humanity, for their base and criminal neglect in this particular. On the banks of this river, which are high from the receptacle up, are a number of small settlements, mostly called towns, and distinguished by very large high sounding names. It is a notorious fact that all these settlements, which generally consist of at most a half-dozen scattered bamboo huts, for the purpose of giving them importance, are known and designated by such names as are given the largest American cities. Of this class are Lower and Upper Caldwell, Baltimore, Virginia, Kentucky, Clay, Ashland, New York, Millsburg, &c., &c. I have visited all these settlements, and do unhesitatingly say, that I am not able to imagine any more abject state of misery than exists even here on the banks of the St. Paul, the garden spot of Liberia. This, like all the Liberian rivers, is navigable for canoes, only a few miles inland. Millsburg is the head of navigation, and the seat of the M.E. Missionary operations, than which, there exists no greater humbug. This New York settlement is the one, about which there has been so much noise made by Colonization agents and newspapers, for some years back. It consists of one one-story frame house, fourteen by sixteen feet, which is everywhere known as the big-house, and four very small bamboo huts; and, indeed, this description is about applicable to all these settlements, pompous in their representations, insignificant in their reality. Two men on the banks of this river, have labored hard to clear the land, and make coffee and sugar farms. I allude to Mr. Blacklidge and Mr. Hooper; but they have been unsuccessful hitherto, and will ultimately be forced to renounce their task, owing to the impossibility of clearing the land of bush.

Cape Mount is a bold high promontory, forty miles northward of Monrovia, and presents a handsome prospect from the coast. There are no civilized settlements there, and it being the principal seat of those interminable native wars, offers but few inducements to settlers. Marshall, forty miles south-east of Monrovia, is a settlement of a few colonists who are fast retrograding, and assimilating themselves with the natives in their customs and habits. They are scarcely superior to them in anything now, and the same ratio of deterioration will, in a short time, render it impossible for the most astute to discern between them. These are all the settlements or places of any interest in Messurado, or Montserrado County, and my estimate of its colonist population does not exceed two thousand eight hundred, allowing it the very most it is entitled to.

CHAPTER III.

Bassa County. Bombastic Municipal Government of Buchanan. Population.

Bassa county embraces four little settlements immediately on the beach, containing altogether, less than eight hundred of a population. The largest of them was formerly called Bassa, but is now known by the dignified title of the City of Buchanan, and is chiefly distinguished for the bushes growing in its streets, and the long list of offices in its municipal government. They have a Mayor, Select and Common Council, Policemen, Aldermen, Watchmen, and in fact, they have monopolized every name in the vocabulary of municipal, civil, and military offices—hence, it is not uncommon for one man to have vested in him, in a small way, the honors and responsibilities of a number of those stations. Here reside some of those great men who write windy letters to the Colonization papers, about the progress they have made in agriculture, &c., at the very time that they are dependent on the uncultivated natives for the rice and cassada they eat.

From reading their bombastic reports, one would suppose that it was a place of some consequence, while it really is a starved-up little village, too poor to have even an apology for a court house or jail. Fishtown is the next in importance, and with Celina and Bexley, make up the entire settled portions of Bassa county, remarkable only for the bombast and ignorance of its inhabitants. Colonist population all told, will not foot up eight hundred.

CHAPTER IV.

Sinoe County—(not from personal observation). Number of votes polled. Population. Total Population.

As I did not visit Sinoe county, I cannot speak from personal observation, but from what I could gather from persons who had been there, and among others, Senator Morris and Mr. Mitchel, the representatives, it is of a piece with the other two counties. There is but one settlement, Greenville. The houses are nearly all built of bamboo and mud, and in the last Presidential election, an exciting campaign, they polled less than one hundred and eighty votes; and for the intelligence and thrift of its inhabitants, I judge by those representatives, who were below even the Liberian average. Population cannot exceed eight hundred.

These three Counties, and this meagre population of four thousand and four hundred, compose all that is of that mean farce known as the Republic of Liberia.

CHAPTER V.

Geographical Situation. Water, &c. Heat. Wet and dry Seasons. Tornadoes.

Liberia is situated between the fifth and seventh degrees of north latitude, and about the tenth meridian west longitude. The climate is extremely hot, the thermometer ranging at from ninety-four to ninety-eight in the shade. The seasons are divided into wet and dry—the wet commences in May and lasts till November, during which time it rains almost unceasingly, and in such torrents as we Northerners cannot imagine. During the dry season which lasts the balance of the year, it seldom rains at all. The sun being directly over their heads, pours down on them the rays of his heat without stint.

Tornadoes, or the most violent and appalling storms of wind, thunder and lightning, are of almost daily occurrence.

The water is miserable stuff, having a foul taste, fully luke-warm when it comes out of the well or spring. This article, which is so necessary to the comfort and health of a people, seems particularly disagreeable and ill-suited to us. It is however made a little more palatable by putting it in earthen jars, and setting it aside in the shade several hours to cool. Think you, who are quaffing the sparkling waters from these pure mountain streams, what those poor souls would give for one cooling draught.

CHAPTER VI.

Face of the Country. Swamp. All the high land named. Timber scarce. High land inaccessible.

The face of the country is one magnificent swamp, grown over with mangrove and dragon's blood bushes, interspersed here and there with a point of land sufficiently high on which to form a settlement. The Cape at Monrovia is one of these. Cape Mount is another, so is part of the banks of the St. Paul and Junk rivers, and except these, there is very little other land there free from the inundations of the tide which rises all over it twice a day, and at its ebb, leaves the most foul and sickening miasma conceivable. A great deal of the disease of the country is produced by the effluvia arising from these swamps. On every prominence of land sufficiently high, there is a native settle-ment, and meagre as is the number of civilized persons there, all things considered, there is not room for a great many more.

The land is very fertile, yet it does not produce any timber of consequence. It is true that camwood, rosewood, wismore, gum, and some other varieties do grow there, but so sparsely that it would not average one tree on a mile.

There is observable however, from the coast, the Kong mountains, which indicate high land, and possibly a good country; but
they are at present inaccessible to Liberia, because the navigation of the rivers is interrupted by the falls or rapids rendering
it impossible to take a canoe into the upper country. It is impracticable to make roads there, because they have not the where-
withal necessary. If the roads were made they would have to be
re-opened every month, owing to the dense and rapid growth of
the brush—and that upper country does not belong to Liberia.

CHAPTER VII.

Agriculture. No farming at all. Dense and rapid growth of the
Bush. Rice and Cassada the only staples. Colonists dependent on
the Natives for Food. Fruits, &c.

It is amusing to one who knows, to read the windy letters from
some of the Liberians, respecting the Agricultural resources and
progress of that country. There positively is not, nor never has
been a plow, a horse, or a yoke of oxen, used in all the country.
No man there has now or ever had, five acres of land cleared
and in cultivation, and I am one of those who believe that it
is impossible to clear the land, owing to the dense and rapid
growth of the bush. The nearest description that I can give of
this bush is to call it a bramble, but as there is nothing grows
in this country like it, I cannot convey to the reader a very clear
idea of it. Suffice it to say, that nothing can exceed the density
and rapidity of its growth. Every thing grows thorny and crooked,
and the natives, when they want to plant their rice, find it easier
to clear a new piece than to plant the same place over again two
years in succession. Rice and cassada is their only staples. The
latter is a coarse, tough, clammy, tasteless root, which nothing
but dire necessity would induce a man to eat. Sweet potatoes do
grow there, but to a very small extent, and these miserable creatures (the colonists), are actually dependent on the naked natives for their rice and cassada.

Of fruits, they have the plantain, banana, orange, lemon, pine-
apple, sour-sop, sweet-sop, tamarind, cocoa nut, &c. Coffee and

sugar would grow very abundantly, but for some reason the amount produced has been very small, totally inadequate to the demands of that small colony.

CHAPTER VIII.

Causes which bring Disease. Cannot escape the Fever. Frightful Mortality. Diseases following in its train. Craw-Craw. Jiggers. Sleeping Disease. Old Sores, &c.

The unhealthfulness of that climate is proverbial, superinduced by the low, swampy situation of the country; the extreme constant heat of the sun, and the continual decay of vegetable matter. The diseases which might naturally be expected to arise from exposure to these influences, present themselves to all new comers to an alarming extent. Every colonist *must* get the fever. And do not, reader, for one moment harbor the fancy that you could escape it, or that it is light or trivial.—It is a dread, stern reality, and although not generally so suddenly fatal as is the cholera, yellow fever, plague, &c., it is no less sure in its effects, varied however, very considerably in its phenomena, by the period of residence and circumstances of the patient. Hence, the mortality to poor emigrants is so very large, proved from the fact that of over twenty-seven thousand sent there since 1820, there are less than five thousand there now, while if it were a healthy country, the emigrants and their natural increase, would now number more than forty thousand. The period of acclimation varies in different persons from two to five years. While passing through the fever, a man becomes a frightful maniac, and realizes perhaps, the most horrid suffering which it is possible for human nature to endure. And even if he recovers from the fever, he must invariably pass through a series of other diseases; some, the most loathsome imaginable—for instance, the craw-craw; the flesh becomes a mass of corruption. I have seen people afflicted with it who were walking carrions. The jiggers is another of those diseases produced by an insect which deposits its eggs in the flesh, which incubates and forms ulcers, from which live things crawl, and the mildest of the fevers follows. The sleeping disease produces a lethargy from which no efforts will rouse the patient, and after months of passive, dreamy unconsciousness, he sleeps himself away, never more to feel the pains of earth. Such is the climate, that if a *colonist* gets a flesh-wound, a mere scratch, it never heals.—There are scores of people now in Liberia, afflicted with sores horrid to look at—some of very long standing, which, if they were in this climate, nature herself would heal. Reader, I am not dealing in fiction, but relating to you things as they occurred to me there, and which you will find to your cost, if ever you are foolish enough to be persuaded by Colonization agents, to go there. And in this connection, I will say that the mortality among the males is greater than among females, the census showing that in point of numbers the women stand as two and a half to one man. This is sufficiently accounted for by the fact, that the men must expose themselves to the weather more than the women, and exposure there inevitably brings death.

CHAPTER IX.

Government. Republic a burlesque. Bargain with the Colonization Society. Persons cannot leave without a Passport. Public notice. Copy of Passport. Imprisonment of Debtors. Armstrong Sold. Whipping Post, &c. &c.

Republic, as it is called, its laws are a burlesque on a free country. The Government is in league with the Colonization Society. It is the part of the Society to send emigrants there, and the part of the Government to keep them there when sent; and arbitrary and un-christian as is that compact, its provisions are rigidly and unswervingly enforced. One of their statute laws forbids all captains, owners, and agents of vessels, from taking away any individual out of that Republic, under a penalty of five hundred dollars, without a passport obtained from the Secretary of State. And if a man wish to leave that country, he must first give a ten days' public notice of that intention, and if, at the end of that

time, no one objects to his going, he must then make application to the Secretary of State. That functionary, in obedience to
his instructions, is not very willing to grant them; and never, unless he has sufficient reason to believe that the applicant designs
coming back. If he can make sufficient influence, and friends to
back up his petition, and remove the doubts of that worthy dignitary, he can procure one as I did.

Knowing the obstacles that stand in the way of procuring passports, I had steadily pursued a course of deception, by giving out
the impression that I only wanted to return for my family, and
would, during my visit to the United States, exert myself to induce as many as possible to emigrate with me; and having really
created the impression, I asked Gen. John N. Lewis (who, at the
same time, fills the offices of Commander-in-Chief of all his Excellency's military forces, Secretary of State, Baptist Missionary,
and Commission Merchant), if it was absolutely necessary that I
should put up a public notice, &c. He said it was; that for himself, he felt willing, in my case, to dispense with it, but the President was inexorable on that subject, and had ordered him to
be very particular as to whom he granted passports, as they had
been several times deceived. I accordingly gave the required notice, and at the end of ten days, on the payment of fifty cents, I
received my passport, a month before an opportunity offered to
leave; and the reader may rest assured, that during the balance
of my stay there, I conducted myself with precision, and concealed my opinions carefully, lest something should eke out adverse to the President's liking, and prevent my escape.

Here is a copy of that important document; the body of the
original is in the hand-writing of the President, and signed by
Gen. Lewis, as Secretary of State, by which the reader will perceive that I was granted permission to visit the United States.

"DEPARTMENT OF STATE, ⎱
"*Monrovia, March 12th, 1854.* ⎰

"The bearer hereof, William Nesbit, a citizen of Liberia, having applied for a Passport to visit the United States of North

America: and having complied with the law regulating Passports, is hereby permitted to do so, without hindrance or molestation.

[SEAL.] "Given under my hand and the seal of the Republic, this twelfth day of March, in the year of our Lord one thousand eight hundred and fifty-four, and of the Republic the seventh."

"J. N. LEWIS,
"*Secretary of State.*"

But I venture to say, that not one in a hundred that used every exertion in their power to get away, were successful. Numerous instances were related to me, of persons who, if they could have succeeded in making good their exit from that prison-house, would long ago have spread these facts before the world; but lacking prudence to conceal their real opinion of things around them, were coldly denied the liberty of going when and where they pleased; and are now, by virtue of that unholy compact, and the tyranny of those rulers, doomed to pass the remainder of their miserable existence there, completely fastened in the talons of their destroyers.

They have also laws allowing imprisonment for debt, and the public sale of a debtor to the highest bidder, to work out the amount of his indebtedness. I saw an example of that law, myself. A colonist named Armstrong, who is himself a slave-holder, was sold for debt at Monrovia, and was, at the time I left that place, working out the term of his servitude. And there is nothing more common than to punish offenders at the public whipping-post, and in that way wipe out their crimes; in fact that is the only mode of punishment at all practicable, as there is but one jail in the country (that at Monrovia). And numerous other similar specimens of the wisdom of their rulers, and the freedom and magnanimity of their government, are daily exhibited, constituting it as very a tyranny as ever disgraced the earth. Of course, the manner of conducting the government is of an exact piece with all their other impudent pretensions. They assume to be republic, to have copied their forms and laws from the United States. And to give color to it, they pretend to have vested their power and authority in executive, legislative, judicial, and all the other departments, cabinets, and bureaus known in the government of nations; and, however strange it may seem to the reader, it is not the less true, that all this famous government, and all this long list of officers, is in the hands of one man, and that man but a tool in the hands of the Colonization Society. It is true that the President, Vice President, six Senators, and nine representatives, are elected by the people. But a little money and patronage do a great deal with such people; and does any sane man think that the Colonization Society, through its active agent, *President Roberts*, does not use these, in order to have the government harmonize with their *wishes?* If any man would read the long list of officers belonging to the Liberian Government, he would read the name of nearly every man there, and yet all these officers are at the beck and call of President Roberts. He is the main-spring of all this machinery, and on him, through the support and connivance of the Colonization Society, de-volves the carrying on and glossing over of as villainous an out-rage as ever was perpetrated on a credulous people.* And I do not deny the consummate skill and ability of that potentate. This is most emphatically the one man power. Beside those officers I have mentioned, the people do not even go through the form of electing any others. All the Judges, Sheriffs, Justices, Con-stables, and every other officer, are appointed by the President. And it is humiliating to me to say it, though it must be said, that the majority of them, even including some of his cabinet offi-cers, *cannot read,* and are totally ignorant of the simplest duties belonging to their stations. Every thing is and must be done by the President. He performs the duties of judge, counsellor, justice, and constable. He receives, disburses, and keeps the accounts; in short, he is the government, the embodiment of Liberia; and when you speak of Liberia, you speak of President Roberts. For the reasons herein given, I predict the speedy downfall of this humbug; but as long as it does exist, although

---

*The tenure of the land is held in the Colonization Society, and the deeds are made through the President, as its agent.

he may not always nominally appear as President, still, possessing superior skill and less soul than any other man there, he will continue to be, behind the screen, the pliant tool in the hands of his master (Rev. J. B. Pinney), as long as the American public choose to shut their eyes, and contribute their money, to the maintenance of this iniquity.

CHAPTER X.

Wild Animals and obnoxious and poisonous Reptiles are numerous. Driver, Bug-a-Bug, &c.

There is, perhaps, no country in the world, more prolific than this, in the number and variety of its wild beasts of prey, obnoxious and poisonous reptiles, and destroying insects. Nature seems to have placed there the most loathsome of her productions. The animal kingdom combines with the elements to render it the most detestable spot on earth. Elephants, leopards and tiger-cats are numerous, often coming into the settlements. Of amphibious animals, they have the hippopotamus and crocodile; and there seems to be no end to the number and variety of the monkey species which fill every tree. Of reptiles and insects, they have the mammoth boa-constrictor, thirty feet in length; the cobra de cabello, the most venomous of all snakes; and every species that has any affinity to that family, finds there its legitimate home. Lizards and centipedes, a foot in length, and the tarantula or hairy spider, very poisonous, and numerous. The driver is of the black-ant species, not larger than the ordinary ant, but differing entirely in their habits; they eat nothing but flesh, and when they go forth in search of food, they attack indiscriminately every living thing that is in their way; man, beast and reptile, must give way before them. They are in such immense droves, that when they surround an object, it matters little whether it be a man, an elephant, or a boa-constrictor; escape from them is impossible, and they never leave it while a morsel of flesh remains on its bones. The bug-a-bug, or termite, a white ant, eats up all their houses, furniture, fences, and every thing that is manufactured of wood. They are in such innumerable quantities, that a very considerable portion of the country is taken up with their habitations, which are of clay, and twenty feet or more in height. Besides these, there are an infinite variety of others, so numerous that you cannot look any where without seeing them; they are in your food, in the water you drink, and imagination cannot exaggerate them in their numbers, or in the horror they inspire.

CHAPTER XI.

Slavery. Slavery exists. Its severity. Badly fed. Seperate huts for the Slaves. Bought from Parents. Sometimes run away. Second President. Manner of civilizing the Natives.

That slavery exists in Liberia, is too true. I would, for the sake of humanity, and the honor of the Colonization Society, that it were otherwise. But slavery as abject, and far more merciless than is to be found almost any where else, exists there universally. There is not one who does not own more or less slaves. They are mostly manumitted slaves themselves, and have felt the blighting effects of slavery here, only to go there to become masters. After my limited powers of description are exhausted, imagination can perhaps finish the picture of the condition of the *Slave's Slave*. A parallel to the Liberian system of slavery is scarcely to be found on the American continent; certainly no where else but on the least favored plantations. Slavery here is severe servitude, generally with plenty to eat; but in Liberia, they have the same tasks to perform, the same stripes to endure, severer masters to please, without sufficient clothing to deserve the name, nor enough rice and cassado, which are the slaves' only food, to satisfy their appetites. They need not, like Oliver Twist, ask for more; their only chance for a full meal, is to steal it; and in that country, theft would be a poor dependence; and as to meat, the slave must content himself if he can catch a monkey, a snake, a crocodile, lizard, rat, or something of this kind, which they often do, and devour it with a gusto, that would astonish and disgust the poorest-fed slaves in the United States. As in the slave states of this country, the slaves occupy small buildings near to their masters' residence, known as the "negro quarters," so their imitators in Liberia, notwithstanding the masters mostly live in bamboo huts themselves, many of them not sufficient to protect the pious patriarchs from the weather, let the colonist himself be barefoot, and three parts naked, let him feel the gnawings of want ever so keenly, still he is never too poor to own slaves, and to have a hut for them at a short distance from his own; and so exact have they been in carrying out the customs and feelings of their exemplers in this country, that the slave is never allowed to eat or sleep in the master's house, or hut, as the case may be. These slaves are generally obtained by purchase from the native parents, after arriving at such size and age as to be able to labor, at prices varying from eight to fifteen dollars. After the private transaction between the master and parents, the courts, at the instance of the master, go through some mummery which fastens the fetters upon the purchased child during his natural life. But I am glad to say that there are many, the laws of Liberia to the contrary, notwithstanding, who run away to the bush; once there, and he is safe. Like the slaves in this country, they run away, re-associate with their brother natives, and defy the powers that would enslave them. Still, there is no lack of slaves; the low price at which they can be bought, makes it a matter of economy to the master, when one of his slaves run away, to buy another, rather than attempt to reclaim the runaway. There is, however, one means much resorted to, to prevent slaves from running away, and its potency is astonishing. I allude to a slave owned by James M'Gill, familiarly called the "second President"; who, though a slave himself, exerts a powerful influence over his native brethren. When a master wishes to obtain the help of this individual, to enable him to retain his slaves, he makes the "second president" a dosh (gift), and informs him what he wants him to do. This potent dignitary forthwith gives the slaves a harangue in their native language, addressing both their hopes and their fears; and being superstitious, this appliance generally accomplishes the object of its design. How long it will require the Liberian colonists to civilize and christianize the idolatrous natives, is yet an unsettled question. It is, however, certain, that if the cruelist slavery on which the sun ever shone—if wars brought on to raise the price of fire-arms and ammunitions—if drunkenness causes them to increase the sale and the price of rum—if all the vices of civilization, without any of its virtues, in any one of these, or all of them combined, can christianize Africa, then the work is in good hands, and I have no doubt will be carried forward; slowly, perhaps, but sure, as that Liberia continues to be a decoy for the colored people of this country.

The colonist once entrapped into this hell on earth, finds, to his dismay, that he cannot return at will, and it is natural that he should try to make the best of a bad bargain; so the manumitted slave, who always thought his master supremely happy, undertakes to procure happiness for himself, by the same means. With a few trinkets, rum, tobacco, &c. he buys a slave, and sets up tyrant on his own hook. They profess to have broken up the foreign slave trade, which is far from the truth; but suppose they had done so, is that *even* a blessing, under the circumstances? I would a thousand times rather be a slave in the United States than in Liberia.

CHAPTER XII.

Missionaries.

We are used to reading very encouraging accounts of Missionary exertions and successes among the natives of Liberia, and any one not conversant with the real workings of the system, would be led to believe that the Missionaries there had been in the hands of God, very widely instrumental in spreading his gospel, and its blessings, among those idolatrous tribes, and that the effects of their labors would be readily observable to the beholder, in their renouncing their pagan rites and customs, and preferring and practicing, at least, some of the habits of civilization. But what are the facts as presented to one, resident among them.—There are hordes of Missionaries there, some of them of very fair attainments, supported and pampered by benevolent donations of means, by the American public. Indeed, there cannot be less than two hundred persons there, receiving salaries as Missionaries, whose only object seems to be, to gull and mislead their patrons, respecting the progress of their work, and to their sins of omission and commission, are to be charged the whole wrong of bolstering up Liberia. If the Missionaries would only tell the truth, and not for the sake of individual gains, deceive the public, one fair, unvarnished statement, from them, would so thoroughly disgust the people of the United States, that the Missionary, as well as the Colonization Societies, would die for want of sustenance, in one short month. They have really done nothing in the way of civilizing and christianizing Africa. I know that this subject is too grave to trifle about; and I speak advisedly, when I say, that there are not twenty civilized and converted natives in all the colony. Not one native, even in Monrovia, out of every hundred, ever goes to church, or attends on any other duties, in the least degree indicating a desire for, or knowledge of civilization, or christianity. They (the Missionaries) have, to a man, turned traders; some even are engaged in dealing out rum and fire-arms. All their pretended religious demonstrations are confined among the colonists, and I verily believe, that the Missionary and Colonization enterprise, conducted as they have been, are an injury to that country; and they, from their wanton perversion of the advantages of knowledge, have contaminated the natives, and sunk them still lower. There are, however, some two or three who have been more honest in their habits— Mrs. Wilkins, of White-Plains Mission, a manual-labor school, devoted exclusively to the education of female natives—this old lady has labored assiduously for twenty-three years, with a zeal worthy of the cause, and such is their tenacity to their ancient customs and traditions, that there is not *one* of all the number that she has brought up, and educated, and taught the right way, but who have gone back to the bush, and divested themselves of their clothing, and every other remembrance of civilization, and are now practicing every abomination belonging to heathenism. The old lady, having fruitlessly toiled amongst them, the best years of her life, was forced to relinquish her task, in disgust, and returned home to the States a year ago. Any other Missionaries there, who are doing any good at all, have their labors directed exclusively amongst the colonists, not deigning to hold religious converse with the natives. I will offer the following incidents, to show the manner in which these Missionaries deal with the natives. Palm Oil, being one of the chief commodities of the country, and being very bulky, dirty, and difficult to handle, I, as a trader, was at a loss to make out what great profit there was in dealing in it, seeing that the price at which it was bought and sold, was 33 cents per gallon, and had steadily refused to purchase any, until I was initiated into the secrets of the loss and gain of the trade, by Rev. Mr. Hill, a Missionary of the Baptist church, at Marshall, receiving a salary as such, from the Baptist Board of Foreign Missions, in this county. "These people" (the natives), said Mr. Hill, "have no ideas of weight and measure, and when we buy from them, we use a gallon measure that holds a gallon and a half, and in this way, pay ourselves for our trouble; and in weighing camwood, we always take enough to make it cheap." The Rev. Mr. Burns, the resident Bishop, or Superintendent of the M.E. Church, on seeing some of us feeding our natives with meat, remonstrating with us, said they were not used to that kind of treatment, and it would spoil them; and I might cite numerous similar instances, did I deem it necessary.

CHAPTER XIII.

Poor Emigrants. Their Condition. Prospects. Ultimate Fate. Discontent. Conversation with Tucker.

The chances for the poor emigrant to Liberia, are exceedingly slim—he cannot escape the fever—that, is a fixed fact, and it is equally true, that there is no disease to which human flesh is heir, more terrible in its effects. But, suppose he is fortunate, and lives through it—what are his prospects then. At the end of six months he finds himself turned off by the Colonization Society, thrown on his own resources, in a country that can afford him no possible employment, but paddling a canoe at twenty-five cents a day; and it would be at the imminent risk of his life, that he would expose himself to the scorching rays of the sun, and, in the nature of things, he could not have cleared and cultivated any land. He sees that nineteen twentieths of his neighbors are living in the most abject state of misery and want; that he is living in a mean, pusillanimous government, having for its only object, the decoy of the unsuspecting—that he is surrounded by, and must daily mingle with hordes of naked natives, whose habits his children will be sure to imbibe, rendering it certain, that however successful he may be, his children will deteriorate, and finally relapse back to heathenism. Having living witnesses constantly before him of the blighting effects of the climate and food, on the mental, physical, and moral powers, and knowing what he has lost by going there, he becomes dejected and desponding, and realizes that he has cast his lot in a hell on earth. He has no other alternative, but to turn in with those who have preceded him, and by hook and by crook, raise a little rum, tobacco, and cotton cloth, brass trinkets, &c., and start on what is called bush trading. Necessity compels him to leave his conscience behind him, and he soon finds himself stooping to means that he would have scorned before. Many of these poor souls told me with tears in their eyes, that they would gladly return to the worst form of slavery in the United States, rather than remain in that place of torment. A large number of the colonist women have even been reduced to the extremity of marrying, or taking up with naked native men, and are living with them in shameless co-habitation; and to estimate this degradation properly, it is necessary to know, that nothing can exceed the supreme contempt with which the colonists always regard the natives.

Perhaps I cannot better illustrate to the reader, the real condition, mentally and physically, of this class of emigrants, after a few years residence there, than by relating a conversation with Mr. Tucker, of Marshall, who is about a fair sample of old Liberians. He was one of the few who has passed through the ordeal of their horrid diseases, got used to eating cassada, and was, according to the Colonization rule, elevated. He had grown prematurely old and decrepit, and, as will be seen, his mental faculties were not much improved. Being anxious to learn as much of men and things in that country, as possible, one day I asked him: Mr. Tucker, have you been in this country long?

T. Yes, sir, a long time.

N. How many years?

T. About ten or fifteen years.

N. Can't you tell more closely than that, which it is, ten or fifteen?

T. No sir, indeed I can't tell how long I have been here; I was young when I came; I am old now, and you will not find many Liberians who can tell how old they are, or how long they have been here.

After listening to him relate some national affair, in which he had taken part, I questioned him as to what time it occurred. He seemed surprised, that we, who lately came from the States, should be so particular about dates, &c. and with a good deal of feeling, remarked:—"My dear friend, when you have been in this country long enough to have eaten all the bread and meat you brought with you, when anything occurs, you will not be able to remember whether it was last week, last month or last year."

CHAPTER XIV.

Military and Naval Forces. Parades, Dress and Cannon. Schooner Lark. Naval Officers. Prison Ship Agility, &c.

The bombastic reports of President Roberts, and others, respecting their military, their army, their navy, &c. are supremely ridiculous. No where else, is so complete a farce exhibited, as at a military parade in Liberia. I witnessed one of these exhibitions in Monrovia, on the occasion of the inauguration of the President, and again at Marshall, on the regular muster day, prescribed by law; and certainly, there never was exhibited in the most ridiculous back-woods militia training, taking into the account, corn-stalks, tin pans, mushroom patriotism, and all, anything at all approximating in fantastical bombast, a parade in Liberia. I would that I were gifted with sufficient descriptive powers, to picture such a scene properly, to the reader, but am satisfied, that nothing but actual observation will enable any one to realize it. A heterogeneous company, of every hue and color, size and shape, two-thirds of them without either shoes or hat, quite a number without even an apology for a shirt, or anything else to hide their nakedness, but a tattered pair of pants, while here and there stands a fellow decked out in all the parapher-nalia of a cast-off British uniform, armed, cap-a-pie with a bam-boo stick, and knowing nothing, whatever, of military evolutions, except what they have chanced to pick up, on witnessing a pa-rade here. These are the flower of the Liberian army—the im-mediate satellites around his Excellency, President Roberts—and I am only induced to hold them up to ridicule, because I wish to give a correct picture of things as they exist there. They have a number of cannon, some of them quite formidable weap-ons, lying about the streets of the different settlements. Only two in the whole country are mounted; the rest are all lying about uncovered, and without care, forming an excellent harbor for snakes, &c. Indeed, so weak and defenceless is this mean hum-bug, that were the American and British Governments to with-draw their squadron from the coast, the natives, who always re-gard the colonists as intruders, would come on them, and by the preponderance of their numbers, wipe out this little plague-spot, by driving them into the sea.

The naval fleet of Liberia, has only one small vessel, the schoo-ner Lark, six guns, presented to them by the British Govern-ment.—They, have, however, a numerous array of naval officers; Commodores, Captains, Lieutenants, Boatswains, Midshipmen, &c., which probably make up for the deficiency of vessels. I have never been able to learn that they did any effective service, other than to furnish a prison ship for the punishment of criminals. They do boast that she is a fast sailer, that no slaver visiting that coast can catch her, and relate numerous instances in which she gave the slavers leg-bail, proving beyond cavil, her superior agility, when pursued. As there is no one there who understands navigation, she never ventures out of sight of land, but sails up and down the coast once in a while, with what object, does not appear very clearly.

CHAPTER XV.

Probable Fate of Liberia. American and English Squadrons support it. Obstacles in its way. Senator Russel's opinion, &c.

Liberia cannot succeed! It is now only a fraud; and as soon as the American and English people withdraw their support, it will irresistibly fall back to its native heathenism. If the mortality there is so great, what is to keep it up when emigration shall cease? If the tendency of the colonists is to retrograde, what will preserve its pretentions to civilization? So weak are they, that I have often heard them admit, that if the American and English squadrons were withdrawn, which alone hold the natives in check, they could not preserve their nationality for one week. The natives would come upon them, and sweep them as with an avalanche into the ocean. The Colonization and Missionary Societies have, perhaps, done all that could be done. They have spent a vast amount of valuable lives and treasure, and have used every artifice to bolster it up. Still it does not advance; and, conceived as it was in sin, and having no great work to do, no high destiny to fulfil, it must irresistibly fall. The enterprizing Yankee, in the fullness of his pride, may point to the present and prospective greatness of this country, and claim that they have overcome more and greater difficulties than stand in the way of emigration to Liberia, but the facts will not justify that. When the Pilgrim Fathers sought these shores, they found a congenial clime, bountiful by nature, and they had only to make peace with their neighbors, and enjoy its full fruition. But it is not so with us; the climate is inhospitable; the air is filled with pestilence; the soil will not produce such food as we can live on; the impossibility of having beasts of burden. These and numberless other insurmountable obstacles, entirely preclude its progress. It does not possess any of the elements of greatness, and therefore cannot advance. And, indeed, I am not aware that there is any country on the globe, in the same latitude, and exposed to the same influences, against which these objections would not apply with full force; and the people of Liberia are not ignorant of the wrong done them in sending them there. They feel it as worse than slavery itself; I have no hesitation in saying, that aside from those that are receiving legal salaries from the Missionary and Colonization Societies, there is not one man who does not indulge in execrations, loud and deep, against this institution, that has thus forced them from the land of their birth, a congenial climate, food adapted to them, and placed them in that far-off land of wretchedness and desolation, cut off from them the possibility to return, and abandon them to despair and woe; all, too, under color of philanthropy. And there are not wanting, even those who are feeding at the crib, honest enough to verbally speak the truth. Senator Russell, who is also an Episcopal clergyman, who has received largely of Pinney's bounties, made use of the following singular expression: "All colonizationists will go to *hell;* but Governor Pinney is the best white man alive!"

CHAPTER XVI.

Manners, Customs, &c. of the Natives.

The natives of that country, in point of numbers, as compared with the colonists, stand as thirty to one, are well formed, of black color, medium size, and tolerably regular features, very lazy, rude, and ignorant, filthy and disgusting in their habits; have their own laws and kings, totally disregarding the pusillanimous pretensions of the Colonial Government, which they consider a usurpation which they will rid themselves of some day. The mass of them do not wear any clothes at all, but appear in all the pride and beauty of nature, unadorned. The most of those living immediately in the settlements, wear a small breech-cloth, made out of one yard of calico; but it is very common to see men, and women even, in the best colonial settlements, as naked as when they came into the world. If they have any ideas

of religion at all, it is of the darkest and most irredeemable pa-
ganism; full of idolatry and superstition, they attribute all their
mishaps to the influence of evil spirits, witches, &c. Every native
wears his *gree-gree,* which is a piece of writing, generally in Arabic,
in a bag made of leather, ornamented with crocodile skin, &c.
around his neck; they regard its power as potent in counteract-
ing these evil spirits, witches, fetisch, &c. and such is their superstition, and so tenaciously do they hold to their notions, that
they would just as soon part with life itself as with their gree-
grees. These are furnished them by their gree-gree men or
priests, who are generally of their own nation. Sometimes, however, they are renegade colonists, and perform some tricks in
jugglery to show and maintain their power. They are polygamists
to the greatest extent, and have as many wives as they are able
to buy; and as all their wealth is invested in women, of course
he that has the most wives, is the greatest man. Some have two
or three, some a dozen; King Bamboo has sixty; others more
than a hundred. One colonist named Early, went there as a missionary, abandoned his legitimate wife, bought ten native wives,
seven of whom had children by him, set up a town for himself,
and became a great man among them; and numerous other
similar cases exist there at this time. These women they buy,
while young, of their parents, at prices ranging at from ten to
fifteen dollars. They are slaves, absolutely the property of the
husband or master, and they sell them or hire them out, not
having the most remote idea of chastity. I know of one king on
Junk river, that gave one of his wives to his own son, and she
bore children to both of them. The women perform all the labor; the men only cut the bush, the women burn it, hoe the
ground, plant the rice, and harvest it. Hence, the man that has
a great number of wives, becomes a very important personage.
They always live in little towns or villages, in huts built of bamboo, sometimes covered with mud, and some of them showing
some taste in their construction. If a man has a great number of
wives, he builds a town of his own, and sets up for himself; paying
tribute, however, to a king of that tribe, who reigns over a large
territory. In the center of the town is a large building, used as a

kitchen for the whole community. Here they cook their chop, and then gather in groups, each family around their own cooking utensils; and with a large wooden spoon, or with their fingers, devour it. A favorite dish among them is dumboy; this is made by pounding the cassada to a consistence like dough, making soup, generally out of snake, monkey, crocodile, or whatever is handiest, to give it a flavor; they then break it off in chunks, and swallow it, it being too tough to chew. When their children are one week old, they cram them as full of rice as they will hold, and lay them in the sun several hours, and if they live through that, they are worth raising; if they die, there are no regrets. They have few diseases among them, and the most common remedy is to grease themselves with palm-oil and lay in the sun.

The natives do not regard death as a natural consequence, the common lot of all; but when one of their number dies, they think that some one else has made a witch or fetish of him; and summoning a council, they accuse all who were supposed to be at enmity with him, and any who cannot establish their innocence, must pass through the ordeal of drinking sassy-wood. This is a fatal poison, and is the arbiter of nearly all their crimes; if he can eject it from his stomach, he lives, and is innocent; if it remains on his stomach, he dies, and is declared guilty. Twice a year they hold their great councils, or palavers, in the gree-gree bush; here they pass their laws, settle their disputes, &c. One of their greatest events is initiating their young men, and making them palaver men, which always ends with feasting and rejoicing. Women are never, on any consideration, allowed to enter the gree-gree bush.

Their females are taken, when quite young, to the devil bush, a kind of nunnery, and placed in charge of an old woman, or matron, whose duty it is to bring them up according to their ancient customs and traditions. They remain here till they have acquired their education, and are sold. When one of their great men dies, they bury him in some conspicuous part of the town, in great splendor; having hired mourners, they get up the most hideous yells and lamentations; but when a commoner dies, they take him to some swamp or island, and turning an old canoe over him, leave his carcass to be devoured by the wild beasts and reptiles.

Taken as a whole, I believe the native Africans are the happiest people in existence; verifying the adage that, "If ignorance is bliss, 'tis folly to be wise!" They pass their whole time in frolic and revelry, singing and dancing; their only wants are rum, pipe and tobacco (and of these only enough for their immediate use), and these supplied, seated in their canoe, on their native waters, they make the welkin ring again with their merriment. They have a rude drum and harp, and though I have slept in native towns, so constant is their amusements, that I cannot form a conjecture as to what part of the twenty-four hours they devote to sleeping. They are very hospitable to strangers, and their custom is to make a dosh (gift) to their visitors, and expect one in return; and though dishonest themselves, in dealing, they are worsted by the superior knavery of the colonists.

CHAPTER XVII.

Domestic Animals. Small size of Cattle. No Horses or other beasts of burden.

Of domestic animals, they have a few beeves of a very diminutive size, certainly not larger than our six weeks old calves, and of quaint appearance; and with such immense horns, as to make one think that the best part of the beef had grown to horns. There is no more exciting event takes place in Monrovia, than the butchering of a beef, which rarely happens, owing to their scarcity. The poor starved colonists become frantic, each one desirous to taste meat once more; and the supply not being the one-tenth part equal to the demand, they pull away at, and pell mell each other; the strongest, securing the prize. They have a few sheep, with hair instead of wool—goats as highly prized for their meat as the sheep. They have a few very diminutive hogs. There is not one horse now, in the Republic—there was one when I went there, of a nondescript species; a size larger than Gen. Tom Thumb's Shetland ponies, and having some affinity to the horse, mule, or jack-ass; and indeed it was difficult, from looking at him, to tell which class he approximated most nearly; but alas! and unfortunately for his owner, and for Liberia, he died—leaving not one vestige of his kind behind him. It is impossible to introduce domestic animals there; all attempts to that end, so far, have proved failures, for the reason that every living creature taken there, must pass through the acclimating fever, which has always, thus far, proved fatal. They have some chickens, and a very few turkeys and geese.

CHAPTER XVIII.

[The following Letters, will corroborate my statements, in many particulars.]

MARSHALL, Nov. 26th, 1854.

Dear Sir:—I received your letter on the 29th inst., at 3 o'clock, and felt so glad, that I sat on the counter from that until daylight, and read it, and drank rum. Sir, you say in your letter, that I gave you too short a statement of things here; I had, and still have, a reason for concealing my opinions; I am in Liberia, and cannot leave without a passport, and that is difficult to procure, and no vessel would take me without one. There are no roads here to travel in, and it is five or six months, before I expect to get away; and if I write you anything disagreeable to the powers here, the news might get back in time to prevent me from getting away. But I will say this much, that it is *hell* by the mile. Mr. Nesbit *don't tell* any *lie* about this country; the sixteenth part has never yet been told—he did not stay long enough to detest it right: laboring hands work for twenty-five cents per day—I have at this time, twenty-three employed at that price. There are no horses or mules here; I did see the frame of a horse that was brought from the interior, about the size of Judge Gwinn's dog. All the farming is done by the natives—the ploughing is done with a hoe, about two inches broad, and six long—the houses are little huts, built in the woods, and the brush is cleared away about ten feet around. As for towns and cities, there are none here; the city of Monrovia is about half as large as Huntingdon; there are five good houses there, and that is giving it all that is due it. The price of wild land, is fifty cents per acre; if cleared, five dollars. There is no produce raised here, except rice and cassada, and a few sweet potatoes; flour, is out of the question, and there is no meat, other than is wild in the bush. A few weeks ago, a vessel that had been a long time on her voyage, and run short of provisions, put in here for supplies, and they could not furnish them anything but rice and cassada, and not much of that. As to government affairs, I will not venture anything at present, only the fact, that they are not able to govern themselves. The rainy season is awful; it commences in May, and ends in this month; it rained without ceasing, for three weeks so hard, that we could not see outside of the house; and, for the last four months, we have not had ten dry days. I thought I had seen it rain in the States, but find I was mistaken. This is the last letter you will get from me, as I expect, by the first of July, to strike glad hands with you, in Huntingdon.

Respectfully Yours,

CURTIS G. CARR.

To Levi Chaplin, Huntingdon, Pa.

MARSHALL, Nov. 28th, 1854.

Dear Sir:—The receipt of your letter, gave me more pleasure than anything else, since I have been in this country. My health is at present, very good; but, it would astonish you to see the food we live on; flour and meat are entirely out of the question—the last flour that was brought here, sold for fifteen cents per pound; meat, thirty-one cents per pound; so that the only food we can get here, is rice and cassada, and that is very hard living. As to the government, the people pretend to elect the President and Congress; all the rest are appointed by the President. There are some few men here, who seem to have some intelligence, but they are scarce. I took part in an election for representative, and neither the judges nor inspectors could read. As to agriculture, I have not seen anything like an excuse for farming. There is not one man in this country who has five acres of land cleared and in cultivation—the only implement is the hoe, and they manage to raise a little rice.—This place is made up of the wrong material, to ever make a prosperous country. They are mostly emancipated slaves, and when their six months is out, and they are turned off the public, they are so free, that they do not make much exertion to get along, for want of a master; and mostly become worthless vagabonds, and make their living by intrigue, robbing the natives of their little produce. Two-thirds of the emigrants have gone back, and are no better than the natives, and seem satisfied with rice and palm oil. The natives here are a well-formed people—dark complexion— and those in the bush, go entirely naked. Some of those in the American settlements, wear a little breech-cloth, made out of one yard of calico; they feed on all kinds of vermin and reptiles, and are very lazy; the men merely cut down the bush, and burn it—the women do all the other labor. The wages for a laboring man here, when he can get anything to do, is twenty-five cents a day; and work is very scarce at that. The houses here are generally huts, built of bamboo, about ten by twelve feet, covered with leaves. There are, however, a few small brick and frame houses, occupied by the nobles of the land. Respecting the seasons here, we have six months that are miserably hot and dry, seldom raining at all; and then six months rain, that scarcely ceases during that time. Of wild animals, and poisonous reptiles, and tormenting insects, we have almost any variety and number. But I will close, saying, that taken altogether, this is the worst place any poor man could come to. If a man has money, he can make out to live, but if he is poor, he must die, and be put up in a mat, and thrown in the ground. That is the way they put away the poor.

Respectfully, &c.

JOSEPH P. BROOKS.

To Mr. Levi Chaplin.

MARSHALL, Jan. 7th, 1855.

My Dear Cousin:—I take this opportunity of writing a few lines, to let you know that we are all well at present, and hope that

these few lines may find you in the same state of health. Times
are very hard here; we have not seen flour for three months, nor
meat—nothing but rice, and very little of that. We have to work
hard, to do anything like a business at the mill. Things do not
work well; I think Mr. Nesbit gave you a very fair account of
Liberia—I tell you, it is hard times. Mother, and all of us, but
father, want to go back to the States. Chickens are selling at
twenty-five cents a piece; eggs, thirty-seven and a half cents per
dozen; rice, two dollars per bushel. When Mr. Nesbit writes his
pamphlet, I wish you would please send me one; I would like to
see what he says about this country. Emigrants to this country
never get over the fever; those that have been here twenty years,
still have the fever; the children of colonists born here, are not
healthy. I never came as near being starved, as I have since we
have been here; we can get nothing but dry rice and cassada. If
you were here one day, you would be satisfied to return again to
the States, as soon as possible. The city of Monrovia has not one
pavement in it; the streets are grown up with weeds, leaving
nothing but a narrow path to walk in, and it is dangerous to go
out at night, for fear of snakes. They have one vessel of war here,
the schooner Lark, six guns; Commodore Cooper, is the com-
mander, and when any one commits any crime, he is tied up at
the whipping-post, and whipped; and they imprison him on the
Lark, and repeat the dose of whipping every day, till the term of
his imprisonment is out. They once met a slaver, and hailed him
to stop; he accordingly laid to, and told Capt. Cooper, if he came
near, he would present him with a cannon ball. Capt. Cooper
made all haste back to Monrovia, to ask the President if he
should fight. That is a sample of their spunk. * * * * Tell grand-
mother that we are all very glad that she did not come out with
us, as we did not want her to suffer with us. No more at present;
but remain,

    Sincerely, your Cousin,

                           JAMES H. DEPUTIE.

To Hannibal Molson.

MARSHALL, Liberia, ⎱
Nov. 29th, 1854. ⎰

MRS. MARY ANN SCOTT:—

Dear Madam—I embrace this opportunity to write to you, sincerely hoping that these lines may find you, and all your family, enjoying good health. I am as well as people get the first five years they are here, but I have not one-half the strength that I had in the States. I landed here on the 19th of December, 1853, and did not get the fever till the 7th March, following. I was not able to work any until the 1st of May; I then worked at carpentering for the Enterprise Company. We then got the saw-mill in operation, and they gave me a situation as sawyer, at $19 per month, in which situation I have continued ever since. We cannot get any meat or bread here, at any price. There has not been any flour in Liberia, for at least two months, and the only chance we have of getting a taste of meat, is once in a while, when the natives bring in a deer from the bush. We have to live on rice alone, nearly all the time, and you may know that that goes hard with me. I hope that the Liberia fever has got out of Mr. Scott, and that he will forever renounce the notion of coming here. If he had come here, he would certainly have died. When he saw the suffering into which he had brought his family, he would certainly have grieved, and grief coupled with fever, inevitably produces death. Tell all the people you see, not to come to torment, before they die, for when they come here, they are coming to torment. More than half that come here, die in a short time, and all that escape immediate death, suffer unspeakable misery, all their lives. I live in a little town called Marshall, forty miles from Monrovia. We are surrounded with wild beasts of numerous kinds; elephants, from four to twelve feet high; tiger-cats, wild dogs, deers, porcupines, monkeys, baboons and snakes, from four to forty feet in length. The people are very willing to eat any of these animals and reptiles, because they cannot get anything else. If it was not for the little rice raised by the natives, the people would certainly starve.—Many a time when I am setting down to such stuff as we can get here, I think of the good meals of victuals I have eaten in your house. The paths are about eighteen inches wide, grown up on both sides with bush, and we walk one before the other, tandem fashion, afraid to set down our feet, on account of the snakes.

If you have a suit before a Justice of the Peace, and can show two dollars, before the other man, you will be sure of gaining the suit. I can make the best man in the Colony, perjure himself, for five bushels of rice. There are not two christians, or honest men, in all Liberia. Some of the constables cannot read their names in print, and it is hard work for some of the lawyers to write their names. They are the meanest people that ever breathed. Samuel Williams and D. Kelly, are quite sick; old Charles Deputie, is lying at the point of death. If they were at home, they would all stay there. There is the most rueful state of things existing here, that ever mankind heard of. I really hope to get back to the States, by May or June next. I will close with a disconsolate heart.

Your Friend,

EDMUND BROWN.

MARSHALL, Liberia, ⎱
Dec. 6th, 1854. ⎰

MY DEAR FRIEND:—I take my pen in hand to drop you these lines to inform you that we are yet alive; but, alas! none but God, and he alone, knows what we have suffered since we have been here. We have not only suffered sickness, but we have suffered for provisions. Since we have been off the public, we have had little to eat but rice and cassada—not one mouthful of bread have we had for three months; a little coffee now and then— sometimes a little tea and sugar—is all we can get; so you may judge that times are hard with us. The saw-mill is all our dependence, and I do not believe they will succeed with it. They do not get to work till nine or ten o'clock, for the want of steam; they can't get the wood to burn well. I wish you could see how they work, and see if it is like the saw-mills in the States. But, O Lord, I do not want you or any body else to come to this place of torment. Oh, my friend, I can't describe my feelings when I hear my children, every day that they are able to eat anything, crying for bread, and there is none to give them. Deputie's health is very bad; and I don't know how he can expect to be well, or do well, after deceiving his family so. I did not think he would have treated me so. O, if I had never come here.

We are now living at Marshall, a little town about 60 miles from Monrovia. We moved on the first of October. Deputie tells people that the reason we moved so soon was that the insects were so bad there that we could not stay; and it is true, if insects they can be called. We saw a snake in our cupboard four feet long, one under our bureau six feet long, and one night one got in my bed; I can't tell how long it was; by the time I got a light, it was gone. I never saw such rats as were in that place—some almost as large as cats; they bit me several times in bed, and eat the bed-clothes upon the beds in which we were sleeping. You, nor any other person but those who have been here, ever saw such lizards, drivers, roaches, bugs, ants, &c. &c. I can't call half of the names of the destroyers that infest the houses here. All our family have very bad health—all sick nearly every day. I don't know when I will be able to get home, but I hope to come before long. Pray for me, that the Lord may so prosper me as to bring me once more to my native land.

MARY ANN DEPUTIE.

[*Extract of a letter from* JOHN H. HARRIS, *dated Monrovia, Nov. 10th, 1854, in reply to a letter from me. He says:*]

The reading of your letter, and the definition you gave of Liberian miseries, created no little comment; and from some of the interested, some anathemas for your future state. The company, however, are more incensed against you for deceiving, relative to your coming back. Some say that you could have secured your passage without subterfuge; but for my part, I conceive more truth than poetry in what you have said; but as I am in Rome, without any hope of getting out for at least one year, I must sing mum, and not rail out against things as I find them here. But I do say this: that no person has any business to come here, unless they have sufficient means, so as to leave it if they do not like it, or they may have a wailing equal to that of Rachael for her children, and with about as much hope of being comforted. All must suffer here, even those that are well prepared; and the poor, the mass of the emigrants, find it a harder road to travel than Jordan's cold stream; for, after being here six months, the time that the Colonization Society keeps you, you find yourself just one hundred per cent worse off than you were the day you landed. This cannot be explained so well by letter, as experience proves it to any one who wishes to try it. I do not say this to deter any one from coming; for that there is money to be made here, is an undeniable fact, but that is the only aspect in which I consider this country at all bearable. And I would not interfere with the right of every one seeing it themselves, and drawing their own conclusions.

JOHN H. HARRIS

———————————

[*The following is an extract from a letter, written by* MR. J. H. H. *one of the party who went out to Liberia with the Pennsylvania Company, dated March 30th, '55, sent to a friend of his in Greensburg:*]

"You asked me whether it were true what a certain correspondent had written in regard to Liberia as it is. Well, there is more truth in it than many of the old settlers would like to admit. And I must confess, moreover, that its modifications are more bland than I could couch for publication. But one should not make expositions of their country that are detrimental to her interests. This comes under the head of "*truth must not be told at all times*"; but with candor I always endeavor to address my friends. I have seen barbarous cruelties inflicted upon the aborigines by the Americans; whether the crime justifies the act, I am not able to say; but there is the same relation existing with many, as there is in the South between master and slave, with as much seeming authority; but it is not so with all; for I have seen acts of humanity here amongst the African-Americans, that would put the Anglo-

Saxons of the United States to the blush, with all their wealth and intelligence. The food of the natives in the American families, is principally rice, palm oil and cassada, and they are satisfied if they get that. With many, meat is a rarity; and their dress, in many of the families, is a breech-clout that barely covers their secret parts. This is revolting to society. The authorities have enacted laws requiring American families to clothe the natives living with them; but as it is never enforced, it becomes optional. There is also a species of servitude among the traders that savors strongly of slavery. An interior head man, or petty king, will come to them for trade; he may have some three or four boys with him, that he has either stolen on the path (for there are no roads), or else captured in war; these he leaves as security with them for the return of produce for the goods; the probability is he will never come back; therefore, they become theirs, to work, feed and clothe, as they see proper. This the law does not recognize as valid, yet it is tolerated, and hard is sometimes their lot; and with many of the colonists here, they think they are naturally and morally superior; as superior to the native as the master thinks he is to his slave in the States. There is also another feeling existing here which is dangerous in its nature, and detrimental to the prosperity of the country, and that is the prejudice existing, politically, *and socially with some,* between the old settlers and new-comers. I am unable to say what was the first cause of it. It is said that a certain clique of the old-comers, who have always been in power, are afraid, by the late influx, of the power being wrested from them, and their emoluments, if any, will be curtailed; therefore, they tried to enact laws disfranchising the new-comers for two years, but did not succeed. This feud has made two parties in politics; but some of the old administrationists have declared that if the new party do gain the election in the coming contest for President, they will contest the right to the chair, even at the point of sword and bayonet. The voice of the people was overruled in one of the Leeward settlements for a Mayor lately; but the new-comers becoming greatly indignant at the result, rose *en masse,* and swore by their Halidom to have justice, and they got it by reinstating the rightful one. So, you perceive there are other things besides the country itself to contend with in coming here; and naught but money and a determined will can conquer; that is, providing the fever lets you live. But I am wearying your patience. Times have been very dull with us for some time; we have had no goods from the States for some six months, and our mill meeting with several accidents, has delayed us much, so that our money matters have been, and are, in as critical a crisis as some merchants in the United States. We have all been more or less sick."

———————

[*Previously writing from Monrovia to his wife, under date of March 6th, 1854, the same gentleman makes the following statements.*]

"You are aware, that what little means I had left from illness, had been invested in our company, and as dividends are only declared yearly, I am left at present, in an almost penniless condition; but even the means of my going or sending for you, might be easily obviated, were there not other matters for us to reflect upon, and which requires greater consideration; and that is, our coming to a new country that is solely dependent upon foreign countries, for almost every article of sustenance, and where there is not one single article of house-keeping affairs manufactured; therefore, everything that we would need, I should have to get from the States; even the most trifling articles in the States, are a big item here, and to come here without every necessary thing, is to step into want and misery, which can only be realized, by seeing some poor souls here in that predicament. And, Love, however hard it may seem, or the separation be, yet, I must honestly confess, that I am not able to get the necessary wants now, for our mutual comfort; for it is madness, as would be like the actings of a simpleton, to come here without them. Therefore, dearest, for our own future comfort and happiness, do humbly submit to our separation a few months longer, when, I trust to be able to come myself, for you. These are painful reflections, but it is better to put up with a few sacrifices now, than that our whole future bliss should be empoisoned by our indiscreetness. Besides, I have not yet undergone the fever, and there is no telling what may be its results, for they say it is not very merciful, when it is so long taking hold. This letter is painful to me to write; therefore, I cannot write more now. I promised to give your father an account of the affairs of the country, but I do not feel much able now, besides, he can receive from Mr. Nesbit, a more satisfactory account than I can write."

NOTE.

Gratified at my good fortune in making my escape from Liberia, I resumed my former business, willing to forgive the Colonization Society for the deep wrong done me, in robbing me of my means; for, by the confidence which I placed in their base falsehoods, I was induced to emigrate there, and thus lost the fruits of my industry and economy; willing to forgive their stool-pigeons (colored men) who decoyed me there, and being averse to controversy, probably never would have appeared before the public with these pages, had I not been assailed by a publication in the Philadelphia *Public Ledger,* of the 26th of February last, as a falsifier, simply because I did not suppress my opinions; but, in my limited sphere, when asked, I verbally related the true condition of Liberia. The editors of the paper *refused* to publish my reply; and I feel it a duty I owe to myself, and to suffering humanity, that I should lay these plain unvarnished truths before them, in the hope that the Colonization agents will apply their zeal, and the people contribute their money to more worthy objects. I will only say in reply to that article, that I plead guilty to the charge of having deceived the Liberians. It was necessary that I should do so, in order to procure a passport; and I leave it to any sane man, if he would not have done the same? Two-thirds of the balance of that article is bombast, got up to deceive the unwary. Talk of building a rail-road in Liberia! The idea is simply ridiculous!

WILLIAM NESBIT.

Hollidaysburg, Pa. June, 1855.

FOUR YEARS
IN LIBERIA

A

SKETCH

OF THE

LIFE

OF THE

REV. SAMUEL WILLIAMS.

[BY THE REV. SAMUEL WILLIAMS]

WITH REMARKS

ON THE

Missions, Manners and Customs of the Natives
of Western Africa.

TOGETHER WITH AN

ANSWER TO NESBIT'S BOOK.

1857

INTRODUCTORY.

I have read over the following pages (with the exception of the Answer to Nesbit's book), and I can candidly commend them as containing just and reliable information on the subjects of remark. The description of the Vey country and people, adjacent to Cape Mount, is particularly interesting; as this is a country but little known, and yet is inhabited by one of the finest races of people on the western coast.

Whoever purchases and reads this little work, will find himself repaid by its perusal. But besides this, he will contribute to assist a worthy man whose health has given way in the missionary work in Liberia, and has come to his native land to recruit it; and then to return again to his great missionary work. I know him personally, and believe him to be worthy of all confidence and sympathy. I commend him to the kindness of the friends of Christian civilization in Africa, and hope they will buy and read his little work. It will do good.

J. P. DURBIN,
Cor. Sec. Mis. Soc. of the M.E. Church.

Philadelphia, August, 1857.

[EDITOR's NOTE: Publication data carried on the original title page of Williams's *Four Years in Liberia* reads "Philadelphia: King & Baird, Printers, No. 607 Sansom Street. 1857."]

FOUR YEARS IN LIBERIA.

I WAS born in York county, in the State of Pennsylvania, in the year 1813. My father, whose name I bear, was a laboring man; he was respected by all who knew him. When I was nine years of age he moved to Harrisburg, Dauphin county, Pennsylvania. It was here that I formed my earliest associations. I was put out the first year of our residence to learn the business of a barber, which business I learned with great ease, and became quite an expert workman in a short time. My master moved from the State before I had served out my time, and I was left to my own will at the age of fourteen. By the advice of my father I went to live with a Mr. H. Vashon, with whom I remained over a year. I then went to Lancaster, and remained until I thought I was master of my profession. I returned to Harrisburg, but did not remain long in my old place. I was of rather a roving disposition, and I went to Huntingdon, and from that to Pittsburg, and after remaining in that city for one year I returned to Harrisburg, where I remained one winter. I then went up the river and found my way to Lewisburg, where I remained for about two years. I married there at the early age of twenty years. I did not remain in this place long after I was married, but returned to Pittsburg, and from thence moved to Johnstown. When I moved to this latter place I had become tired of a roving life, and thought I would settle myself for life. Johnstown at this time was but a small town, and I thought that I could make a living in it, and grow up with the place. In this I was not mistaken. I opened a shop and succeeded in business beyond my expectation.

I had up to the time of my settling in Johnstown, never thought of my condition as a man, and it was not until the year 1838, when the people of Pennsylvania voted for the amended constitution, that I really felt that I had not my rights in common with other men. I had ever since I had arrived at the age of twenty-one years voted at the elections; but at the election of that year, for some cause which I never could understand, I was not allowed to put my vote into the ballot-box. This was very grievous to me; and it was the more so, because this election was to determine whether I should vote in my native State again. I was dissatisfied, and was never afterwards reconciled to my lot, although my course was such here, and had always been everywhere, that I secured the respect of my neighbors and townsmen. I cannot say that I ever was mistreated in any place. My word became my bond in business, and wherever I went I met with a welcome. As far as my civil rights were concerned, I knew no difference; but my political rights were taken away, not by my own townsmen, but by a large majority of the people of the State. I, however, bore up against this until the Fugitive Slave Bill passed. I then concluded that I would find a new home some place in the world where the black man could be free.

Notwithstanding all the respect that was shown me by the citizens, yet I felt myself oppressed. I could have free privilege in all the churches; there was no negro pew for me in any church in the place, but I was treated with politeness and respect in them all. Yet there were times when I was oppressed, and one of those times was on election day; I felt that I was as good a man as there was in town, yet I dare not deposit a vote. I could talk, and I had my influence over a certain class of voters (yes, I say it boldly that I made more than one vote on election days), yet I could not put in one myself. This grieved me, and I could not see when the thing was to be any better. Another source of oppression to me was, I would sometimes go from home. Now my popularity, if it may be so called, was not only in my own town, or in the neighboring towns, but, whenever I would go beyond the circle of my acquaintances, I could see that things were changed, and frequently I would be sent in the kitchen to eat my meals when traveling. I was once ordered out of the first-class car to take a seat in the Jim Crow car. These things galled me, and after many years reflection on the subject, I came to the conclusion, if there was a free spot in all God's earth, I would seek that place.

I made inquiries about Canada, and found that it was not free from this wicked prejudice. Where was I to go? I had read much of Liberia, although I was a violent Abolitionist, and had been ever since converted to that faith by my friend Vashon. But I wanted a home where I could be free. I began to reflect seriously upon the subject of going to Africa, and I found that I could do so without infringing upon my Abolition principles; and I am just as strong in the faith to-day as ever I was in all my life. I always believed that there was many good Colonizationists, yet I thought that I might live in Liberia and be happy. So, in the year 1852, after having resided in Johnstown for near sixteen years, I concluded to visit Liberia and see it for myself, and if I found that it was or could be a country, I thought of casting in my lot with its citizens, and help to make it. I therefore began to get ready at once for my voyage. I made up my mind in March, and expected to start in October. I disposed of my business to a Mr. Wilson Patterson, a very worthy colored man, and set about in good earnest to prepare. When the citizens saw that I was in earnest, they agreed to help me, that the expense should not come on me entirely; and they were very liberal; they gave me nearly two hundred dollars, which sum defrayed the bulk of my expenses; and on the first of November I bid all my friends good-bye, and took the cars for Baltimore, but was delayed there for some four weeks in consequence of the vessel not being ready. On the 27th of that month I set sail, in company with Mr. Charles Deputie of Hollidaysburg, as visitors to Liberia. We were passengers on the same vessel that carried Bishop Scott out to hold the Liberia Conference in 1853. We all were professors of the religion of Christ; and more than that, were all Methodists, and not to be turned from our principles. More than this, I hope that we were all Christians. I must say that I found the Bishop a very pleasant companion. Brother Horne was also one of the cabin passengers, and we had a most delightful voyage after the sea-sickness had subsided. We had religious worship regularly all the way to Africa. The Bishop acted as preacher in charge, and gave out the Sabbath appointments; and I was somewhat surprised the second Sabbath at sea that I was to preach in the afternoon. I did so; and I believe that I gave satisfaction. I did the best I could, and was satisfied thus far with myself, yet I knew that it was a feeble effort. Mr. Horne had preached in the morning, and he had given us a practical discourse; and not only practical, but learned, for he is a learned man. He is now the Principal of Monrovia Seminary, and is much beloved by all who know him. This voyage terminated as the most of voyages do, without any thing very interesting to relate. We came to anchor off Monrovia on the sixth day of January, 1853.

I was favorably impressed with the country the first day that I landed. I was well treated by the citizens, and found them kind, and disposed to entertain strangers. I met two of my old acquaintance, Mr. Wm. Finley and Mrs. Rev. D. A. Wilson, the latter had been a resident of Johnstown and was now a missionary. Mr. Wilson was the principal in the Alexander High School, and was doing a good work in the Presbyterian ranks.

I was at church on the Sabbath following my arrival at Monrovia, and listened to Bishop Scott. He preached quite an able sermon. In the afternoon Brother Horne preached; the next Sabbath I preached in the afternoon. During the week I was much delighted in a trip up the St. Paul's; I saw many improved places, and a most beautiful river with high banks, and a good soil. I remained at Monrovia about two weeks and then went down the coast as far as Cape Palmas. After remaining on the coast until the 17th of March, I left very well satisfied with what I had seen in Africa, and reported favorably when I got home. I will here give that report, that those who have not seen it may read it now.

NOTES ON LIBERIA.

Liberia is located on the western shore of Africa, between the third and seventh degrees of north latitude. The land, in a general way, near the sea, is low and sandy, but back ten or twelve miles in the interior it becomes more elevated and the soil much better. There are a number of small rivers flowing into the sea within the confines of Liberia, the principal of which are the Grand Sesters,

St. Paul's, St. Johns, Junk, Sinoe, and Cape Mount. The St. Paul's is a fine stream: near its mouth it divides into two rivers—one is called Stockton Creek, and upon this branch stands Monrovia. The mouth is shallow, and large vessels cannot get over its bar, but small craft, of from ten to twenty tons burthen, pass over safely. Up this river are the settlements of Virginia, Upper and Lower Caldwell, and Millsburg; all fine settlements. I visited the first three, but did not get so far as Millsburg.

Monrovia has about fifteen hundred inhabitants, and is a beautifully located place, on a high elevation. It has a commanding view of the sea on two sides. I spent twenty-one days in the town and surrounding country, and think, every thing considered, it is a fine place.

Grand Bassa County comes next. Buchanan, the county-seat, is situated on the left bank of the St. John's, and the village of Edina is on the right hand. There is not the same appearance of thrift here that is seen in the upper settlements of the St. Paul's. Bexley is a promising settlement, about six miles up the river, and the citizens are getting along very well. Sinoe county is the last in the Republic, and Greenville is its county-town. The people manifest quite a spirit of enterprise. Greenville is situated at the mouth of the Sinoe river, and is beautifully laid out, its streets running at right angles. I was up the river, and visited the settlements, with which I was much pleased. Lexington is the last settlement made. It has not been in progress more than two years, but the inhabitants show a spirit of industry, and have got quite a clearing made in the forest. I walked across from this place to Louisiana, and saw there another most beautiful settlement. Every thing seemed to be in a thriving condition, and many of the farms were in a good state of cultivation here as well as in Lexington.

My choice of all the settlements that I saw is on the St. Paul's. The lands are principally taken up near the river, but there is an abundance of vacant land back from the river, which I have no doubt is as good, if not better, than that on the banks of the river. From all the information, however, that I could get, I believe the best site for a new settlement is on the Junk river. There emigrants would have the choice of land, inasmuch as there is no settlement as yet made. My plan is, when we go to Africa, to land at Monrovia, where we will have the advantage of the medical advice, which is of great importance to all new settlers. There we could remain until we were acclimated, and then our men might explore the country, and make their locations. They might improve them, and by the time the families were in a situation to remove, be ready to receive them. To go directly to the country would subject us to many inconveniences that we might avoid by being six or eight months in the town. Before commencing to farm, many of the necessaries of life would have to be obtained at the town, and we must learn the nature of native trade, on which we must depend for many things.

The productions of Liberia are very numerous; and if men, after they have got a start, will only be industrious, there is no danger about a living. They can raise cassada, sweet potatoes, and yams, which will answer much better for bread than wheat in that climate. They can buy rice from the natives, although this article is sometimes very dear; yet if emigrants are properly provided with articles of native trade, they can always buy at a fair price. Every emigrant ought to be able, before going out to Liberia, to procure some leaf tobacco, a box or two of clay pipes, a quantity of fish hooks, and a few pieces of blue cotton cloth; all of which is money with the natives, and you can buy with these what you cannot get for silver or gold.

The productions of Liberia are numerous; yet, in my opinion, the articles raised for exportation should be confined to coffee, indigo, arrow-root, ginger, and bird-pepper. My advice to friends in our Pennsylvania expedition would be to confine themselves to the raising of these five articles—and let them do so on a large scale, and they would soon find themselves in the possession of ease if not wealth, for all of these articles will command a ready sale in a foreign market, and they can be raised with comparatively little labor. Coffee and arrow-root grow best in a sandy soil; indigo grows everywhere, but if care is not exercised it becomes troublesome. I am told that the method of preparing this weed for market is very simple, and a considerable income might be realized from the exportation of it alone.

Pepper and ginger could also be made articles of profit to the producers of them. I am sorry to say that there is not as much attention paid to the growing of those articles as ought to be, and as soon will be. The people, as yet, do not know the value of them. As soon as they find that they can make more by a careful attention to their cultivation than by their present mode of trade and traffic, they will receive the attention they ought.

The first want of Liberia that we will mention, is that of a proper mode of fencing. Common wood fences are found not to answer the purpose, in consequence of the destructive nature of the bug-a-bug. This little insect is very troublesome at present. They will destroy any common wood fence that can be made, in the short space of two years. The people have tried hedges, but, in all cases, they are found to grow too large. Stone is too dear for the common use. But I am in hopes that it will be found that, when the country becomes generally under a state of cultivation, this troublesome insect will, in a great degree, disappear.

The next want of this country is beasts of burden. They have no way for transportation of goods or other things but by natives, and this is a very slow and ineffectual way. This difficulty will in a great degree disappear as fences are introduced. It is now more for the want of fences than any other cause that they have not horses, asses and oxen. All these animals will live and thrive well in Liberia. During my short stay there, I saw them all, and they looked well. The ass is as large as that of any other country, but the horse is much smaller than our American horses. It is about like what is known in this country as the Indian pony. The oxen, also, are very small. Generally, the cattle of Liberia grow to be about the size of our two yearlings, but I saw some larger and of a good medium size; these, however, are not common. None of these beasts can be kept in any number, for the want of fences. As soon as a plan of fencing can be introduced, beasts of all useful kinds will be raised in abundance.

The morals of Liberia are as good, perhaps, as those of any other country. A very large majority of the inhabitants are members of some religious body. The Methodist, Baptist, Presbyterian and Episcopalian are the religious bodies established, but the Methodists stand first as regards numbers. Their number is more than all the rest together, and I met many good, warm, old-fashioned Methodists. I was permitted to preach several times while in Liberia, and felt that the Lord was in our presence. I had the honor to preach to a number of distinguished persons, among whom was the President and lady, the Vice President, and others. I must confess that I felt some fear in getting up before the great ones of Liberia. But the Lord was with me, and I have not had more liberty for years than on that occasion.

There remains much yet to be done in Liberia. It is in the midst of heathenism. There are thousands who are yet without the knowledge of a Saviour; and, although they are doing considerable for the purpose of enlightening the heathen, yet it is as a drop in the bucket to what is wanted. This ought to induce holy men to embark for this land. This colony now is as a candle in a thick fog, whose light is seen but for a step. Every man could and ought to be a missionary, whether employed by the Board of Foreign Missions or not. His example and his influence ought all to go to persuade the natives of the truth of religion. Too many of the colonists forget this, and only think for themselves and of money, instead of doing something to promote the gospel. They take advantage of the natives, and by so doing injure the cause of Christ. I trust that a large emigration soon will go to Liberia which has the cause of Christ fully at heart, and be induced, for the love they have for their Master's cause, to labor for the enlightenment of the native Africans. I believe that much more could be done for them than is now doing.

All emigrants ought, in going to Liberia, to have some means, and ought not to be entirely dependent on the Society for their support. Although they are supported for six months, yet this is not sufficient, as all may expect to be more or less sick the first six months after going to Africa, and in consequence of which they are not in a proper frame of body or mind to make any preparations for the future. But if they had some means of their own, they, at the end of the six months, will have something to depend upon. Each family should have not less than two hundred dollars, which, if laid out in the States in tobacco, pipes, blue cotton cloth, &c., would answer at double that amount in Africa. The African fever may be regarded in about the same light as our American fever and ague. I saw several who were laboring under its influence, and the symptoms were about the same. The only difference, perhaps, is that the African fever is not as regular in its attacks as that of the American: but after the emigrants are once through the acclimation, they usually enjoy as good health in Liberia as in any other place. The citizens look very healthy, and if prudence and caution are exercised, there is but little to fear from the fever. Out of all the emigrants that went out last fall—three hundred and seventy—only sixteen had died up to the time of my leaving, and four of these were very old persons, and seven young children; which leaves only five that can properly be said to have died by the diseases of the land, and one of these brought it on by his own imprudence.

The climate of Liberia is tropical, and, consequently, it is warm. During my stay, I kept a regular note of the degree of heat, and the thermometer varied only seven degrees; it ranged from eighty-one degrees to eighty-eight degrees; eighty-one the lowest and eighty-eight the highest that I saw while on the coast of Africa. But this was always in the shade; to go into the sun there was a great difference. The sun in the heat of the day was very oppressive, and it was imprudent to be out from 10 A.M. to 3 P.M.; but I was out all hours of the day, and in three instances walked during all these hours, and found no other inconvenience or effect but a plentiful perspiration. On one or two excursions I had my son with me, and he stood it manfully. That day we walked about six miles, which is considered in Liberia a good walk. On another occasion I walked five miles in the middle of the day, and at another time I started at seven o'clock in the morning, and walked until two in the afternoon, many miles into the interior, and all this produced no bad effect on me. Although it is very warm, yet in-doors or in the shade it is quite pleasant, in consequence of the delightful breeze that is constantly blowing. It was during the dry season that I was in Liberia; but it is not to be supposed that it does not rain during this season of the year. It rained frequently during my stay in the country, and some very heavy showers. I was in the country seventy-one days, and I suppose I saw at least ten or fifteen good showers and one tornado. However, the tornado was after I left for home. I will assure any one that it was no plaything as it presented itself to us aboard the ship.

The fruits of this country are not so numerous nor so delightful as those of our own country. They have the orange, lemon, lime, soursop, guava, pawpaw, mango, plum, pine apple, and many others of less importance.

The fresh meats are nearly the same as we get in our own market, with the exception of goat meat. They have beef, pork, mutton, and venison of a very good quality. Chickens, ducks, and sometimes turkeys are brought to market. Fresh fish are to be had in great abundance. Mackerel are caught at Monrovia, and they are very good indeed.

A country would be a paradise indeed if there were no objections to be urged against it, and I have some to urge against Liberia. The first I would name is the naked condition of the natives. They are in town in vast numbers, and they have nothing in the world upon them but a cloth around their loins. Men and women go dressed in nearly the same style. This custom might be stopped, for the colonists have all the law-making in their hands, and they could easily pass a law making it unlawful for them to come to town without a covering upon them. Why this is not done, for the life of me, I cannot see. But when once the country is filled up with people from the Northern States, they surely will have an eye to this matter.

The next objection that I find to Liberia, is the indolence or seeming indolence of many of the colonists. There is not in the country as much industry as ought to be. Very many of the lots in the city of Monrovia are wholly neglected, and suffered to grow up with weeds and bushes, when, if they were cultivated, they would yield enough, almost, for the support of the families occupying them. This is to be attributed more to the kind of people who have settled them than to any other cause. They are principally emancipated slaves, who do not appreciate freedom in its proper light, but think that when once free they are at liberty to be industrious or otherwise, and many choose to be lazy. Now, if, in my opinion, the Northerners could be induced to go to Liberia, we would soon find quite a different state of things. The great majority of the present colonists are from the South, and have adopted southern habits, the state of society being more southern than any thing else. For instance, all love to have a servant to wait upon them, both gentlemen and ladies. If it is but to carry a lantern, or to carry a fish, it must be done by a servant.

Another objection is, the preference given to native labor over that of Americans. Many of the colonists are in want of work to make something to enable them to get the comforts of life, but the natives are employed in preference, because they can live on twenty-five cents per day, while the colonists must have seventy-five cents. Now, this is wrong. Let all the poor Americans be employed by the rich, and let them by these means be helpers to each other, and this will advance the interests of the country to a very great extent. It would do away with the necessity of all emigrants having money to start with. The present mode of traffic and trade I condemn; not that it does the individual any harm morally, but because it is depriving the soil of so many tillers. To build up a great nation, the soil must be brought into active employment. It must be tilled, and its productions thrown into market—the income of which must enrich the country. All settlements must have their traders; but in Liberia nearly every man is a trader. If he is a farmer, he associates with this native trade, and very frequently he has to neglect the one for the other.

Wants of emigrants going to Liberia. You are told not to take with you any thing for housekeeping; that you can get every thing there in the shape of furniture. My advice, however, is to take along every thing you possibly can, as every thing is difficult to be obtained in Africa. Every family ought to be provided with bed-steads, tables, chairs; and, in a word, every thing that is needed in this country you will need in Liberia, unless I might except feather-beds. All who have these would do well to sell them, and buy in their stead good hair mattrasses. Do not be prevailed upon to go without the things for housekeeping, as you will be sorry after it is too late. Every thing in the shape of household furniture or kitchen utensils are very high. They cost four times what they would in the States. You ought to be provided with one barrel of salt beef and one of pork. Take shoes enough for one year. You ought to have a keg of good butter, to serve until you get accustomed to the palm oil, after which you would rather have it. It would be well if each family could take a barrel of flour to serve them until they become accustomed to rice and other African productions.

Here I must end my advice and my report of what I have seen. Much that is to me deeply interesting I must omit. It only remains for me to return my sincere thanks to those whose friendship has cheered me in undertaking a voyage fraught with anxiety and peril, but which has richly repaid me. I see in Liberia the elements of a great State. From her borders I behold an influence issuing which shall yet elevate my race in the future to that proud position which it once held in the past. Although my birth-place, and the birth-land of my fathers, and endeared to me as holding the bones of a now sainted parent, it is my wish only to remain in the United States until a company can be organized which shall go out together, taking with them a saw-mill and an apparatus for making iron—ore yielding, in Liberia, 90 per cent. In a few months longer, I trust, I shall go to the home of my fathers, there to aid in upbuilding a new republic, and in founding a mighty empire. Would to God I could persuade my brethren everywhere to go with me, so that, after being aliens and exiles, like Israel in Egypt, for so many long years, we might at least die in the land of our fathers.

SAMUEL WILLIAMS.

There was quite an excitement raised after this report was published. I received letters from all parts of the State, some making inquiries, some applauding me for my adventures, and some abusing me for trying to deceive the people; some I answered and some remains to be answered yet. The first week after I came home several called from distant towns to see me, and to make inquiry respecting my impressions. I gave to all what was the honest convictions of my mind in the matter, and told them that for me and my family we would go to Liberia; others might do as they please. It was proposed by several that we should raise a joint stock company. I agreed to the proposal, which was the worst thing that I ever did in all my life. My plan was, in the first place, to go in copartnership with men who could each raise a little money and reside in Africa as merchants; but I was persuaded out of this. I thought that a saw mill would do well in the country (and I yet believe that one could do well, but it will have to be on a different plan from that which we took with us). There were four of us who were very anxious for Africa: Chas. Deputie, Thomas Lilason, John H. M. Harris, and myself. We four commenced to raise a company, and succeeded, as the public know. The Pennsylvania Colonization Society loaned us enough to purchase our saw mill, and we raised amongst the company some sixteen hundred dollars, which was laid out in goods, with a credit of near that much more. We got all in readiness to go to our new home in Africa. The company consisted of John H. M. Harris, Wm. Nesbit, Thomas Lilason, Chas. Deputie, Alfred Truman, Curtis G. Carr, David Kelly, Elias A. Briar, Wm. Thomas and myself. Briar and Thomas remained behind; Briar came out the next fall. Thus equipped, we repaired to New York to take the vessel that was to sail on the 1st of November, but we were detained in New York until the 10th. On the afternoon of that day we left the pier that we had laid by and commenced our voyage for Liberia. Mr. Pinney accompanied us out into the bay, and, after he had made all necessary arrangements, he bid us good bye, wishing us a prosperous voyage and a happy home in Africa. We soon got under way. Our women suffered much from sea sickness for some three weeks, for we had very rough weather during all that time. After this we had a very pleasant trip to the coast. We found that Mr. Pinney had laid in an ample supply of everything that was necessary for our comfort. We had all kinds of vegetables and fresh meats. I do not believe that there was ever an emigration that was better fitted out than we were, and yet, with all this, some was disposed to complain; so that it is impossible for one man to please everybody in a company, even small as ours was. We enjoyed ourselves very much aboard ship—we had our debates and other amusements—and the captain seemed glad that we were all so happy; his name was Miller, and a better man, I think, could not be found to carry emigrants than he. Every attention was paid to the sick, both of the cabin and steerage; and frequently he would have the sick women brought from below and placed in the cabin, that they might have the more air. I was much pleased with him; his officers also were very kind to us all. The first mate's name was Hatch, and the second's McGill; both did all that they could to make us comfortable and happy, and happy we were. After spending forty days on the voyage we, on the night of the 18th of December, dropped anchor opposite the Light House on the Monrovia Heights, and the next morning all was bustle to get ready to go ashore. A number of gentlemen called off in the morning to see us, as they had been looking for us for some days. All expressed their satisfaction at finding us in such good health and spirits. We all got ashore by three o'clock in the afternoon, and I believe that every one was well pleased with the town, unless it was Mr. Nesbit. I heard him remark, after seeing it, that it was rather a one horse town; but even he forgot that it was a one horse town after we got our goods opened and had sold for some two or three days. It seemed that money drove all notions out of his head about either one or two horse towns.

We were now in Liberia, and had to begin to take care of ourselves. One of the first steps, after our goods were opened and the families comfortable, was to look out a location for the saw mill, when it would come out, as we expected it in a very short time. In this, however, we were mistaken, as it did not get out until the first of April. In the meantime we had selected for its location a place on the Junk river, at or near Marshall, in the midst of a fine timber district, and supposed that we would have no difficulty in getting the lumber to market after it was sawed; but in this we were greatly disappointed. We found that to get it from this place to Monrovia or Bassa it would cost as much as to freight it from the States; and hence, we were greatly crippled in our plans. The erection of the mill was a very expensive operation, and this, in connection with our not getting the lumber to market, were the principal causes of our failure. We had expended a large amount of our means in the erection of the mill that should have been remitted to our creditors in the States, and expected to replace it when the mill would get into operation; but here we failed, because there was no means of transportation but by way of the river and in canoes, and then it had to be carried four miles, across the summit or dividing ridge that divided the Junk waters from those of Monrovia, which was a very slow and expensive operation. Our lumber accumulated on our hands at the mill, until a considerable quantity spoiled during the rainy season. Our stock of goods was getting low and we strained every nerve to remit to our merchants in Philadelphia what was due, that we might get another stock. We succeeded in raising all the money that we owed our dry goods merchant, which was a considerable bill, and wrote to him our circumstances, and hoped in a short time to receive a new lot of goods, which, if we had, we would have recovered from our embarrassed circumstances. But instead of the goods we received a letter that the firm had failed shortly after we had remitted. This at once struck terror among all our men. Now began difficulty for me. Some of the company began to complain against me for bringing them to Africa, and I was abused; they said I had made wrong statements to them concerning this country. But strange to say, that while we were in flourishing circumstances, I had told all truth, and was one of the best of men. At one of the meetings of the company they gave me a vote of thanks, and could scarcely find language to express their delight at what I had done for them; but when circumstances changed I was the sole cause of all their misfortunes. These things grieved me much, to think that those who I had looked upon as my best friends should now try and attach all the blame to me for our misfortune, when the whole thing was a train of circumstances out of my power to control. It was unfortunate in the first place that we brought the saw mill to the country; but I did not do so, nor was it my advice. My plan was to associate myself with two of the present members and put our means together and come as merchants; but one of these men was the most anxious that we should bring the mill. It was equally unfortunate that it was located on the Junk; but I did not do this, it was done by the committee; to be sure I was one of that committee, and I was in favor of putting it on the Junk; but I was but one man, and the committee consisted of five, and every man was in favor of it being just where it was put. But as soon as we failed in our expectation I was blamed for every fault that had been committed, and for what were not faults. I was hurt and grieved at all this, and if the men alone had been my accusers I would not have thought so hard, but their wives also complained against me. I thought of Moses, how very unpleasant he and Aaron must have felt when the whole camp of Israel rebelled against them. I retired from all business of the company, resigned my office and went to my farm, and have had nothing more to do with the affair since, more than to give my advice, and once or twice helped them out of a hard place by making small advancements for them. My means, that I put into the concern, I consider all gone; and let it go, but let me have peace. After our failure in getting goods I proposed to go at once to the States, and, by the aid of my friends, I felt that I could yet save the company, but they would not consent that I should go; they struggled for a while, like a drowning man, and at last ceased.

As far as our mercantile operations were concerned, we were dead. The saw mill still struggled on, and is yet gasping, but never can recover. In the first place it is the wrong kind of a mill for the country: the expenses attending the working of it are too great, unless it could be done by native labor, which cannot be procured at all. And as I stated before, the difficulty of transportation is too great; so that upon the whole it finally must go down. Having given a brief but faithful statement of our business affairs, I will now say something in relation to the country.

Liberia, like all other countries, is not a paradise. If it were, men would not be so hard to persuade to come to it, but would seek to partake of the fruits of the garden. Nor is it on the other hand a purgatory; but like all other lands, it has its sweets and its bitters, its sorrows and its pleasures, its life and its death. Yes,

death has found its way into the peaceful regions of Western
Africa. In America I have seen husband and wife parted; children snatched from the embraces of their parents, and friend
fall by the side of friend. Death sometimes makes awful havoc
among the living, and strikes consternation and alarm unto
thousands that she spares. See them flying from the monster,
leaving home, property, business and friends, and fleeing for
terror!—what is the matter? DEATH is in town, in my neighborhood, yea in my house! Steamboats crowded, cars packed all in
confusion, and what does all this mean?—DEATH, death is here!

And let me inform my reader that death is in Liberia, though
not so terrible as in other countries. There is no great occasion
of alarm; there are no sweeping epidemics. The cholera has
never yet visited her shores; the yellow fever has not yet made its
appearance in Liberia; the small-pox is but seldom seen; the
measles, the scarlet-fever, the typhus fever, and a host of other
diseases, do not infest her shores. And yet we have said that
death is here; yes, it is here, and friend must part from friend,
brother from sister, and husband from wife. We have witnessed
this in Liberia as well as in America, and where shall we go where
the monster is not, and where is it not the enemy of man? They
have found that all the gold of California or Australia could not
bribe it to remain from those rich regions. The power of Russia,
or England, or America, or all combined, cannot conquer it,
and keep it out of their territories. And why is it expected that
death ought not to visit Liberia? It is not expected, but by the
enemies of Liberia; and they do not expect this, but argue it.
And when one dies in Liberia, what a wonder! Oh, how awful!
And the friends who have been left in America, mourn over the
fate of those that died in Liberia. But if they had remained in
America and died, it would not have been anything out of the
usual course of events. But how awful because they died in Liberia. Foolish creatures who reason thus. Why not die in Liberia
as well as in America? Death is but the common lot of us all
whether here or there. One of our good citizens visited the
States a short time ago and died in New York; but his friends do
not reflect on America as being the cause of his death, and ad-

vise all others to remain in Liberia, for fear, if they go to New York, they will die. No, some unforseen cause led to his death, and no reflections upon any one or place. But, say the enemies of Liberia, the acclimating fever is what destroys our friends that go to Liberia. Well, out of the fifty that came out in the emigration with me, there were but two died with the acclimating fever; and one of these was at the advanced age of eighty-six years. Although up to this time, there are ten dead, all the rest have died with other complaints: one from the effects of salivation; one from pleurisy; one from dropsy. Now, why all this hue and cry? But I admit that some emigrations suffer more than others, and the reason is simply this: some come here that will have their own way in spite of all that doctor or agent or any other person can do to prevent. And those are they that suffer most. But I do say that where proper care is taken by the emigrant, but few die. I will also remark that some locations are more healthy than others; and those who choose for themselves in coming to Liberia, ought to be particular on this point, and find out the most healthy location and settle there. I would here say, that Cape Mount is unquestionably the healthiest in all the country. Emigrants coming here have scarcely any fever, and a great many escape altogether. It is a beautiful place. I have visited a number of the settlements since residing in the country, and I pronounce all in a prosperous condition. In some of them agriculture is beginning to be carried on to a considerable degree. The St. Paul's farmers are in general, industrious and prosperous. Many very fine plantations are to be seen. Amongst which we will name Jordon's, Richardson's, Outland, Blacklidge and others, who have as good sugar plantations as I ever saw in the neighborhood of New Orleans. They are not as yet making as good an article of sugar as they do on the Mississippi, but the molasses is superior to Orleans molasses. Several fine coffee farms are to be seen also along the banks of the river; and, I think, as far as my judgment goes, that the people of this region are doing as well as they could possibly do any where. I spent some days along the river in December last, and was highly delighted with the prospects of a great and rich community in a short time.

Junk settlement is progressing but slowly. They have not had any increase from emigration since the first Marshall family: hence the name. I will say of this region, that a family can live cheaper than in any other part of Liberia that I know anything about. Here you are in a good farming community (native farming). Rice grows in abundance, and can be had in the proper rice season for about thirty cents per kroo or half bushel. Cassadas grow in great abundance, and can be bought for almost nothing. I am speaking of things in general. The last year has been an exception to the general rule; there has been an unusual scarcity both of rice and cassada, and both were much dearer than usual. The Junk river is one of the best in the republic for fish. The large mullet is taken here in great abundance, and is a superior fish; it eats much like the shad when fresh—it is by far the best fish in this country. There is also an abundance of oysters of the very best quality, and easy to catch. The principal food of the citizens in the dry season are fish and oysters. I lived on this fare for some two and a half years, and was no ways tired of it. Had things been left to my choice, I would have gladly remained at Marshall. The people of this settlement are the most happy people that I ever saw, they are sure of enough to eat, and that seems to be all they care for; they make no effort to improve the place or the land, but eat fish and oysters, cassada and rice, and talk politics. They all trade a little, and are an exception to all others. I am glad to learn that the universal practice of native trade that existed a few years ago, is fast getting into disrepute among the thinking portion of the people, and they are encouraging agriculture in its stead. And the time is not far in the distance when men will generally see that this practice is not to their advantage nor the advantage of the country.

On the whole our beloved little republic is on the advance; and in spite of all that can be done by her enemies in the United States, she will grow into greatness; although a Nesbit and a Delany, a Purvis, and a host of others have sworn that she shall

not prosper. She will let them see that they have not the power
to stop her progress. Her churches, her schools, her benevolent
societies, all tell to the world that she lives in the age of improvement, and cannot be held back by designing men, neither white
nor black. She is now reckoned among the nations of the earth;
and who is he that can tell what is in the future for her. Carthage
was once smaller than Liberia, and to what greatness did she rise
in five centuries. Liberia is on the same continent, and after a
lapse of some two thousand years, who knows but that another as
great as Carthage is to arise, to give laws to the nations in Africa,
if not to foreign nations? We have plenty of nations within our
own limits that we can and will give laws to, and teach them the
customs of civilized life, and they are already beginning to look
up to us for this; and it is not unfrequent that we are called upon
to settle their disputes and wars, which we always do in an ami-
cable way, and make all parties satisfied.

The time will come when Liberia will be regarded in a far
different light, with such men at her helm as she has had to
guide her since her national existence. She must advance, and
that rapidly. Roberts, who was the man for the times, has no superior as a ruler of a young nation; and it seems providential
that he should be here to take hold at the very time of all others
that he was most needed. He is called old Gruff—gruff as he
may be, he knows how to rule, and when all things seems to be
in a fair channel to prosperity, he leaves or vacates his chair. In
other words, he refuses to be renominated, but leaves it for another, who was providentially spared from the merciless hand of
the savage, to be the chief magistrate of this young nation. And
why do men fight against God? for can it not be easily seen that
God has this young nation under his fostering care? Stephen A.
Benson, the mild and unassuming, if he has any fault it is that of
diffidence. He does not desire to take the honors that is due
him. He is a Christian, a gentleman, and a statesman. I was present at a meeting between him on the part of the government,
and a number of the chiefs of the Vey country, and I was delighted to see with what calmness and decision he talked the
Palaver. He was settling a difficulty between themselves. And

when they would grow noisy and angry at each other, he could bring them to order with the utmost ease. Now all that Liberia wants to secure her future greatness, is to keep men like these always in office, and not to let politics get the better of their judgment, but always vote for the best and ablest men, and all will be right and the country grow. In a century from this time, the offspring of her now most inveterate enemies amongst the colored race will be seeking protection under her wings. Yes, though men may talk and write and threaten, yet they cannot stop the advancement of truth, liberty and civilization. These things will advance in spite of all the combined powers of the world or hell.

Shortly after my arrival in Liberia I became connected with the missionary operations; and, after spending one year in this labor, I became much interested in it, and came to the conclusion to spend the remainder of my days in the cause; although it is a work that is attended in some cases with much labor and exposure, and that at small pay as far as pecuniary pay goes; yet, it is a most delightful work to those who have the worth of souls at heart; and this I trust that I have. My first appointment was at Marshall, to take charge of the small society there. Here I labored for two years; and I do most sincerely hope that I was the instrument, in God's hands, of doing some good, both to the settlers and the surrounding natives. I can look back to this field of labor with feelings of delight, and at the place with sorrow. It was here that I had many seasons with a few good brethren and sisters. And this is the place that contains the remains of a beloved wife. But then I reflect that she did not die as do those who have no hope, but in the full confidence of a Redeemer's love. Her ashes rest in a grove near the Methodist Episcopal Church, where she will remain until she and I shall be summoned by the great trumpet's sound. May my last days be as peaceful as hers.

After spending two years in this charge, Conference, in its wisdom, thought fit to remove me from that to my present station at Cape Mount, although I would rather have remained where I was. But I am a believer in the itinerant plan, and as far

as civilized communities are concerned, I believe there is no
plan like it. But for the native work I do think that a preacher
who is accepted of them ought not to be removed, until death
removes him; he should learn their language, live among them,
and become one of them.

But to return, I of course, after my appointment was read out,
made all possible haste to get to my new field of labor, and arrived at Cape Mount on the 7th of January, 1857, and found all
peaceable among the brethren. But my labors are not confined
to the settlement, but I have all the accessible part of the Vey
country to attend to. And I must say here, in the language of
sacred writ, "the harvest truly is great, but the laborers are few."
This is a very interesting country. The natives are in the advance
of their neighbors of the leeward coast at least fifty years. I have
made several excursions among them, and was truly astonished
to find so much intelligence. But as it has been the universal
custom for ages gone by, to get all off a stranger that they can, it
remains to a great degree the same yet amongst this people.
They are shrewd in trade, and the man that gets any thing off
them pays for it. But yet these people are very anxious to be
instructed, and any of the chiefs would be willing to allow a
school to be established in his town for the purpose of instruct-
ing his children.

Among other places I visited Gordonama, an interior town,
situated twenty-five miles from the coast. I found the path or
rather the water course much obstructed by roots, logs and
trees; and after spending part of two days in getting to the head
of navigation, I at last arrived there, and then walked about four
and a half hours to get to the town. It was dark when I arrived,
and could see but little; so I got supper and went to bed for the
night. I got up early in the morning and was astonished at what
I saw. The house that I lodged in was the largest in the place,
and it was truly a fine house. It was on the public square where
all the town meetings are held. They held a meeting the night
that I was there, and I was much interested with the affair. About
seven o'clock the big bell suspended at one end of the house in
which I lodged, was rung, and a boy could be heard proclaiming

through the street, and calling all the people together. I went to the piazza and took a seat to see what was to be done. A young man, that spoke English very well, came and seated himself by my side, and told me that the people were called to hear words from the king, who was absent at that time. It was concerning a report that a neighboring town was preparing to make war on this town, and he warned his people to be ready; that they should call all the people from the small towns, and from the farms, and should keep a strict watch; and if any thing happened, that they should dispatch a herald to him immediately. This was about the amount of the address, which was given by a young man of beautiful countenance. His mien was erect while he was addressing the people. Speaking of the bravery of his townsmen and the feats they had done in wars, he became most intensely excited. He would throw up his arms and his head, and his whole gesture was grand and vehement. When about to conclude, he threw up his spear in the air and yelled in the most wild and frightful manner, that alarmed me no little. The yell was responded to by the whole assembly. And now came fun: The banjos struck up, and the drum began to play, and all was commotion. The whole company fell into a regular dance. No women are allowed at these meetings. I was somewhat amused at several very old men, who were so old that they could not get their feet up, would stand still, and all animation, lift the heel and try to keep time to the music. After spending twenty or thirty minutes in this way, the whole company dispersed, and in a few minutes more all was still throughout the town, with the exception of the sentinel's call. I thought while thus looking at the proceeding of this evening, if this people could be brought into civilized habits, what a noble people they would be. The Vey people are surely a superior people, and a remarkably good looking set of men.

I took a stroll around town, and I saw much industry. The people were spinning and weaving, and making crockery ware; it presented quite a business appearance. I stopped to notice how the women spun their cotton, and was astonished at the simplicity of the machine. It was nothing more than a stick with a socket on the one end, and a split in the other; the socket end went down, and an oyster shell served to let it spin in; the cotton thread was fastened to the stick or spindle, and the operator would start it with the thumb and finger, and while the speed would keep up, she would make the best of her time in letting out the thread, and when the speed would cease, she would wind up what she had let out and start it again. Thus by a continuous application of thumb and finger, the speed would be kept up all day, and quite an amount of thread made. I next stopped in a weaver's shop, and this was about as strange as the spinning. He has his reeds and gears as any other weaver, but they are of a diminutive size; the reeds are not more than from four to six inches in width, and hence they do not make any cloth wider than this. But to make up this deficiency, they will sew piece to piece, until they have it as wide as they may want it. I have seen some most beautiful cloths made in this rude way, and they are quite an article of trade on the coast.

After looking at all the curiosities, I returned to my room to await breakfast, and in due time there was brought me a large bowl of rice and palaver sauce, and a pitcher of cold water. I took breakfast, and then walked out to take a look at the suspension bridge that crossed the river, or creek. I had crossed it the evening before, but I could not see what it was like, as it was dark; when I approached it now, I saw a bridge constructed on the same principle on which that of Roebling's Wire Suspension Bridges are constructed. Here vines are used instead of wire: vine after vine has been laid across the river, until it has become of sufficient strength, and then the whole is wrapped with another vine, which forms it into a body of some five or six inches in diameter. After the two side pieces are thus put up, they have then worked it with a kind of basket work, and completed it by ties from the centre, that pass to either side, and fasten to a tree. Take the bridge as a whole, it is about one of the greatest curiosities that I have met with in Africa. The stream over which the bridge passes, is sixty or eighty feet wide.

It was here that a great massacre took place a few years ago. Gordonama was at war with some of the people in that region;

the enemy thought to steal a march upon the people of Gordonama, and came in a body. But the king of this place was on the look out, and had his spies stationed in all directions; when the enemy approached near to the crossing place, they found that a recent rain had swelled the stream bank full, and they were reduced to the necessity of resorting to the bridge as a crossing place. The spies were on the alert, and waited until the whole army was across, with the exception of what was then on the bridge; it was sufficient to contain some forty or fifty. At this juncture, the ambuscade rushed out, and with one slash of the cutlass they severed the ties of the bridge at the one end, and let the whole thing down into the stream with all that was on it; and the stream being bank full, there was no chance for any to escape. But some forty or fifty fell victims to this scheme. The residue of the army seeing what had befallen their comrades, were filled with consternation, and began to fly for their lives. George Kain, the king of Gordonama, pursued, and great was the slaughter that day; many of the drowned floated down the river and out at the bar-mouth. This struck terror into all the enemies of Kain, and he had peace for a considerable time.

After viewing this bridge, I returned to my lodgings, and received the head men of the city, to have a talk with them about the prospects for mission operations among them. I met some six or eight of the principal men, and they gave me much encouragement. They told me that Kain was very favorable to every thing that would give his people knowledge, and for that purpose he had a Mandingo God-man in his town. I told them that our God palaver was much better than the Mandingo's, and our books would learn them more sense. These head men were all willing that operations should be commenced in their town, with the exception of one. He was the chief warrior, and was called a Softly man. It was said of him, that he could approach an army of any number without being perceived. He had the power to blind the eyes of all, and walk amongst the enemy and see all they were doing and depart, and no one could be the wiser. I, of course, believed as much of this as I pleased; but this man was opposed to my coming to the town as a preacher or a teacher—he thought that they did not need my instruction, and would not have any thing to say to me afterwards. But by the rest of these head-men I was treated with much kindness. They told me that I should make myself easy, as this was my town.

My house was continually beset by a host of women and children, who were led there by curiosity to see the white God-man, as they called me. I was perhaps the first preacher that had ever visited this place, and they all wondered, no doubt, what was to be the result of my visit. After the consultation with the chiefs, I invited them all to come in the evening and hear me talk God-palaver; and when the evening came, the room which was about twenty feet square, was filled with those that wished to hear what was to be said. After all was seated on the floor, or on such things as they could get to set upon, I told them by an interpreter, that before I talked to them, I must talk to God; and to do this, I told them they must all get on their knees. I was obeyed, and all of us knelt down before God in this heathen town, and perhaps the most for the first time in all their lives. I prayed to the great Giver of all good to meet me on this occasion, and give the words that I was about to utter, power to reach the hearts of this poor benighted people, and while I thus prayed, the spirit of the Lord came upon me, and I was much blessed, and felt greatly encouraged to talk to this people. After prayer, I spoke to them of God's power, and of his mercy and goodness. They seemed to sanction all that I said, and listened with the utmost attention. I spoke about twenty minutes, and after I was done, they all seemed pleased with what they had heard. I concluded the exercise with prayer, and dismissed the congregation. I was so much encouraged by what I had seen, and the impressions that I thought were made, that I made up my mind to attend to this people regularly. And although the distance was great, yet I hoped to be able to visit them at least once a month. This visit was made in the latter end of January, 1857. But in my arrangements I was frustrated. I was not in good health at the time I paid this visit, and on going home my health became so very poor, that I thought it prudent to remain in the settlement, and confine my labors to it. But I had frequent opportunities to talk with the natives, and I met Kain when he came down on business with the government, and had frequent conversations with him on the subject of a mission at his place; he is perfectly willing that it should be, and indeed is anxious to have a school in his town, and promises to protect the Missionary whoever he may be. He himself is fond of talking on the subject of the Christian religion, and while in the settlement he visited the Church several times. He often calls at my house to converse with me, and of course I always turn the subject of conversation upon religion. He is quite intelligent, and speaks English very well.

I consider the town of Gordonama of more importance as a mission post than any other place in my knowledge; and I am quite extensively acquainted in the Bassa country, having lived in it for upwards of two years. This place is important on account of its large population. Kain tells me that he can muster for the field five hundred and sixty men, which would make the population at least fifteen hundred. Now, in this number, there are many that are at least half civilized, having lived with the settlers when young. Many speak English very well, and it would not take a great deal of labor to secure their influence at least; and, in some cases, some of this class might embrace religion, which would advance the cause very much.

Again, this place would be of great importance, because, that missionaries residing here, could receive their supplies with much more ease than from any other large town that I know of. They can be brought within twelve or fifteen miles of the town, and then it can be packed by natives from this place for a small amount.

Another reason that I would give, which in my opinion adds importance to the place—it is a kind of depot to the interior trade—the interior people bring their stuff thus far and barter it with this people and return home. It is but seldom that the bushman ever beholds the sea coast. This is law; and this law is made by the people of Gordonama and the neighboring towns. It certainly is very unjust, and ought to be done away. Now, the missionary would be able to exert an influence to have this matter set right; and more than this, those bushmen would hear the gospel, and would carry the tidings of it into the interior with them, and excite the people of their region to have the like operation among them. It would prove a great key to the vast Goula and Mandingo countries.

I feel confident that if there was a judicious effort made and proper men employed for this work, that success would attend. But it wants men that are not afraid to die; that would not turn aside from duty at every seeming difficulty. They must be brave men—men that have the cause of Christ much at heart—men that are willing to make every sacrifice that is required of them for the work's sake. I am in great hopes that the time is not far off when there will be a move in this—when the Board of Missions to which I am attached, may take the matter in hand, and plant Christianity in the great interior of Western Africa. The expenses attending a missionary operation in the interior would not be as great as on the coast. In the first place, they could build much cheaper. The buildings, of course, would be of a different kind; yet they could make very comfortable houses for one-fourth of what it would cost in Liberia. For instance, I built a mission house for the conference at Marshall, which is in the old settlement, at the cost of seven hundred dollars. This house was thirty feet by thirty-two, and perhaps will last twenty years. I built another mission house, on the native plan of building, at Cape Mount, twenty-four feet by thirty-six, and quite as comfortable as the former, at the cost of one hundred dollars; and this house will last at least, in careful hands, ten years. So, for seven hundred dollars, we will have a house for seventy years instead of twenty. Thus, could the mission build all her houses in the interior, and missionaries could live fully as cheap in the interior as on the coast; they could buy the country produce for one half the coast price, and could afford to pay a little more for what they import.

I trust in God that this country's redemption draws nigh. Oh! that God may inspire the hearts of many to lay hold of this important work; and may every one that enlists, enlist with the motto of a sainted Cox as their watchword: "Though a thousand fall, let not Africa be abandoned." There are many more important places in this region that might be occupied with profit. Medenia is a most beautiful little place, and its head man quite a gentleman; but not so favorable to the preaching of the gospel amongst his people. There is Sugary, another small place owned by King Sandfish, an old man of at least eighty years; his head and beard as white as wool; he is very pleasant in his manners, and quite a friend to the Liberians, and does much for them. He is a very strict Mahometan, but yet he allows any one to come to his town and preach the Christian religion. I visited his place once, and expect to make it one of my regular preaching places.

The natives of this portion of Africa are a very strange and singular people, and their customs are perhaps different from all others. First we notice them in their agricultural pursuits. In the month of January this operation commences by cutting down all the small bushes that grow on the land that they wish to cultivate. This is done with an instrument that they call a bill-hook. This instrument is not large, and it is crooked at the end like the hawk's bill, hence it derives its name. With this instrument it is surprising the amount of work they will do in a day. After all the small bush is cut, they let it lay for some time to dry before felling the larger trees upon it. After it is sufficiently dry, then they begin to cut what they call the big stick. This is the tree that is too large to be cut with a bill-hook; this they do with a country made axe. This weapon would make our backwoods-man laugh if it was handed to him to clear his forest with. The country blacksmith has not yet learned to put an eye in an axe, and hence to avoid this difficulty he puts the eye in the handle. He thinks it much easier to put a hole through wood than through iron. The axe is about two inches wide at the bit, and tapers towards the pole, until it runs off to a sharp point; they then procure a good solid stick that has a knot at the end, and then they burn a hole in this end through the knot, and the axe is stuck through this hole. It is then ready for operation. With this machine they go to work upon the big stick. The sapling they fell with great ease; but when they come to a large tree, they begin to make preparations to attack its upper branches.

To do this, they build a scaffold alongside so that they can get up to the small part of the tree, and here they cut, as they believe that the wood is much softer up from what it is at the ground. If the tree is very large, they will climb up and cut off all the branches, limb by limb. They have no care how matters look, so that they remove the shade from the ground. After all the big sticks have been cut and trimmed down so that they will lay close to the earth, they then rest; having done all the work of cutting, they now wait for the sun to do its part in drying the whole mass and preparing it for the flames. After some three or four weeks of dry weather they apply the torch, and with the wind blowing fresh from the sea, it soon communicates to every part of the cut district and consumes all the leaves and small branches, with all the insects that might have been on the soil. While the fire is burning the men are singing to some favorite idol or god to help the flames to do its work, for upon this depends the hope of success in reaping a crop.

It is a fact that rice does not grow well on land that is not burnt. I know this from experience. Many a poor fellow, after all the labor that he has expended in cutting his farm, when he attempts to burn it sees all his labor lost, the fire refusing to do its part; that man is doomed to be hungry for one whole year. This was the cause of the hard times that we have had for the last two years in Liberia; the farms were all cut as usual, but the rains set in before the farms were dry enough to burn, and in some districts, in consequence of this, there was nearly starvation produced. If it had not been for the bountiful provisions of Providence in planting the palm tree, many hundreds would have starved. It did not alone affect the countryman, but the colonist too was the sufferer. Formerly, he could buy his rice for one dollar per bushel, but now the price rose in proportion to the demand, and he had to pay four dollars. Cassada, too, rises in proportion. Formerly, he could get it for twelve and-a-half cents, now he pays fifty. Thus, hard times were universal in all the land. After the burning operation, then comes the planting process. This is done by the women with a small hoe, which is called the rice hoe. This thing is about as large as a large blade of a Congress penknife, and is stuck into a stick about eighteen inches long. With this is done the ploughing that is done in these parts. After the rice is scattered over the ground, then this instrument is used in scratching it under. It is a very tedious process. Often there will be in one field of about five acres some ten or twelve women, and of all the singing and noise that was ever heard, are heard on these occasions. After this operation is over, then there is a season of comparative leisure. All that is now to be done is to keep the pigeons from picking up the seed that has been planted, until it has come up. Then there is nothing to do until the rice begins to fill. It then requires all the children about the town that can scare a bird to be on the spot to keep off the rice bird. This little creature is a greater annoyance to the rice grower than any other thing that he has to contend with. They come in great numbers, and will choose a tree in the vicinity, and here they rally, after being repulsed from the field, and will again dart down by thousands, and if some one is not on the spot to drive them away, in an incredible short time they will have destroyed all the rice in the place where they light. They do not take the grain, but they suck the milk from the grain and leave it altogether worthless, so that it is necessary to have a sentinel at every point to prevent the enemy from doing the work of destruction.

When the rice is ripe, and it commences to ripen in the latter end of July, then all hands are required in the field every day, men, women and children, and all supplied with knives to cut rice. They do not use the sickle as they do in America, but each uses a small knife; and he takes the rice, stock by stock, and holds it in his hand until he has cut a handful. It is then given into the hands of the tier, who goes around and collects it from the cutters; and when there is a sufficient amount, it is tied up with a rattan string and stuck upon a stump until evening, when all hands each takes his part and carries it to the rice kitchen. Here it is laid up loosely for a day or two, that it may dry out before packing. It is then packed away in the kitchen, and fires kept under it until it becomes perfectly dry. Here it remains until taken down to be threshed out for use.

After the harvest is all housed, then comes what would be called in old Pennsylvania, a harvest home. Every body gives themselves up to frolicking and amusement, and this season continues until the next cutting time. Great care is taken that all work may be out of the way. Their houses have been repaired in the forepart of the season; their canoes have been dug out, and all is leisure to be devoted to amusement. This is the great season of visiting, banjo picking, drumming and dancing. This season too is appropriated to burying their dead. It is a season of universal joy and plenty.

If a person of distinction die, they are laid carefully away until they get time to bury him. This time is always chosen in the season when there is plenty, as it is a matter of the greatest importance to the friends to know that everybody has plenty on these occasions. The body that had been laid away will be produced, although it may have laid for a month, and may be handled with perfect impunity. I remember while at Junk, that a man with whom I was well acquainted, came to me and told me that his brother was dead, and wanted me to have him a coffin made. I felt sorry for his loss, as he had been a very good friend of mine, and asked him when his brother died, supposing that he had died that morning or the previous night; but, judge my astonishment, when I was told by my friend that he had died four days past. Said I, you just now come for a coffin! why did you not come as soon as he died? I was told that he had been busy cutting farm, and had not the time until now. And where is your dead brother all this time? said I. He told me he had shut him up in the house where he died, and left him until he got time to bury him in a becoming way. Hence he wished a coffin made in American style. I recommended him to the manager of the saw mill, who had one made for him.

I notice this circumstance, to show that there is no unpleasant smell arising from dead bodies. If the dead to be buried is a king, there will be a great gathering of all the neighbouring kings, head men and worthies in all the country, and every one will bring with him a large amount of rice and other provisions. Some will bring sheep and goats, and fowls will be brought in abundance; wash bowls, cloth, and every kind of country money that they may have, is brought to this great feast of the dead. The corpse will then be brought, and if there has no part been stolen, it will be deposited in its long resting place, and every person of distinction, will deposit in the grave a small portion of the goods brought. But they are very careful not to spare much as a sacrifice. The balance of the goods is bartered among the crowd. The rice is cooked, the goats are killed, the fowls are dressed and made into soup, and they will have a feast on this occasion that will be remembered until another king dies. After the feast, the whole winds up with a grand play, and this is done to perfection.

The African huntsman is a person of some importance among his people. All the small game, or in other words, animals, belong to the man who kills them. There is no special law concerning them. But there is what is called grand meat, or king's meat. This cannot be touched until it is first brought and presented to the king, and through him to the people, after he is served. A Leopard is one of this kind. The man who is fortunate enough to kill one of these animals, is considered a mighty man. When he kills one, he procures the assistance of some of his comrades to bring it to town; they approach the town quietly until they get very near, and then they begin to yell and rush into the centre or square, and they here throw down their burden, when they stop; the proud huntsman takes his seat on the beast, and begins to relate a story in which he has but little regard for truth. He says, that while walking leisurely through the bush, he by chance came upon this small bit of an animal, and not knowing what it was, he of course shot it, and brought it to the king to see if he could give it a name. When the king steps up, feels proud that he can impart the required information, and in all the dignity of an African chieftain, he says that this is a LEOPARD. And when the multitude hear the name, they all roar in a shout, that the king's meat has been killed. The man who brought in the Leopard, keeps his seat upon the body of the monster, until the king advances and gives him his dash, which generally consists of two fathoms—or four yards of white cloth, a little powder, and a few gun flints. The king then retires, and the citizens generally advance and each tender him something; some a head of tobacco, powder, or whatever they may have. After this ceremony has been gone through with, the victor arises, and the king advances to receive the prize, which is done with considerable formality. The king orders a scaffold to be erected, and the Leopard is hoisted upon it and set upright, and perhaps a large country cloth is put upon him, and a cap on his head; and in this way is he decorated to receive the honors of the town. Every man then gets his gun, and there is, perhaps, two or three rounds of blank cartridges discharged; then the drum and the banjo are produced, and all the warriors, guns in hand, have a dance around their fallen foe. After this is concluded, the beast is taken down from his elevated station, and the king appoints some one to skin him; this done, the king takes the head, and gives the balance of the meat to the people. Then commences a scene of confusion, which lasts but for a few minutes; every one rushes to obtain a piece of this delicious luxury; knives are glistening and clattering. Each one cuts for himself, and many leave the scene wounded, and perhaps without any of the meat to pay for the trouble of contending. If an individual becomes wounded by his neighbour in an affray of this kind, he has no redress.

The Devil Bush is an institution that exists amongst the Africans, which seems to be of the most ancient date, and it is something that the outsider understands as little about as any other practice among them. It is known that an institution of this kind does exist; but what is done in the bush is a mystery that many of the curious have tried in vain to solve. The place chosen for this bush, is the most wild and fearful in all the neighborhood, and there seems to be a sacredness attached to all places of this kind, and none but those who belong to the institution dare approach it. If a woman is known to have been in this place, the law demands that she must die; and even after they have been abandoned, they will not allow any one to encroach upon them. I would not like to be the man that should be found cutting a bush on one of these old Devil Bushes. I would expect to pay the forfeit with my life; they would find some way to poison me.

The women too have their secret order, which is called the Greegree Bush. Here they meet once a year, and they are as particular as the men are about theirs, and will not allow a man to approach their holy place. Here all the young maidens are taken before they are disposed of for wives, and it is considered an everlasting dishonor to grow up and not to know the secrets of the Greegree Bush. There are but few that are permitted thus to escape knowing, as the old women attend to all the youngsters, and do not ask for their consent to go to this place, but take them by force, and initiate them in the secrets of the order.

I have said that after the rice is cut and safely housed, that it is a season of luxury. It truly is the case, and it seems that they know no bounds to their pleasures. But it is one continued feasting, singing and dancing. The town will make what is called a big play, and all its neighbours are free to come and partake. If the head-man is wealthy, he will have a bullock killed on the occasion, and sheep and goats in abundance; rice and palavar sauce, dumboy, and all the country dishes, are in profusion, and all perfectly free for all that comes, whether it be a countryman or an American; all are well treated, and they eat, talk, and sleep all day, and sing, drum and dance all night; and thus are several days spent. In a short time, another king or head-man will make a feast of the same kind, and of course does not wish to be outdone by his neighbour; every nerve will be strained to be at least up with the last entertainment of the kind. And thus it is for about three or four months. No work is done that can possibly be left undone during this season.

The native Africans have no great variety of dishes of food; their most common dish is rice and palavar sauce. This dish is simple; the rice is boiled and lifted in a bowl. A sauce is prepared made out of ochre or ochre leaves. This is put into a mortar and beat until it is formed into a pulp; it is then dressed with a little hot palm oil and boiled chicken or fish, and served up on top of the rice, which makes the whole a very rich dish. Many is the bowl that I have enjoyed after a fatiguing walk to get to a town. Another favorite dish is the dumboy. This is made by boiling the cassada, and then beating them in the mortar until they are formed into something like light dough. They then prepare a soup, made out of fish, or fowl, or flesh, as the case may be, which is seasoned very hot with pepper; you then take the soup and pour it over the dumboy, and it is ready to be eaten. This is a very good dish, and one that is much used, both among the Bassa and Vey people, and which I used whenever I could get it.

The religion of the natives is a subject which is hard to define. To tell what are their religious views, would be impossible, they are so mixed with superstition. However, they all believe in a God that made all things, and they pray to this Being. But they are perfectly ignorant on every other fundamental doctrine of the Bible. They believe in a devil, and they worship him also. They have their religion filled with the most strange ideas. They have no knowledge of the resurrection, and this doctrine is altogether new to them, and they scarcely know how to understand it. Yet they are disposed to give heed to all that a preacher says, and they think it impossible for a God-man to lie.

There is not a more kind people in the world than they. If a stranger comes to one of their towns, every effort is put forth to make him happy. The first care is to provide for his necessities, and a woman is called and the rice given out, the fowl killed, and in a short time a bowl of rice will be brought, and another containing the soup, and set before the stranger. It matters not how urgent may be the business, nothing can be done until after the parties have eaten. The best house in the town is set aside for the accommodation of the guest, and everybody seems happy to be the servant of the stranger. Of course they expect something in return. This is a universal custom as far as I have heard. The dash seems only to be the ancient custom handed down to this age; it prevailed universally in the eastern country, and the queen of Sheba, when she came to see Solomon, brought gifts with her. I always give the headman a small dash when I go to his town, either to preach or otherwise, and it has its effect, although I once thought differently. But at the present, any one that wishes to be esteemed and popular amongst these people, must give them. It will get an audience by far the easiest. It is amongst this simple people that it is my lot to labor in the ministry. What care is required that my deportment may be such that the gospel may not be blamed! It requires much prayer and faith that God may plant His word that His servant sows. There is perhaps no class of men in the world that needs the instructions of missionaries more than the poor Africans. When we consider the length of time that they have been in the most abject ignorance and superstition, without one ray of light to lighten their pathway through this world of sin and wretchedness, oh! what diligence, what labor, and what prayer are necessary on the part of those who are sent as the heralds of salvation. How strange that a cause so good and holy, and having for its object the salvation of millions and the glory of God, can be opposed by men who call themselves Christians! But it is even so. They are to be found too in the ranks of colored men, who wish the world to look on them as champions of philanthropy. Yes, they speak great swelling words, and wish to throw every barrier in the way of Africa's enlightenment.

Now, we contend that all those who oppose Liberia oppose the mission operation in Africa. Liberia is the Missionary's protection; and we do say that the operation would be much retarded if Liberia, as a nation, was blotted out. The government exercises an influence over the surrounding country that could not be exerted by any other human means. The natives know very well that if the Missionaries are interrupted they will be held accountable to the government for a breach of treaty; but we argue that the opponents of Liberia affect the Missionary operation in another way, and that is, they strive to prejudice the minds of the pious against this country, and thereby prevent many a good man, who might make a useful Missionary here, from coming. There, no doubt, have been thousands, who were desirous of coming to Liberia, prevented from coming by the influence of the enemies of this country. Now we contend that they are not doing Liberia itself any material harm by this course, but the mission suffers. It wants men, and good men, to shoulder the cross of Christ, and proclaim the glad news of salvation to a perishing multitude. We are bold to say that there are hundreds now in the United States that, if left to the convictions of their own minds, would embrace the first opportunity of coming to this land; but when those convictions are known to the public there are a host that rally in all their strength, and are determined that they shall not go to a country where they could be useful to themselves and to others. They employ every means within their reach to carry out their plans, and very frequently, regardless of all truth, they will assert things of Liberia that were never heard of or thought of before.

One prejudiced man, in a pamphlet, asserts that the Missionaries in Liberia are all, to a man, rum traders. Can God look upon such slander with impunity? we think not. I consider the success of the mission in this field to depend wholly upon Liberia's prosperity; destroy Liberia as a government, and you knock out the prop upon which the Missionary operation leans. But it is clear that God has ordered Liberia's government as a stepping stone to the enlightenment of all this vast coast of dark Africa, and as being a child under his fostering hand. Who then is he that can do it harm? Though hell may rage and vent her spite, yet all the blows aimed at the prosperity of this little republic will fall harmless to the ground. They all have failed to do that which was intended; a Garrison has been fighting against it for more than a quarter of a century, and what has he done to injure Liberia? He has done nothing. And a host of others are now engaged to injure this little nation, but they will all fail as those have done who have gone before them; the reason is they are fighting against God. God has commenced the work of reclaiming Africa and he will finish it in his own good time; and after all the opposition which will be brought to bear against Liberia as a nation by the enemies of civilization, God will take care of it, for He has need of it in carrying out His designs in Africa. He will use it as a means by which the gospel will be sent to the interior of this great country. How this is to be done through the government, yet remains to be seen, but those are the convictions of my mind on this matter. This government is yearly making new treaties with the tribes beyond the limits of Liberia, and in all the treaties the government has respect to religion, and does something to call the minds of the natives to this all important subject. Why then oppose so good a cause?

But we are told that the opposition is not against Liberia but

against the Colonizationists. Now, when we oppose the colonization cause, as an organization, we oppose Liberia, for they are
the friends of Liberia; but I am opposed to some who belong to
the colonization society, but it is because I believe them to be
bad, designing men. But I do not oppose the whole organization
because I believe that there are some bad men in it—I oppose
them as individuals and as dangerous men. I believe that the
time is not far off when many who now oppose this country and
its institutions will see their error, and will yet be the friends of
Liberia—yes, many who now oppose the operations of Liberia
will either come to her embrace themselves or will send their
children to enjoy the blessings of liberty and equality, that the
government holds out to all the oppressed sons of our race in
every clime. They are all invited to come and enjoy the free
institutions of a free government. They will yet see that the hand
of God is in this whole matter, and will rally for the fight against
ignorance and superstition in western Africa. Their weapons are
the word of *truth*, by which the world shall be conquered and
brought humbly at the feet of Jesus to own him conqueror.

Liberia has some delightful spots and desirable homes. Cape
Mount is one of these. I think that, in a search over earth's re-
motest bounds, a more desirable place could not be found. The
cape lifts her proud head far above all the surrounding land,
and seems to look down upon them with a degree of contempt,
and when standing on one of its elevated peaks, with what delight and interest is the mind entertained. While thus standing,
the eye takes in at a single glance the broad expanse of the Atlantic that lies stretched out before you; and by turning to the
south you can see the vast valley that lies between the two capes,
Cape Mount and Cape Mesurado. In this valley are thousands of
human beings who are yet to be brought to a Saviour's love. In
the month of March the prospect is truly animating; here, for
miles, you will see the smoke raising from the burning farms;
cloud after cloud will rise up and take its place among the mists
of the atmosphere, while, perhaps, your ear will be saluted by
many a song, arising from those whose habitation is at the foot
of the mountain. After the eye and ear have been abundantly
feasted by looking to the south, you turn to the north, and, at

the foot of this same mount, you will see the place that was selected by the notorious Canot as the seat of his accursed traffic.
Here his polluted soul would revel in all the evils of the hellish
slave trade; here the mind can contemplate the horror and suffering that attended this horrible iniquity. Imagine, while gazing down the mountain's side, that you see his barracoon yet
standing, and, within its precints, hundreds of human beings
ready to be shipped off to be sold, and that too, to a people
professing to be christians. Hear them scream as brother is torn
from brother, and sister from sister, and all from their once
happy home! Let the mind follow the large canoe as it conveys
them out of the mouth of the river and over the bar. Look at
her as she is struggling with the breakers as they roll to the
shore—you tremble for the safety of the inmates; perhaps there
are hundreds in it, and all chained one to the other! Ah, that
fearful breaker, see how high it rides! can the canoe live through
this? All is suspense; but on rolls the breaker until it meets the
canoe. She is upset—its poor victims struggle but struggle in
vain—they disappear to become food for the monsters of the
deep. And this is but one of the atrocities of this practice. Within
the walls of the barracoon hundreds are murdered—the weak,
the old and the infirm, who will not command a price from the
slave ship; these, with many an infant, are sent to a premature
grave. Oh, how can a wretch, such as Canot and hundreds of
others, ever expect to find mercy at the hands of a just God? But
you may extend the view from where you stand far up the coast,
and can see Sodama, in the place where the Gallinas empties its
proud current into the ocean. This is Cape Mount; it has proved
itself to be the very best place in all the republic for emigrants
to acclimate; they may pass through the change here almost im-
perceptibly. I would say to all coming to this delightful country,
first stop at Cape Mount and spend one year, and then you will
be prepared to go where your inclination may lead you—you
will have passed through the fever, or nearly so, by that time.

ANSWER TO NESBIT'S BOOK.

In reading the work put out by Mr. Wm. Nesbit, there is so much to claim attention that I scarcely know where to begin to answer his tirade and misrepresentation of the country that I claim as my home. But I will begin with his description of the face of the country. Page 23, he says, the face is one magnificent swamp, and wishes to convey the idea that the whole country is inundated. Now, Mr. Nesbit knows very well that this is not a true statement. I acknowledge that there are swamps on the coast as there are on our southern coasts, but I do not acknowledge that the coast of Liberia is any more subject to these than the coasts of Louisiana or Florida; but, to the contrary, the swamps do not extend near as far interior as the swamps do in the southern part of America. Those swamps do not extend more than four miles back, and after leaving the sea that distance, you leave all Mangroves and Dragon Bloods. Mr. Nesbit knew this, for he, with myself, travelled nearly one entire day in the vicinity of the New York settlement, in Liberia, and we, in that day's travel, neither saw Mangrove nor Dragon Blood; what is true concerning that location is true of all the country, after going about four miles inland. He says, that the land is very fertile but does not produce any timber. In this, Mr. Nesbit has made a wrong statement, for, instead of the country not producing any timber, I do most positively assert that in those districts, where the natives have not cut down or destroyed the timber in making their farms, that the largest timber I ever saw grows in great abundance. I myself have measured a tree that measured one hundred and two feet in circumference. There are many more of this kind through the

[EDITOR'S NOTE: This "Answer" was originally published as the final chapter of Williams's *Four Years in Liberia*.]

country. I do not mention this that the public should think that this is a fair sample of the forest timber, but I will say that the undestroyed forest is larger in its growth than the forests of the United States. He speaks of the camwood, rosewood, &c. Camwood does not grow in any abundance near the coast, from the fact that all that was handy or near has long since been cut down and sent to market, and the natives did not know how to propagate it, but rosewood does grow in abundance; also, wismore is as plenty as the oak or maple is in this country.

Mr. Nesbit speaks of the Kong Mountains being seen from the coast. In this he is about as near right as in the most of his composition. The Kong Mountains are situated some two or three hundred miles in the interior; judge if they could be seen from the coast! But the hills that he supposed to be the Kong Mountains are an extensive range running along the coast as far as I have travelled, and are not more than from thirty to forty miles from the sea. I have been to them and have stood on them and viewed the country for many miles from them. He (Mr. Nesbit) must have made up his opinion of Liberia while his brain was excited by the fever, and while a hill seemed to him to be the great Kong Mountain.

I am not able to state how far our country extends into the interior, but of one thing I am sure, that we can go as far inland as we wish. To prove this, Mr. Seys has formed a new settlement some fifty or sixty miles back from Monrovia. Whether this upper country belongs to Liberia or not proves that we have access to it, which is all that we wish, and proves Mr. Nesbit in the wrong.

That there is not, nor never has been, five acres cleared by any one man, is too absurd for me to notice. Every body will contradict this that has been to Liberia; I might name many that have five, ten, or twenty acres cleared and planted.

I wish to call particular attention to the 9th chapter of Mr. Nesbit's book, where he desires to make the impression that when once in Liberia you are forever shut up, and all possibility of getting away is cut off. This is untrue, and a libel upon our laws and our free institutions. That we have a law regulating passports is true, and what nation that has it not? He says that all ship masters, &c., are forbidden to take away any one without a passport—this is true—but, what does all this amount to? Simply this, to prevent fraud from being practised by those wishing to come away. Nesbit says, that if any one chooses to object to an applicant getting a passport it cannot be had; but he does not tell us on what conditions those objections could be made effectual. Now, the truth is, that we have but one law on this matter and that is, that any individual wishing to leave Liberia must be free from debt, and if this is the case there is no one in all Africa that could prevent his passport, or his coming away; but if, on the other hand, he owes his neighbor, and is unwilling to pay it before going, the creditor can enter a protest against his getting a passport. This is the whole of the affair. If Mr. Nesbit did lie and act the deceiver with General Lewis—there was not the least occasion for it; but that he did lie and deceive his friends and partners in business is most true. For the purpose of procuring means to bring him home, he told his friends that he would be back in the fall, and that he would bring out some goods with him. On the strength of this assertion the company loaned Mr. Nesbit one hundred dollars, which he has not returned; so his object can be seen for lying himself out of the country.

Mr. Nesbit attacks Mr. President Roberts. I am not disposed to fight his battles, but I do say that he has attacked him most unmanly. In my opinion, and not mine alone, the world has but few greater men than *Joseph J. Roberts,* and he is not only great but he is as good as he is great. He would spurn to do an act such as Nesbit charges him with; but the world knows the man, and I am certain that but few thinks the less of him on account of any thing that is said of him in Nesbit's work.

He speaks of beasts of prey, reptiles, &c. We have a variety of these things, but Mr. Nesbit puts the worst construction on this as he does on every thing else. Now, that the "driver" is so much of a monster as he would have everybody to fear is certainly not true. They would indeed be fearful if we would lie down and have our hands and feet tied, but we can keep out of the way of the driver as well as any thing else that is hurtful. As for serpents we have them, but not in the number that one would be led to suppose from the reading of Nesbit's book. I can say that during all the time that I spent in Liberia, which is nearly a year for every month that Mr. Nesbit did, I have not seen more snakes than I would have seen if I had remained in Johnstown. Thus he exaggerates the truth and makes it horrifying to the timid and unsuspecting.

Again, he says, that we have slavery in Liberia. Now I do most solemnly declare that Nesbit lied in making this assertion. Upon the contrary, our laws make it a criminal act for any Liberian to receive a native in any way that he might be held as a slave. The Liberians cannot receive them as apprentices unless they take them before the proper court and have them bound as such, and every one, as soon as he or she is of man's or woman's age, can leave at will and go where they please. Nearly all have natives as helps in their families, and this is as it should be; but I confess that black people are no better than white people, as many, when they have power, abuse it, and so it is with some in Liberia; wicked persons there do abuse the native youths. But why does Mr. Nesbit condemn the whole country and accuse all as slave holders, because a few abuse their power? There is no fairness in the man, but he seems willing to say or do any thing to carry his point.

Mr. Nesbit next attacks the Missionaries, and wishes the world to look upon them as a set of swindlers, traders, and liars; he also represents them as rumsellers. Now I think it hardly necessary to notice this, as I feel assured that there are none who believe these assertions, unless it is some one who has no more soul than what he (Nesbit) has, and if this is all the impression he has made it is scarcely worth answering.

He further says that the Missionaries have done nothing. I am free to admit that they have not done as much as they or their friends would like them to have done. But why did not Mr. Nesbit give the true cause why there was not more done amongst the natives? I do not pretend to say that the Ministers in Africa are a better set of men than preachers are in other lands, but I will say that they will compare favorably with any other part of the world for uprightness of deportment, zeal and piety; but the real cause why there seems to be but little doing amongst the natives of Africa is, that they are, perhaps, of all other people, the most superstitious. They have their religious rites unto which they adhere with the utmost tenacity. It is not only a wicked heart against which we have to contend, as Missionaries, but all the practices and inventions that wicked men could devise for thousands of years. The Devil Bush is one of these things against which the Missionary has to contend; their system of gree-grees is another—polygamy is another. Now if Mr. Nesbit had known any thing about these things he would have came to the same conclusion that I have come to, viz: that the Missionaries have done wonders.

When he (Nesbit) says that there are not twenty natives who are civilized and converted in all the republic, he forgot the settlement of New Georgia, where there are over fifty civilized natives in that one place. I am very sure, if it were possible for me to pass round and take account of all in the republic, I should find many more—yes, more than twenty, more than forty. In my charge of last year I left five native members, who were as good members as any other, but the truth is, that after the native is civilized he becomes a Liberian, and a stranger does not know him from the rest of the Liberian citizens, unless personally acquainted.

As regards rum-selling amongst the Missionaries, I do not know of any thing of the kind, and I question very much if Mr. Nesbit did, but to the contrary I do know that the body to which I belong, are, to a man, opposed to it, and if a brother would use to excess or advocate the traffic of rum amongst us, he would be hissed out of Conference. I further believe that all the other denominations are equally strict in this matter.

There are men of the highest attainments engaged in Missionary operations. I will name a few and let the world judge if these men could be guilty of the base conduct that Nesbit has ascribed to them: Bishop Payne, Rev. Scott, and Rev. Hoffman, of the Protestant Episcopal Church; Rev. D. A. Wilson, Rev. E. T. Williams, of the Presbyterian, and Rev. J. W. Horne, and others, of the M.E. Church. These are all white men who had no interest in going to Africa but that of promoting their Master's cause—yet these have to be classed in Nesbit's book as traders and rum-sellers.

As for the palm oil story I shall not say any thing, as I do not

know about the measure used by the merchants. I think that
there would be profit enough on this article without resorting
to any thing of this kind. Mr. Nesbit could not see where the
money was to be made, although he bought his goods at Monrovia and took them to Marshall and there sold them at one
hundred per cent, and yet he cannot see how there was any
thing to be made on buying palm oil—quite short-sighted!

Although Mr. Nesbit prophesies the speedy downfall of our
little republic, she has not yet fallen, nor is there any likeli-
hood that she will, for she is steadily advancing. He says this will
occur when emigration shall stop, but when is that to be? It does
not look much like stopping as yet, when there are, every six
months, more emigrants offered than can be taken over. Perhaps he supposed that the publication of his pamphlet would
stop it at once, but this is only to some extent in Pennsylvania;
however, I hope that, even in this part of the world, the people
may see right sometimes, and move to Liberia, there to help to
build up a great nation.

Concerning native customs and manners, in chapter 16, I
think that everybody will allow me to know more than Mr. N., as
his stay was only four months, and a portion of that time he was
sick, and I was there nearly four years, and have been more or
less amongst them while in Africa. Their customs are very different from those of the Liberians; they have their own laws—
where their laws do not conflict with ours—and I ask is this
strange? surely not. Did not the United States allow the Indians
the same, and why does not Mr. Nesbit rally out against them for
this folly, if folly it be? No, this is not his object, he wishes to
make Liberia look small and contemptible, but I think that he
has failed in this. He says that it is a common thing to see the
natives naked. Now, I question whether he ever saw a grown native entirely naked—if he has he saw more than I ever did; although it is quite common, when you visit their villages, to see
their children, up to the age of ten or twelve years, running
naked, but the men and women are as susceptible of shame as
Mr. N. or any other person. How Mr. N. saw so much more than
any other person that ever was in Africa I cannot conceive. He

is not the first that got away from that country, and I suppose others have been as truthful, and yet, strange to say, he saw more, heard more, and learned more than any other one man. Can it be that he is the only honest man that ever came from Liberia?

Mr. Nesbit should have taken more pains to have informed himself of the natives and the Liberians, before writing and giving to the world for truth that which he knew nothing about. He asserts that such of the natives as are guilty of making a witch must die. This was once the law: but it is not practised now in or about Liberia. Our influence has put this abominable practice down, and if it is done at all it must be done very secretly. Instead of the natives having no regard for our laws, they have the utmost respect and fear of offending us, and are also very careful to avoid all appearance of disobedience. It is a frequent occurrence for them to refer their matters of dispute to our magistrates, and feel that whatever may be the decision that it is right, and they are satisfied.

I believe that the coloured portion of the Missionaries are as far in the advance as the colored preachers in America. I do know that the Liberian Methodist Conference is, as a body, far ahead of any colored Conference in the United States; they will compare favorably with any white Conference. We have men of talent: we have a BURNS, PAYNE, THOMPSON, MATTHEWS, GROSSE, ROBERTS, WILSON, TYLER, and A. D. WILLIAMS. Many of these are ornaments to Liberia, and would be stars anywhere, where there is no prejudice to keep them down. I should not omit the good and holy father COKER, who took his life in his hands and came out from Baltimore some seven years ago. These are men of honor and would scorn a mean act sooner than he who tries to injure them.

As it regards the 14th chapter, it is something that will do no harm and I shall not consume time to give it much notice. I would, however, say that the whole affair is an attempt at ridicule, and has but little truth in it. As for Commodores, Lieutenants, Boatswains, these are titles altogether unknown in relation to the Liberian government Schooner Lark. It has its captain, mates and purser, and perhaps two or three midshipmen. I assert that our military operations are conducted with as much propriety as any other people, although we may not know much about military tactics. Our companies' operations have been witnessed by naval officers both of the British and the American squadron, and they have universally been praised for their skill as soldiers. I am quite certain that those natives, who have been hostile, have long since came to the conclusion that the Liberians understood their business; and if Mr. Nesbit was to try their skill I am inclined to believe that he too would come to the same conclusion.

Chapter 15. I here assert and am not afraid of any successful contradiction, that neither the English nor the American squadron has any influence to prevent the natives from coming down upon us if they were so disposed; but they know to their sorrow the strength of the Liberian arms. We have nothing to fear from any internal enemy. The natives are divided into tribes, and these tribes into factions, and it is as impossible for them to concentrate their forces against us as it was for Mr. Nesbit to tell the truth concerning us. Their local interests forbid this. I am not vain enough to suppose that if the whole native force of Liberia could be brought to bear against it at once, that it could stand successfully the attack, for it is estimated that they number three hundred thousand, while that of Liberia is not over twelve thousand. But this never can be—circumstances forbid it, and while one or two tribes may combine against us, we, on the other hand, can obtain other natives to assist us. The history of the world goes to prove this usage and our history confirms it. As far as the squadrons are concerned, we could live very well without them, although we feel thankful to the governments for them, and shall ever treat their officers as the representatives of the greatest nations on earth.

I am now done with Mr. Nesbit, and I leave the public to judge who has had the best chance to know the truth in the matter—he in four months or myself in four years. As to veracity, I claim at least to be as good as he, and think that when I was a citizen of this State I stood as fair. Unless there is something in the climate of Liberia that degenerates the character of every one that goes there, I yet would be considered truthful. Now the facts in the case as it regards Mr. Nesbit is about this: He went to Liberia at an expense, perhaps, of some two or three hundred dollars, and did not like the country, for which I did not, nor do I yet, blame him. But why, if he did not like it, did he not come away with honor and not misrepresent every thing that he saw? Well, he was out of pocket and wished to make it good, and conferring with M. R. Delany, a most inveterate hater of colonization and all its doings, was advised to publish this book, and, of course, what Mr. Nesbit did not think of Mr. Delany could. This thing was thus concocted and set afloat for the purpose of making Mr. Nesbit's pocket whole again.

I find by travelling in this State and conversing with some of the best colored men in it, that the statements of Mr. N. are not believed as fully as they once were. A number of the citizens of Pittsburg and Allegheny assured me that they believed that Mr. Nesbit told many things that were not truthful, and when I explained matters to them as they really are, they seemed to be satisfied. All I would ask would be for any good man from Pennsylvania to go to Liberia and spend one year, and come back, and I believe that he would corroborate my statements in every particular, and condemn that of Nesbit's in many instances.

I give to the world this brief sketch, and have only further to say that all who read it may depend on it for truth; although it is plain and simple, yet it may be relied on by all, for it is not my object to deceive. I have no interest in this land—Liberia is my home and I expect to end my days in it. I cannot think that it is for the best interests of Liberia to misrepresent things or to give to them false colors. The world knows us and knows from whence we came. The people of this country have sense enough to know how much to expect from us in the short time we have been in existence. No one, who has the right use of his reason, expects that we should be now as far advanced as the United States. We have been an independent government but ten years and have had everything to contend against, yet, with all the difficulties, we have honorably sustained ourselves, and are growing into importance as fast as any reasonable man could expect. It never was expected by the friends of Liberia that it would grow into manhood in a day or a year; but her growth has been steady and sure, with as little mortality as any other country ever was settled with.

FIVE LETTERS

ON

LIBERIAN

COLONIZATION

(1851–1863)

AUGUSTUS WASHINGTON

INCLUDING A

BIOGRAPHICAL SKETCH

OF

AUGUSTUS WASHINGTON

BY

WILSON JEREMIAH MOSES

BIOGRAPHICAL SKETCH OF AUGUSTUS WASHINGTON

Augustus Washington, an "unmixed representative of the colored race," was born around 1820 in Trenton, New Jersey, where he remained until the age of sixteen.* Little is known of his early life, but by his early twenties he had achieved enough education to do some teaching; he wrote of "engagements connected with my school" in a letter printed in the *Colored American,* July 31, 1841. Around that time he was active in the abolitionist, temperance, and black suffrage movements, attending meetings in Brooklyn and Buffalo, New York, and in Trenton and Princeton, New Jersey. With financial assistance from New York abolitionist Lewis Tappan, he studied informally for two years at Dartmouth College, circa 1842–44. Described in Martin Delany's *Condition . . . of the Colored People* as an "artist of fine taste and perception," by 1852 Washington had established a successful busi-

*[EDITOR's NOTE: David O. White, in "Augustus Washington, Black Daguerrotypist," *Connecticut Historical Society Bulletin,* January 1974, places Washington's mother in the undefined category of "Asian." Other authors have echoed White on this, although a foot-noted version of this article deposited in the Connecticut Historical Society does not document the race of Washington's mother, nor does it specify what is meant by "Asian." A contemporary source, published in the *Colonization Herald* and reprinted in the *Maryland Colonization Journal* (September 1859), speaks of Washington as "an unmixed representative of the colored race." See the editors' introduction to the letter from Washington printed in the *Colonization Herald* and reprinted here on pages 213ff.]

ness as a daguerreotypist in Hartford, Connecticut, and was "patronized by all classes." An amateur violinist, he brought a violin with him on his trip to Liberia and played it aboard ship, to the evident discomfort of Daniel Peterson. It is likely, however, that this was not so much a reflection of the level of his accomplishment as an indication of the limitations of Peterson's tolerance for lighthearted amusements.

Washington showed an interest in African missionary work as early as his 1841 letter in the *Colored American*, where he expressed his disapproval of the American Colonization Society. As the following letters reveal, he eventually overcame his misgivings concerning colonization and migrated with his family to Liberia in November 1853. In a letter published in the October 1855 *African Repository*, he stated that he arrived in Liberia with "less than $500 in cash, but $275 in goods for sale, and . . . $500 worth of Daguerrean materials." He taught Greek and Latin at the Alexander High School in the Liberian capital of Monrovia for fifteen months and continued to ply his trade as a daguerreotypist, which by June 1855 had brought him "about thirteen hundred dollars." He also ran a "store and auction and commission business [which] paid no great profit, but partly supported [his] family." By the summer of 1855, Washington had built two houses in Monrovia, both of which he rented out, and he had also established a farm twenty miles up the St. Paul River. Convinced that "the true interest of Liberia consisted in the development of her agricultural and mineral resources," he later established himself in the settlement of Careysburg as a sugar and cane farmer and river merchant. He occasionally resided in the neighboring countries of Gambia and Sierra Leone, where he engaged in commerce. Washington was elected to the Liberian national legislature during the 1850s, and by the end of the decade he had been appointed to a judgeship.

The first of the documents reprinted here, Washington's letter of July 3, 1851, is unique for its refinement of style and the evenhandedness of its author, who is able to discuss procolonization and anticolonization arguments with equal fairness. These qualities place it among the most convincing arguments for colonization written by a black man in the antebellum period. It was reprinted in several colonization journals, and Carter G. Woodson included it in his memorable volume, *The Mind of the Negro as Reflected in Letters Written During the Crisis, 1800–1860* (Washington, D.C.: Association for the Study of Afro-American Life and History, 1926).

—*Wilson J. Moses*

THOUGHTS ON THE AMERICAN COLONIZATION SOCIETY, 1851 AUGUSTUS WASHINGTON

HARTFORD, July 3, 1851

As the infant Republic of Liberia is now attracting the attention of the enlightened nations, and the press of both England and America, I may hope that a communication in regard to that country, and the Afric-Americans in this, may not be deemed a subject intrusive nor foreign to the public interest. And I am encouraged by the just and liberal course you have taken in favor of the proposed line of steamers to the Western Coast of Africa, and also the boldness with which you have lately urged the propriety and interest of some of the colored people emigrating from our crowded cities to less populous parts of this country, as the great West, or to Africa, or any other place where they may secure an equality of rights and liberty, with a mind unfettered and space to rise. Besides, as your paper is generally read by the progressive and more liberal portion of white Americans and some of the most intelligent of the colored, I may also hope to be confirmed in my present sentiments and measures, or driven to new and better convictions. I do not wish to be thought extravagant, when I affirm what I believe to be true, that I have seen no act in your public career as an editor, statesman and philanthropist, more noble and praiseworthy than that of turning your pen and influence to an African colonization and civilization, after finding that you could not secure for the

[EDITOR'S NOTE: Augustus Washington's *Thoughts on the American Colonization Society* first appeared in the official journal of the American Colonization Society, *African Repository* 27: 259–65.]

black man in America those inalienable rights to which he, with
other oppressed nations, is entitled, and for which you have
heretofore labored. Though the colored people may not appreciate your kind efforts, and those of many other good and true
men who pursue your course, we trust you will not on account
of present opposition be weary in well-doing. Though dark the
day, and fearful as is the tide oppression is rolling over us, we are
certain that it is but the presage of a more glorious morrow. We
do not despair. We thank God that notwithstanding all the powerful combinations to crush us to the earth, as long as the Bible
with its religion endures, there will ever be a large number of
the American people whose prayers, sympathies and influence
will defend us here, and assist and encourage our brethern who
have sought, or may in future seek liberty on a foreign shore. If
these no other reward awaits, the time is not distant when they
shall receive at least the thanks and benedictions of a grateful
people, "redeemed, regenerated, and disenthralled by the genius of universal emancipation." Ever since the annexation of
Texas, and the success and triumph of American arms on the
plains of Mexico, I have been looking in vain for some home for
Afric-Americans more congenial for their feelings and prejudice
than Liberia. The Canadas, the West Indies, Mexico, British Guiana, and other parts of South America, have all been brought
under review. And yet I have been unable to get rid of a conviction long since entertained and often expressed, that if the colored people of this country ever find a home on earth for the
development of their manhood and intellect, it will first be in
Liberia or some other part of Africa. A continent larger than
North America is lying waste for want of the hand of science and
industry. A land whose bowels are filled with mineral and agricultural wealth, and on whose bosom reposes in exuberance
and wild extravagance all the fruits and productions of a tropical
clime. The providence of God will not permit a land so rich in
all the elements of wealth and greatness to remain much longer
without civilized inhabitants. Every one who has traced the history of missions in Africa, and watched the progress of that little
Republic of Afric-Americans on the western coast, must be con-

vinced that the colored men are more peculiarly adapted, and must eventually be the means of civilizing, redeeming, and saving that continent, if ever it is done at all. Encouraged and supported by American benevolence and philanthropy, I know no people better suited to this great work—none whose duty more it is. Our servile and degraded condition in this country, the history of the past, and the light that is pouring in upon me from every source, fully convinces me that this is our true, our highest and happiest destiny, and the sooner we commence this glorious work, the sooner will "light spring up in darkness, and the wilderness and the solitary place be glad, and the desert rejoice and blossom as the rose."

I am aware that nothing except the Fugitive Slave Law can be more startling to the free colored citizens of the Northern States, than the fact that any man among them, whom they have regarded as intelligent and sound in faith, should declare his convictions and influence in favor of African Colonization. But the novelty of the thing does not prove it false, nor that he who dare reject a bad education and break loose from long-established prejudices, may not have the most conclusive reasons for such a course.

I am aware, too, of the solemn responsibility of my present position. It must result in some good or great evil. I maintain that, clinging to long-cherished prejudices, and fostering hopes that can never be realized, the leaders of the colored people in this country have failed to discharge a great and important duty to their race. Seeing this, though a mere private business man, with a trembling pen, I come forward alone, joining with friend and foe in moving the wheel of a great enterprise, which, though unpopular with those it designs to benefit, must result eventually in the redemption and enfranchisement of the African race.

With the conviction of a purpose so noble, and an end so beneficent, I cannot notice the misrepresentations, slander, and anathemas, which I must, for a while, endure, even from those whose approbation and good will I would gladly retain. It was no difficult task to have seen, that unless they could force emancipation, and then the perfect, social, and political equality of the races, human nature, human pride and passions, would not allow the Americans to acknowledge the equality and inalienable rights of those who had been their slaves. One or the other must be dominant. For this reason: seven years ago, while a student, I advocated the plan of a separate State for colored Americans—not as a choice, but as a necessity, believing it would be better for our manhood and intellect to be freemen by ourselves, than political slaves with our oppressors. I enlisted at once the aid of a few colored young men, of superior talent and ability; and we were earnestly taking measures to negotiate for a tract of land in Mexico, when the war and its consequences blasted our hopes, and drove us from our purpose. About five years ago I told my excellent friend, George L. Seymour, of Liberia (who, after a residence of some years there, had returned to this city to take out his family), that I knew only one way to develop the faculties of our people in this country, and that by their entire separation from oppression and its influences; and that if I was compelled to abandon my plan of a separate State in America, I would devote my voice, my pen, my heart, and soul, to the cause of Liberia. I have since written to him that he has my heart in Africa now, and in two or three years, if we live, I will shake hands with him on the banks of the St. John.

Ever since a lad of fifteen, it has been my constant study to learn how I might best contribute to elevate the social and political position of the oppressed and unfortunate people with whom I am identified; and while I have endeavored, in my humble way, to plead the cause of three millions of my enslaved countrymen, I have, at the same time, thought it no inconsistency to plead also for the hundred and fifty millions of the native sons of Africa. But every word uttered in her behalf subjects us to the imputation of being a Colonizationist, and covers us with the odium our people attach to such a name; as if something unjust and wicked was naturally associated with the term, when in fact that odium, if such I may call it for the sake of argument, can exist only with those who have forgotten the history of Plymouth Rock and Jamestown, or who are determined not to know the truth, in spite of facts and the evidence of the most

enlightened reason. What is Colonization? For the benefit of
those who treat it with contempt, and think that no good can
come out of it, I may merely remark that the thirteen original
States, previous to the Declaration of Independence, were called
the Colonies of Great Britain, the inhabitants colonists. The
companies and individuals in England that assisted in planting
these colonies were called Colonizationists. These colonists came
from the land of their birth, and forsook their homes, their fire-
sides, their former altars, and the graves of their fathers, to seek
civil and religious liberty among the wild beasts and Indians on
a foreign, bleak, and desolate shore. Oppressed at home, they
emigrated to Holland, and after remaining there twelve years,
returned to England, and found not the hope of rest until they
came to America. That very persecution and oppression of the
mother country planted in America the purest civil and religious institutions the world had ever seen. And now this powerful Republic, by her oppression and injustice to one class of this
people, will plant in Africa a religion and morality more pure,
and liberty more universal, than it has yet been the lot of my
people to enjoy. I never have been of that class who repudiate
everything American. While I shall never make any compromise
with slavery, nor feel indifferent to its blighting, withering effects
on the human intellect and human happiness, I cannot be so
blind as not to see and believe that, in spite of all its corrupting
influences on national character, there is yet piety, virtue, philanthropy, and disinterested benevolence among the American
people; and when, by the progress of free thought and the full
development of her free institutions, our country shall have removed from her national escutcheon that plague-spot of the nation, she will do more than all others in sending the light of
liberty and everlasting love into every portion of the habitable
globe. In our enthusiasm and devotion to any great benevolent
cause, we are generally unwilling to make the best use of men as
we find them, until we have wasted our energies in accomplishing nothing, or a calmer reflection convinces us of our error. It
is well for those to whom this reflection comes not too late. We
have been an unfortunate people. For 400 years the avarice,

fraud, and oppression of Europeans and their descendants have been preying upon the children of Africa and her descendants in America. Says my eloquent correspondent, in writing upon this subject: "I know this was the soil on which I was born; but I have nothing to glorify this as my country. I have no pride of ancestry to point back to. Our forefathers did not come here as did the Pilgrim fathers, in search of a place where they could enjoy civil and religious liberty. No; they were cowardly enough to allow themselves to be brought manacled and fettered as slaves, rather than die on their native shores resisting their oppressors." In the language of Dr. Todd: "If the marks of humanity are not blotted out from this race of miserable men, it is not because oppression has not been sufficiently legalized, and avarice been allowed to pursue its victims till the grave became a sweet asylum."

During the past thirty years, two influential and respectable associations have arisen in our behalf, each claiming to be the most benevolent, and each seemingly opposed to the intentions and purposes of the other.

The American Colonization Society, on the one hand, proposed to benefit us by the indirect means of planting a colony on the western coast of Africa, as an asylum for the free colored people and manumitted slaves of the United States; and by this means also to send the blessings of civilization and religion to the benighted sons of that continent. The principal obstacle in the way of their success has been, that the free colored people, as a body, everywhere, have denounced the whole scheme as wicked and mischievous, and resolved not to leave this country; while those who have gone to that colony, from a state of slavery, as the condition of freedom, have been least able to contribute to the knowledge and greatness of a new country, and impart civilization and the arts and sciences to its heathen inhabitants. This Society was one of the few that are popular in their very beginning. But that which made it most popular with the American public furnished the cause of the opposition of the colored people. They erected a platform so broad, that the worst enemies of the race could stand upon it with the same grace, and undistinguished from the honest and true philanthropist. It could at the same time appeal for support to the piety and benevolence of the North, and to the prejudices and sordid interest of the South. I state this simply as a fact, not for the purpose of finding fault. It is always easier to show one plan faulty than to produce a better one.

Notwithstanding the different and adverse motives that have prompted the friends of Colonization, they certainly have labored perseveringly and unitedly for the accomplishment of one great purpose. And in spite of all our former distrust, we must give them the credit at least of producing as yet the only great practical scheme for the amelioration of the condition of the free colored man and the manumitted slave. They did not profess nor promise to do more. Instead of engaging in clamorous agitations about principles and measures, they turned what men and means they had to the best purpose, and engaged industriously in founding and nurturing a colony for the free colored people, where they have an opportunity of demonstrating their equality with the white race, by seizing upon, combining, and developing all the elements of national greatness by which they are surrounded. Thus far the end is good; we need not stop now to scan their motives.

The Abolitionists, on the other hand, proposed by moral means the immediate emancipation of the slave, and the elevation of the free colored people in the land of their birth. And this they did at a time which tried men's souls. Theirs were a platform on which none dare stand who were not willing to endure scorn, reproach, disgrace, lynch law, and even death for the sake of oppressed Americans. At first, interest, reputation, office nor profit, but the reverse, were the reward of an Abolitionist. Now that Anti-Slavery has become popular with many of the American people, it assumes another name, and is converted into political capital. Even Free-Soilism was not so much designed to make room for our liberties, as to preserve unimpaired the liberties of the whites. The Abolitionists have not yet accomplished any thing which we can see to be so definite and practical. Yet they have divested themselves of personal prejudices, aroused the nation to a sense of its injustice and wrongs toward the colored people, encouraged them in improving and obtaining education here, broken down many arbitrary and proscriptive usages in their treatment, and convinced this nation and England that they are a people capable of moral, social, and political elevation, and entitled to equal rights with any other community. Both of these benevolent societies might perhaps have accomplished more good, if they had wasted less ammunition in firing at each other. While one has formally declared a moral and intellectual inferiority of our race, with an incapacity ever to enjoy the rights and prerogatives of freemen in the land of our birth, the other has declared that hatred to the race and love of slavery were the only motives that prompted the Colonizationists to action. In taking a liberal and more comprehensive view of the whole matter, we believe that whatever may have been the faults, inconsistencies and seeming opposition of either, both have been instrumental in doing much good in their own way; and under the guidance of an allwise Providence, the labors, devotion and sacrifices of both will work together for good, and tend toward a grander and more sublime result than either association at present contemplates.

For our own part, under the existing state of things, we cannot see why any hostility should exist between those who are true Abolitionists and that class of Colonizationists who are such from just and benevolent motives. Nor can we see a reason why a man of pure and enlarged philanthropy may not be in favor of both, unless his devotion to one should cause him to neglect the other. Extremes in any case are always wrong. It is rare to find that all the members of any association, untrammelled by interest, act solely from high moral principle and disinterested benevolence. The history of the world, civil, sacred and profane, shows that some men have, in all ages, espoused popular and benevolent causes, more or less influenced by prejudice or selfishness. Human nature, with its imperfections, remains the same.

Ever since the adoption of the Constitution, the government and people of this country, as a body, have pursued but one policy toward our race. In every contest between the great polit-

ical parties we have been the losers. But this result it is reasonable to expect in a Republic whose Constitution guarantees protection alike to our peculiar and our free institutions—thus
securing the rights and liberties of one class at the expense of
the liberties of another. Besides this, Texas and all the States
that have since come into the Union, have surrounded us with
political embarrassments. Every State that has lately revised or
altered her Constitution, has been more liberal in extending
rights to the white and less so to the colored man. In view of
these facts, I assume as a fixed principle that it is impossible for
us to develop our moral and intellectual capacities as a distinct
people, under our present social and political disabilities; and,
judging by the past and present state of things, there is no reason to hope that we can do it in this country in future.

Let us look a moment at some of the consequences of this
social and political distinction on the entire mass. They are shut
out from all the offices of profit and honor, and from the most
honorable and lucrative pursuits of industry, and confined as a
class to the most menial and servile positions in society. And,
what is worse than all, they are so educated from infancy, and
become so accustomed to this degraded condition, that many of
them seem to love it.

They are excluded in most of the States from all participation
in the government; taxed without their consent, and compelled
to submit to unrighteous laws, strong as the nation that enacts
them, and cruel as the grave.

They are also excluded from every branch of mechanical industry; the work-shop, the factory, the counting-room, and every
avenue to wealth and respectability, is closed aginst them.

Colleges and academies slowly open their doors to them,
when they possess no means to avail themselves of their advantages, and when their social condition has so degraded and de-
moralized them as to destroy all motive or desire to do so.

They are by necessity constant consumers, while they produce comparatively nothing, nor derive profit from the production of others. Shut out from all these advantages, and trained
to fill the lowest condition in society, their teachers and minis-

ters as a class educate them only for the situation to which the
American people have assigned them. And hence too many of
them aspire no higher than the gratification of their passions
and appetites, and cling with deadly tenacity to a country that
hates them and offers them nothing but chains, degradation
and slavery.

Since things are so, it is impossible for them while in this
country to prove to the world the moral and intellectual equality
of the African and their descendants. Before such an experiment can be fairly tested, our colored youth from childhood
must be admitted to a full participation in all the privileges of
our schools, academies and colleges, and to all the immunities
and rights of citizenship, free from every distinction on account
of color, and the degrading influences that ignorance, prejudice
and slavery have heretofore thrown around them.

The same inducments as to white Americans should engage
them in agriculture, commerce, manufactures, the mechanic
arts, and all the pursuits of civilized and enlightened communi
ties. Every man of common intelligence knows this has not been
done; knows, too, it cannot be done, for the first time, in the
United States. In the face of these facts, we are compelled to
admit that the Afric-Americans, in their present state, cannot
compete with the superior energy and cultivated intellect of
long-civilized and Christian Saxons.

And, hence, we are driven to the conclusion that the friendly
and mutual separation of the two races is not only necessary to
the peace, happiness and prosperity of both, but indispensable
to the preservation of the one and the glory of the other. While
we would thus promote the interests of two great continents,
and build up another powerful Republic, as an asylum for the
oppressed, we would, at the same time, gratify national prejudices. We should be the last to admit that the colored man here,
by nature and birth, is inferior in intellect, but by education
and circumstances he may be. We could name many moral and
intelligent colored young men in New York, Philadelphia, and
Boston, whose talents and genius far excel our own, and those
of a majority of the hundreds of Saxon students with whom

we have at different times been associated; men who, if liber-
ally educated, would operate like leaven on our whole people,
waken responses in the unexplored regions of Africa, and pour
new light on the republic of letters; but who, for the want of
means and an unchained intellect, will probably live and die
"unknown, unhonored and unsung."

> "Full many a gem of purest ray serene,
>   The dark unfathomed caves of ocean bear;
>   Full many a flower is born to blush unseen,
>   And waste its sweetness on the desert air."

This may appear ridiculous to those who know the colored
man only as a domestic slave in the South or a political cypher
in the North. But the generations living sixty years hence will
regard him in a very different light. Before that time shall have
arrived, American Christians, as an expiation for the past, have
a great duty to discharge to a prostrate nation, pleading in silent
agony to God,

> "With tears more eloquent than learned tongue
>   Or lyre of purest note."

We too have a great work to perform. To the Anglo and Afric-
American is committed the redemption and salvation of a numerous people, for ages sunk in the lowest depth of superstition
and barbarism. Who but educated and pious colored men are
to lead on the van of the "sacramental host of God's elect" to
conquer by love, and bring Africa, with her tractless regions, under the dominion of our Savior; to baptize her sons at the font
of science and religion, and teach them to chant the praises of
liberty and God, until

> "One song employs all nations; and all cry,
>   'Worthy the Lamb, for he was slain for us!'
>   The dwellers in the vales and on the rocks
>   Shout to each other, and the mountain tops

> From distant mountains catch the flying joy,
> Till, nation after nation taught the strain,
> Earth rolls the rapturous hosanna round."

Whatever may have been the objections to Colonization in former times, I call upon colored people of this country to investigate the subject now under its present auspices. When I consider the kind of treatment they have received from their professed friends in America, I do not blame them in the past for exclaiming, "God deliver us from our friends, and we will take care of our enemies." I can never forget the round of applause that rang through an audience when a talented colored man of New York, in an earnest harangue against Colonization, said: "Mr. President, the Colonizationists want us to go to Liberia if we will; if we won't go there, we may go to hell." It seemed to indicate that they felt there was too much truth in the remark. Their principal objection has been, that men who professed the greatest love for them in Africa, did the most to exclude them here from the means of education, improvement, and every respectable pursuit of industry. And their personal treatment was such as colored men only are made to feel, but none can describe. When the temperance men treated the inebriate as an outcast—a wretch debased and lost—they accomplished nothing, but repelled him from their kind influences; now, when they recognise him as a man and a brother, their efforts are crowned with great success. In keeping with other reforms, I think that colonizationists have become more liberal and kind than formerly. Whether this be true or not, if I can dispose of a single objection, I shall be confident that Afric-Americans are to be benefited more by the cause they advocate and sustain, than by any other practical scheme philanthropy has yet devised. I should have been glad if this Society, consistent with its leading purpose, had done something for the improvement and education of colored youth. And this would have been a great auxiliary to their main object. They have thought that, if they encouraged their education here, they would not go to Africa. This is a mistake! If they would aid and encourage them in obtaining such education as white men receive, they could not keep them in this country. They would entirely unfit them for the debased position they must here occupy. Give me but educated intellect to operate upon, and I can send Liberia more useful men in three months, than I can in five years' labor with society as I find it. I speak only from my own experience, when I say that, during a life of constant struggle and effort, I never have received any sympathy or encouragement in obtaining an education, nor in aspirations to usefulness, from any of the advocates of Colonization, except my noble friend, J. C. Potts, Esq., of Trenton, N.J. Yet from some little acquaintance with many others, I believe they are good and true friends, ready to do any thing for colored Americans that they would for white men in similar circumstances. I have never doubted the good motives and true benevolence of such gentlemen as Benjamin Coates, Theodore Frelinghuysen, A. G. Phelps, J. B. Pinney, John McDonogh, and a host of others, whose sentiments and efforts in our behalf I know only by reading. But slavery and its consequent degradation, together with our social position, have kept us farther apart than if separated by the waters of the Atlantic. However good the men and worthy their cause, it cannot flourish without the co-operation of Afric-Americans here. Our brethren across the Atlantic have been struggling thirty years, and in tears and joy have laid the foundations of a free Republic with civil and religious institutions. They now call on us to assist in sustaining them and participate in their blessings; to aid them to civilize its inhabitants and extend the rising glory of the Lone Star of Africa. We should examine their cause, and if it is just, we should no longer withhold our aid; and especially when, in benefiting them, we must benefit ourselves. If, by my feeble efforts, I shall ever be able to do any thing that shall tell in future blessings on that injured country, it will be very much owing to the sympathy and encouragement received, in the course of my education, from S. H. Cox, D.D., of 1844, and Lewis Tappan, Esq., that unchanging and unflinching advocate of the slave.

But we have never been pledged to any men or set of measures. We must mark out an independent course, and become

the architects of our own fortunes, when neither Colonizationists nor Abolitionists have the power or the will to admit us to
any honorable or profitable means of subsistence in this country. I only regret that I come to the aid of Africa at a time when
I possess less ability to speak or write in her behalf than I did five
years since. Strange as it may appear, whatever may be a colored
man's natural capacity and literary attainments, I believe that, as
soon as he leaves the academic halls to mingle in the only society
he can find in the United States, unless he be a minister or lec-
turer, he must and will retrograde. And for the same reason, just
in proportion as he increases in knowledge, will he become the
more miserable.

"If ignorance is bliss, 'tis folly to be wise."

He who would not rather live anywhere on earth in freedom
than in this country in social and political degradation, has not
attained half the dignity of his manhood. I hope our Government will justly recognise the independence of Liberia, establish
that line of steamers, and thus give Africa a reinforcement of ten
thousand men per annum instead of four hundred.

Pardon my prolixity. The subject and the occasion have compelled me to write more than I expected to. In attempting to be
just to three classes, I expect to please none. While the press and
our whole country is vexed and agitated on subjects pertaining
to us, if I can do nothing more than provoke an inquiry among
Afric-Americans, I shall have the satisfaction of hoping, at least,
that I have contributed something to the interest and happiness
of the citizens of the United States and the people of Africa.

AUGUSTUS WASHINGTON

FIRST SEVEN WEEKS
IN LIBERIA, 1854

Augustus Washington

Monrovia, Liberia
February 8th, 1854

Rev. John Orcutt,

Dear Sir: —You probably expected to hear from me ere this by way of England but you will require no apology when I inform you that at the time the last steamer left this port, January 16th, I was not able to write, having then my first attack of fever, which left me at the close of a week. I only wrote one business letter to your city, with a remittance of $75; and I presume you have heard of my safe arrival from the person to whom I wrote. At some future time, I expect to give you a fair description of the acclimating fever. From experience I can say but little about it now, because during the week I was sick I was not in bed half the time nor was I very sick at any time. The most disagreeable part to me was taking medicine so often during the day to break the fever. But I was in good hands, boarding at that time in the family of Dr. H. J. Roberts, who has the reputation of being the most skillful and successful physician in this section of the country. Except that week, I and my family have enjoyed as good health as it is possible for persons to enjoy any where. While you are nearly freezing, we are enjoying what is here regarded as the warmest season of the year; and yet during the last month the mercury has not risen above 87°, nor fallen below 72°. It is re-

[EDITOR'S NOTE: This letter by Augustus Washington is addressed to the Reverend John Orcutt, Traveling Agent of the American Colonization Society. It first appeared in *African Repository,* June 1854.]

markable that for twenty-five days this month the mercury stood every morning at 80° or 81° and at 2 o'clock p.m. at 84 or 86. This is the season when the harmattan winds blow from the north during the forenoon; and these few mornings when the mercury fell to 72 and 74, was when these winds were blowing very strongly. I enjoyed them very much, but the old settlers complained of cold, and the natives were shivering. I think the Isla de Cuba a very good sea-boat. We encountered three severe storms, and on two occasions many of the company thought we would go to the bottom. When within 400 miles of Monrovia, we lay in a calm for one week; most of the time the ocean was as smooth as a mirror. As we were in the gulf stream several days, unable to get out on account of head winds and storms, we had a good share of sea-sickness. Notwithstanding our detentions, we arrived in the port of Monrovia, on the evening of the 18th of December, and such was the desire to see this land of prom-ise, hope and mystery, that the noise and excitement drove them from our couch of repose. Some I think remained up all night. In the morning we took a view of the cape from our anchorage. It was a beautiful sight to look for the first time in our life on the sunny hills and verdant plains of the only land in which we can feel ourselves truly free. The next morning I was among the first to go ashore, and I soon met with several faces I at once recog-nized. I took breakfast with my friend Dr. Roberts, and then called on Judge Benedict, and a few other citizens.

I soon saw that the people here live in a style of ease, comfort and independence at which they can never expect to arrive in the States.

I also saw cattle, goats, sheep and hogs running at large; and was quite amused to see some native boys pelting them with or-anges. I did not know before that orange trees grew as large as apple trees in the States. Before the street door of the house in which I boarded the first week there were three very large trees bearing several barrels of the ripe sweet oranges, besides coffee trees full of coffee. In the garden were other orange trees, lemons, limes, citron, plums, cabbages, beans, and many things I know not the names of.

Feb. 22. At the time I wrote the above I was expecting the steamers in a few days, but she came two days before her time and I was compelled to await this letter for another opportunity. I send it now by an American trader. I have written only two or three letters to the States as yet, because having had an attack of the fever, my physician requests me not to read nor write, and I do not feel much inclination to write at all unless I can write a great deal. Besides, whenever I am able to work, I can make so much more by my time in taking miniatures that the temptation is to work when I can. I have remitted in another letter today to Mr. Pinney drafts on New York to the amount of $500, which is the avails of about five weeks work at daguerreotyping, I put my price down to what the people consider cheap, $3 for the cheapest picture, and when I am able to work I go to my room and take some 20, 30 or 40 dollars worth of pictures in a day. I have hired boys whom I send to tell as many as I can attend to. The dry season will continue from January 1st to May or June, and then I shall engage in other business. Therefore I have sent $5009 to Mr. Pinney for the purchase of goods. I have a very fine house with a good store under it, and thus I shall be, if I live, for six months in a year an artist, the rest of the time a merchant on a small scale. We can buy many goods from English and American trading vessels, two of which are now in port. I shall send you those views as soon as I am able to take them, and forward them by the next vessel which I expect will leave here in a few weeks. We like the country thus far very much; and should I be able to write, as I desire, a series of letters for the Tribune, you will see there are things here both new and strange.

I cannot encourage any body to come here who has not something of his own to depend on, aside from the aid he gets from the Society. Because every thing here is very dear for poor people. For instance flour 10 cts. a pound, or $13 per barrel; pork is now 25cts. a pound; $29 a barrel; sugar 20cts. per pound; butter 50 often 62 or 75 a single pound; milk 25 cents qt. and so of every thing in proportion.

Thus it is in a country in which enterprising and industrious men can soon become rich. Every thing almost but hard coal is in demand here, and every thing sells. Thus a man needs only a little capital, and that in goods, and he can get along well. But if he does not have something to do with of his own it will go hard with him. There is no use in covering up the dark parts of the picture. More men will come to this country when they know the whole truth than will ever come, when you show them nothing but good. When we get the right kind of men here we will soon make things cheaper, for all these things can be raised in abundance as the samples we have fully prove. You would be surprised to see what quantities of dry goods, groceries and provisions are constantly imported from England and Germany. And only because the people have formed a habit of buying supplies from abroad. If the American people were only liberal enough to establish direct steam communication with us, we should for many years get all of our supplies from America. The English have four steamers touching here, one each way monthly, viz; Forerunner, Faith, Hope, and Charity, quite some significant names. They stop some six or twelve hours and discharge and receive the freight and mails. Thus the most convenient way to get any goods, is from England by these steamers. There are a number of American trading vessels, coming to the coast, but we cannot depend on them for receiving any freight, exports or imports, as their business is trade and private speculation. Consequently our letters must be sent at an expense of 40cts. by the steamers or take a six months cruise along the coast, before they start on their destination. The Liberians are not kindly dealt with by America. She should be the first to extend the hand of recognition, first to acknowledge her independence. But the mail is about to close and I must stop. Remember us kindly to your lady, and in particular to that most noble lady, Mrs. Sigourney, and the several gentlemen, who you know were particularly interested in me. And allow me to express again my sincere thanks for your kindness in assisting us in preparing for our departure.

I remain, your obedient servant.

A. WASHINGTON.

LIBERIA AS IT IS, 1854

Augustus Washington

Monrovia, June 27, 1854

In a residence of six months in Liberia, I have met with nothing so "passing strange" as the fact that no one has made known to the American public the sufferings of Southern emigrants after their arrival here, the paucity of physicians, and in some instances their shameful neglect of duty. I am aware that this cannot be done without incurring the censure of some persons in this country who at present occupy high official stations, who have become influential and comparatively wealthy by conniving at these faults, and who for this have the full confidence of the Agents of the American Colonization Society. I know too that for my presumption in exposing these wrongs as the only means of reform, I must fall under the displeasure of these gentlemen and perhaps of some few illiberal members of the Society. But I have a strong consolation in knowing that here I have the hearts and sympathies of the common people with me—the masses who are poor, whose letters of complaint have been [intercepted] and kept from the public, and whose wrongs have never been redressed. There are thousands of colonizationists in the States, North and South, who contribute their money to the cause with the best and most benevolent motives—men who honestly wish to elevate, christianize and bless Africa, and make free and happy her unfortunate descendants—men who have hearts in the right place and always sympathize with crushed hu-

[EDITOR'S NOTE: Augustus Washington's *Liberia as It Is* first appeared in *Frederick Douglass Paper,* December 15, 1854. It was reprinted in the *New York Tribune,* n.d.]

manity, whether in Greece, Turkey, Hungary, or Africa, and have no desire to send men to these unhappy shores, only sicken and die for want of suitable food and medical attendance, while, if the promise of the Society were truthfully filled, instead of thirty, forty, fifty, and sixty, not more than six per cent of the emigrants would die. These gentlemen have a right to know the facts of the case. Senator Russell declares to me that he has written four times to the agents on the very subject, and has received no satisfaction. A few other citizens have written and some emigrants have done so; but who has ever met with their complaints in any public paper, while some execrable cowards, who complain most of the *Society* and everything American talk one thing here and another thing to the States to please the people, have their letters published in all the papers. Not only public, but even private letters of such persons as President Roberts, Judge Benson, and their adherents, are all given to the public and then a brood of young aspirants for office and colonization patronage follow in the wake of their elder brethren. Even many new comers will write fine things of this country which they never have seen, and of which they have only read.

> They talk of the beauties which they never saw
> And fancy raptures they will never know.

"I would rather be right than President." I shall maintain the cause of God and humanity, and the poor emigrant and native regardless of consequences. I know that by a different course, I could soon grow rich by the suffering and death of those poor people. For, in nearly every town and county, there is a one-man power, for that county; a man may hold all the offices of government and besides be lawyer, merchant, judge, and agent for the Society, and, if he chooses, it is not difficult to turn the money and offices of these people into his own coffers. But if I have health and the same amount of brains, I can become wealthy if that be a virtue without aid from the Colonization Society, this feeble Government, or the men who see their daguerreotypes in the group I have pictured. For every mouthful of beer we get, we are equally dependent on the natives. When they choose to "kick up a row" (which often happens) and make war among themselves, we can get no meat, sometimes for months. We have no regular market; but when a beef is occasionally brought to market, I have seen six different hands pulling at two pounds of beef, while the butcher was carving it up, and, thus quarreling, and playing a regular "grab game" for a little meat, and seldom is there anything like a supply. And why is this? Because scarcely any of the people in this city work, but nearly all sit down and depend on living by trade with the natives and thus, while a few with capital grow rich, most of them live only from hand to mouth. Since all alike depend on the natives for their living, why need anyone fear to do right for the value of the patronage of the Society, or the smiles of a few in transient power? Their policy with the natives has been an unwise one. The latter are not found in our schools, and seldom in our churches. One teacher tells me he has about sixty scholars, but not one native. While they give no encouragement to education among them, fearing they will get power some day, they sell them any quantity of muskets with which to blow out our brains; when a wiser policy would be to make it a penal offense to sell them muskets and powder, but educate them, regard them as men, and incorporate them in community. There is but little regard for poor emigrants, yet I value them most because they are the working men, the bone and sinew of the community. They are the only men that would cultivate the soil and become the producers, and without such the country will only struggle on as now, in poverty, till it meets with some reverse, and falls as a colony into the hands of some European power. Think of the fact. We only live on the seaboard, or a few miles up the rivers. We have put a single road five miles up the rivers. We have not a single road five miles into the interior. All the region behind us is land unknown. The hundreds of tribes in our rear have only to unite, and they can at any time drive us into the ocean. And yet, to hear the windy speeches of our orators, one might suppose that all Africa had been conquered, and our lone star banner unfurled in every country from the Cape of Good Hope to the Mediterranean, from Guardafui to Cape Verde. When I published in *The Tribune* in 1851 my views in favor of African colonization, I could not believe that the opponents of the scheme had uttered so much truth. In that communication the only thing I have since found to regret was my advocacy of the proposed line of steamers to this coast, and this regret is only for the reason that there is as yet no suitable preparation made for emigrants as to comfortable houses, and proper medical attendance by the American Colonization Society nor the United States Government. Still I have charity enough to believe that if the former and latter knew these things as they are, if the Society was not able, the Government itself, for humanity's sake, would do something to aid them. Many of us new comers clapped our hands with joy that the *Shirley,* which has just arrived, brought no emigrants; but our joy was soon turned to sorrow when we learned that the *Sophia Walker* would soon arrive with a large number from Baltimore. Unfortunate wretches! What will they do in the midst of these driving rains packed down in these leaky huts in which gentlemen in the States would not keep their horses and favorite dogs. The state of things here, years ago, in regard to the treatment and suffering of emigrants was heart-rending and almost incredible, and yet no one who had not the means and opportunity to leave the country dared report them. They have greatly changed now for the better, and yet there is a dark chapter that never has been written. All the letters from Liberia, published in papers in the States give too high a coloring to everything pertaining to the country. It is no Paradise, no Elysium, no Eldorado. It is the last refuge of the oppressed colored man, and a country that could as easily have been subjected by the whites, if they had no other, and were thus compelled to make the same sacrifice of thousands of lives. We northern emigrants by the *Isla de Cuba* have fared well enough and thus for ourselves have no very special public complaint. Our sufferings are nothing in comparison. Having some means of our own, we have all resided at the Cape in Monrovia, where we could more easily obtain medical attendance, comfortable houses, and tolerably good food. Besides we have all been within the reach of the kindness of the wealthy class of citizens who have often favored us in sickness by their kind offices, and with suitable and nourishing regimen which our money could not buy. The *Banshee* with two hundred and seventy three emigrants arrived the same day we did, and the agent Mr. Dennis, according to instructions from Washington sent about two hundred of them up the St. Paul's River, crowding as many as possible into the United States Receptacle, and scattering the rest along the banks of the river, into such houses as could be procured. And these are small huts—generally one story high, with only a single room, from ten to twelve feet square, and into which a whole family, from five to twelve or fifteen are placed. Many of these huts are built of twigs interwoven; and plastered outside with common mud. The thatched roofs let down any quantity of water on their beds and often they are compelled to change their positions constantly, and hold their umbrellas to escape being saturated with rain. But what are the facts in regard to this U.S. Receptacle? It is an old, shabby, rickety building, originally designed for the *Pons* captives, and since used by the Colonization Society for the reception and six months residence of emigrants. It is only one story high, with a garret, and is built of brick—It contains twelve pens below and four garret apartments. These rooms (if they deserve such a name) are about six feet by nine, having one small window without glass, which must be closed during the rains and at night, thus making a suitable dungeon for a murderer. Within these rooms, I have seen nothing but an excuse for a bedstead made out of rough saplings lashed together with bark or rope, and stuck up against one side of each stall, about four feet from the floor. I first visited this place, and saw these stalls, about three weeks after my arrival in this country and remarked to my friends, that if I had to stay in one of them, I should surely expect to die. I saw nothing else in these except what the emigrants had brought, and upon this baggage many of them had to make their seats. Some of these stalls contained each whole families of six to ten and fourteen. Dr. Jacob M. Moore, who was employed by the agent here to attend them for the six months, declared to me that they had no place to keep their provisions except under their beds, and there, at any time, you would find their rations of salt beef, salt pork, rotten fish, &c, with all other indescribable necessaries.* Besides this there are always some sick persons in bed. *This fever is no humbug.* It is a stern reality, and of a family of six, after two months they never will find three successive days that all of them are well, short of six or nine months. Thus I maintain that the best house in town, and the best of medical skill, and the best of fresh food are nothing too good for an emigrant if he can afford it, while passing through the raw ordeal of acclimation. But such is the development of hope in the Afric American (the Fowlers will sustain me) that whatever may be the suffering and misery he endures, as soon as he escapes them, he forgets the past, and descants with rapture on the future. Who does not know how miserable, servile and degraded is the condition of the free colored people in the States?—and yet Messrs. Pennington, Frederick Douglass & Co. preach to these people the certainty of elevation and social and political equality in America, while the million, educated free from their prejudices, could not come to such a conclusion in their wildest dreams of philanthropy. The former would accomplish much more good for our race, if they would come over and help us correct the abuses and oppression here, and make this country what it might be, than by staying there and wasting their energics in exhausting efforts, which always avail nothing. I have just taken the pains to measure a hut one story high, with one room and garret, twelve by sixteen feet into which seventeen of the emigrants of the *Banshee* were placed, and in which they remained nearly two months till the fever broke out, when they were separated, leaving ten in the hut. Another hut close by has four persons in one room, twelve by fourteen feet. This is the way they live. We think they have in Mr. H. W. Dennis, an honest, upright faithful and attentive agent; but there are no better houses to be obtained for small rent, and he is not furnished with any money by the Society, but

---

*That is to say, the colonists were forced to keep their food provisions under their beds alongside their chamber pots.

is compelled to trade, and twist many ways to meet the cash payments for the rent, nursing and washing, &c., of the emigrants or compel the Society's creditors to take trade goods and provisions when they do not want them. He has the confidence of this community, and we all think he will do right, and give satisfaction to the emigrants to the full extent of the power and means conferred upon him by the Society. He is the man, perhaps the only man here that does or ever did give his whole attention to this business exclusively. The emigrants by the *Isla de Cuba* have petitioned to the Directors of the New York State Society to send their friends in future to Mr. Dennis; but it seems to me unfair unless they also give him an additional small salary. Such a man, if he were white, possessing the same qualifications, would receive a salary of twelve or fifteen hundred dollars, while now he receives only six or seven hundred. Any man like him can make four times this amount by trade; and I shall be sorry for the poor emigrants if they lose him.

No class of men are more needed in this country than thoroughly educated and skillful physicians. I never have heard of a country in which life is so cheap. But here again is one man power. The Society employ regularly but one physician—Dr. Roberts—whose estimate of poor emigrants is very small. While he will visit some few of the reputed wealthy families of Northern emigrants three times a day uncalled, the majority of the rest can get no attention; and the poor Southern emigrants declare to me that they send, and send, and send again, and he will not see them himself once in two or three weeks, and sometimes in two or three months, but he will send them a boy or heathen native with calomel, oil, and pills, and will doctor them in this way, and if these do not cure, they must die. One poor family, and the single men have been treated in this way. People here generally build houses by piece-meal, occupying some years in completion. The Doctor's time has been absorbed in building his house this year, and I think some years before. Now, in these circumstances the Society should have employed some one to assist him in medical practice. This neglect of duty is partly owing to the want of competition and an independent supervision by some agent or commissioner who is too honest and brave to be influenced in favor of wrong by kind treatment, good wine, or splendid dinners. I have heard this same complaint twice, in whispers in the States, and hundreds of times here. But poor men, as the mass of emigrants are, they dare not make any complaint public against the Society or its agents or against the Government functionaries of this Republic, fearing the loss of daily bread, if not their lives. Thus glaring wrongs have existed here for a long time which the rich grow fat on, and the poor, for their lives dare not meddle with—They tell us we must take men as they are—we must not disturb their passions—we must not arouse their prejudices. To take men as they are in any such sense, is to leave them worse, than you find them; an angel's spear must be had, whose touch will bring the toad to a proper shape, though it start up a devil. I would rather live a serf under the Czar of Russia, than in a country where I must employ a physician in whose carefulness, responsibility, and skill I have no confidence. The want of competition keeps some men always at the point from which they started, and the dependence of the community renders them petty kings. The truth is when emigrants come here by hundreds at a time, Dr. Roberts has more than he can properly attend to, even with the occasional assistance of Dr. J. M. Moore. But this is no reason that he should do less than his duty. In justice to Dr. Roberts, I may here say, that I have no fault to find with him except in his medical practice as the Society's physician. In my intercourse with him as a citizen, I find him kind, generous, and affable as most persons I meet with. Besides, he is yet a young man, and, if he would study and carefully practice, is capable of rising to the head and leading the van, of the medical fraternity in this country. I have no personal quarrel with nor enmity against the Doctor. But individuals have complained of this and other wrongs to the agents of the American Colonization Society in vain. As a last resort, I write this publicly in behalf of many hungry orphan children, and wretched widows, made desolate by the loss of their husbands who have died for want of food or medical attendance, in a strange and foreign land. I do not wish the Society to throw

him overboard, but simply demand a greater degree of attention to poor emigrants—a higher grade of skill and efficiency in
himself, and then pay him a better salary. Because this is a dear
country in which to live comfortably, and the man who gives his
whole attention to any one department of business deserves to
be well paid.

It is a common saying here that we have either a feast or a
famine, and it is no less true in regard to physicians than provisions. Report says that two medical young gentlemen of Boston
are about to sail for this city. We shall give them a hearty welcome, and then we shall have four physicians.—Drs. Roberts,
Moore, Loving and Snowden—the latter two gentlemen will
need considerable practice before they become skillful in the
diseases of this country. We wish them all success, and believe
the interchange of thoughts and the competition for skill will
render them all more efficient. Besides, we shall have Dr. McGill
here, the recent Governor of Cape Palmas, a graduate of the
medical department of Dartmouth, reported to be the most able
physician in Liberia; but as the society would not pay him what
he considered a fair compensation, he has given up practice for
the present and associated himself with his three brothers
known as the firm of McGill Brothers, one of the oldest, most
wealthy, responsible, and respectable mercantile houses in Liberia. I hope that these four physicians will agree upon some
system of administering less medicine to their patients. I think,
for this climate and its peculiar diseases, it will be discovered in
a few years that the milder and simpler systems of hydropathy
and homeopathy will be more effectual than the common allo-
pathic practice.*

I will not harrow up your minds by any accounts of fearful
mortality caused by the want of medical attention and the comforts of life among poor emigrants. Suffice it say that of two hundred of the emigrants of the *Banshee* (which arrived at the time
we did) sent up the St. Paul's river, one third have died, and our
agents, citizens, and physicians are all in controversy about it, in

---

*Water cures and other fads of the nineteenth century.

two party papers, published in this city, called the *Herald* and *Sentinel*. If any colonization papers doubt my statements, let them only dare publish the letters from these papers. It will all come out. Let them only state one fact and comment in future. I have spent one whole day investigating the case of the *Morgan Dix*, which sailed from Baltimore Nov. 1, 1851 and arrived at Bassa with one hundred and fifty one, all well. (See At. Report for Dec. 1851, and April, 1852.) They were then supplied with means— with a saw mill and agricultural implements.—But where are they now? Echo answers, where? Could the grave disgorge those gun boxes into which their corses were buried, it would disclose a horrid tale of the neglect of the physician, agent, or Society— or exhibit the murderous work of sending fresh emigrants to people new districts of country that resemble no place so much as Golgotha. Read and understand that of *these one hundred and fifty one emigrants there are but nine survivors*. Others maintain there are fourteen. Grant that there are fourteen survivors. I challenge the Colonization Society and their agents here and in America to prove that there are more. And all this is the result of sending men to the most unhealthy part of this country, and packing them into old, rickety thatched houses, in which the emigrants tell me they had to hold umbrellas to keep them from the pelting rain. Besides these have but one physician for Bassa and Sinoe, which I think are one hundred and fifty miles apart, and I have too much evidence not to believe that some of the emigrants actually starve and die for want of food and medical care.—But let me speak softly. I well nigh forget that I must buy my goods and provisions in New York, Boston, and Baltimore for my store, and after talking so loudly, I may be troubled to find an agent to discount my drafts, and forward goods in coloniza-tion vessels. Besides, I may be persecuted by a pack of hungry pork-eaters in Liberia. With the physicians I have done at pres-ent. From Dr. Roberts and his particular friends I may expect resentment. But if I can only save from the grave a few poor Southern emigrants and make better the chances of long life to my friends from the North, I am willing the doctor shall pay me for my boldness in any kind of coin he pleases. In justice to the

Society I may say that this case of the *Morgan Dix* is an extraordinary one. The emigrants of the *Isla de Cuba*, in which I came having settled at this place, have lost only three of their number, and seem to be doing well; and the *Banshee*, as I have said, which arrived the same day, lost of her two hundred—sent only fifteen miles up the river—one third. Some of my friends write me and inquire how I like the country. I may say, on the whole, first rate, and if I did not, I could return to the States to morrow, $1,000 better off than when I came here six or seven months ago. I have had three pokers in the fire and God has prospered me with all, although I have been sick at times, as much as three months; wife sick constantly: children well now: I invite my friends to come to Liberia, but take care to have some little means to start with. You can earn it in America easier than in Africa—Where one succeeds with nothing, twenty suffer and die, leaving no mark of their existence.

                                                                A.W.

LETTER FROM
AUGUSTUS WASHINGTON
FROM THE
COLONIZATION HERALD

Many of our readers will remember the author of the sub-joined interesting communication, addressed to Thomas Clegg, Esq., of Manchester, England. Mr. Washington is an unmixed representative of the colored race: and possesses a clear intellect and much good sense. He sailed with his family for Monrovia, Liberia, in November, 1853, having previously resided at Hartford, Conn., where he was successfully engaged for several years in the daguerreotype business. It will be noticed that the statements he now makes after a residence of nearly six years in Liberia, are very different from those he gave through the columns of the New York Tribune soon after his arrival in that country.

And what an excellent opening Liberia presents to colored men of capital and enterprise to join Judge Washington and his like, who have there entered upon the cultivation of the sugar cane for the manufacture of sugar and molasses, and the cultivation of coffee, cotton, &c., thus making that Republic an exporting power for these and other valuable commodities! Cheap labor is to be found in Liberia in any quantity, and nothing but

[EDITOR'S NOTE: This letter from Augustus Washington to Thomas Clegg first appeared in the *Colonization Herald* (n.d.) with an introduction by the editors (included here) and was reprinted in the *Maryland Colonization Journal*, September 1859. Thomas Clegg was "a Manchester cotton spinner involved in promoting cotton cultivation in Africa since 1850," according to historian R. J. M. Blackett. See his *Building an Antislavery Wall* (Baton Rouge: Louisiana State University Press, 1983), 177.]

capital and skillful management is required to be added to the already existing sugar and coffee estates and the commencing cotton farms, to make them immediately and immensely profitable; whilst if the same capitalists were to go to Yoruba they would be lost in a wild region, and their effects would be wasted where no foundations of civilized life exist, and where no commencement of civilization and improvement of the country are yet made. Co-operation, social union and joint efforts are required to settle and improve any new territory. All these will be wanting in Yoruba, whilst they are found in Liberia. We are not opposed to the Yoruba movement, but we prefer the Liberia enterprise, because we are convinced it will be far better for our colored people.

FREETOWN, SIERRA LEONE, June 18, 1859.
Dear Sir:—In September, 1858, while on a visit to the Gambia, I met with a copy of the African published in this city, containing an interesting correspondence (extracted from the Manchester Weekly Advertiser) between yourself and Messrs. J. J. Myers, M. R. Delany, and Ambrose Dudley, Committee of the Mercantile Line of the Free Colored People of British North America. The association is composed of gentlemen, some of whom I formerly knew in the United States. The object of the committee seems to be to solicit your opinions on the subject of their establishing a trading post at some point on the Eastern or Western coast of Africa. The purpose in itself is both wise and commendable; for this is the final result to which all the Africo-American population must inevitably come, or they must perish slowly, but not less effectually, by their heterogenious [sic] contact with the American people. Those who have carefully observed the past, and have the vision to look down the dim vista of time and read the future, will not be slow to hasten to the only permanent refuge left for the black man. In Africa he has "mind unfettered, and space to rise"; here he has full scope for the growth of manhood and the development of all his moral and intellectual capacities. As to business attainments, even in this city, we have a class of native men, but partially educated, not twenty years from

the decks of the slave vessels, whose instructive knowledge of domestic economy, business tact, and skill in financiering, is said to surpass the Jews of Cheapside. I state this fact not so much to commend such a principle, as to show that while there is an opinion entertained by many of the friends of the black man that our people in America are an improvident and prodigal race, we have the other extreme among the Africans in their own native country; and if there is any truth in the opinion of their prodigality and extravagance, it is rather to be ascribed to their long intercourse with the Anglo-Saxon race, while deprived of their freedom, self-reliance, and checked in their career to a higher state in moral and intellectual existence.

At the time of reading your communication, I observed that while you seemed much interested in behalf of those gentlemen seeking a home free from opposition on a foreign shore, you speak of Natal as a place for growing sugar and cotton, but remark that "there you must take all the labor with you, as the Caffirs will only work when it suits them." It will easily be seen that when colonization from America to Africa has been so slow for thirty years past, no system of voluntary emigration could be established which could at once carry labor from the United States to endure the fever and fatigue of the African coast. You remark also, that "there is a good opening for trade in cotton all over the Yoruba country, and near Rabba, Ilorin, Ibadan, and all about the Niger." But you also say that you "fear these people would not let you settle peaceably in the interior if you went there in a body." This statement seems to show in a word the impracticability of a small company effecting a settlement there. You proceed to say—"There is an opening for African labor in Tunis, in North Africa; but as it is in the Turkish dominions, I cannot recommend you to go there as a colony; but it would, in my opinion, be very desirable for the best educated amongst you to go—say a dozen or twenty families together—to different parts of Africa, keeping up a constant communication between one part of the country and another, and being constantly making openings, as circumstances allowed, to send for more from America, and thereby drain away every man of African blood in

America," &c. I hardly need say, that while the plan in itself is good in theory, with the one hundred thousand dollars capital which this company expects to control, it is entirely impracticable. Let facts speak:—

Sierra Leone is only a small territory, twenty miles square. It has been settled some seventy years, and yet she has no jurisdiction beyond the boundaries of her original territory. The people cannot farm; they are crowded for want of land. This they must in future have from the surrounding tribes, or by annexing some part of the adjoining territory of Liberia. And where, I ask, would be the security for the lives, liberty, and property of these interior tribes of civilized Africans and the European merchants, if the Government of England should remove for one year the heavy cannon from this garrison, and the bristling bayonets of her standing forces, seen everywhere in our city? Another fact:—Liberia is less than 300 miles to the leeward of this city, and since the mail steamers have ceased to call at Monrovia, I am compelled to incur an expense of £40, and charter a schooner there to get a passage to Sierra Leone. If this be the expense and difficulty of extension of bounds and of communication between two civilized and Christian settlements speaking the same language, and so contiguous on this coast, and what must be the expenses and chances of intercourse between a civilized people, in detached parties, in Yoruba and the adjacent country?

I did not intend to find fault with your suggestions, because I am confident that they were given in candor, and with an earnest desire to state only what seemed to you best at that time; but as a citizen of Liberia I did take exception, and do now, to the sentiment of the remark that "Liberia is considered so far to be a failure." I did not blame you or your friends in thinking so while you were not posted in the true facts. I at once wished to reply, and show that though the British public might, and with some show of reason, entertain that idea, it was nevertheless without foundation, and there was no facts to prove it. But knowing that facts are stubborn things, that they tell where words fail, I concluded to wait till the maturity of my own crop of cane and cotton, that I might send you with my letter samples of Liberian sugar, cotton, and coffee. I have taken this liberty with you because I know that in England, the United States, and on this entire Western coast, you have long been known as first among the true friends of Africa; and from what I learn from those who have the honor of your personal acquaintance, I am certain that your love of the truth and magnanimity is such, that you would rather have your opinions proved to be founded in error, than give currency to a wrong sentiment; especially one which would have the effect to draw off that generous sympathy and warm interest in our experiment, which has been so long cherished for us by British philanthropists and Christians in all parts of the world. You will find enclosed a bill of lading for four specimens of our produce, viz., one cask, 371 lbs. net, Liberian-made sugar; one barrel, 44 gallons syrup; one small bale, 85 lbs. cotton; also a specimen of hemp or manilla, called by the kroo-men, caffier. A sack of coffee I could not get now. You will please examine these, and see what they promise. Whatever their value may be, you may pass to my credit, together with the amount of enclosed small draft, and remit me the amount in 32-in. prints of 24-yds. Should we in future find a market in England, I do not expect our sugars will pay anything like the prices I am selling at in this city. These are some of our first productions in a rough state, and we of course expect you to be charitable in your judgment.

In respect to the sugar, I may say that the Queen's officers and soldiers at the garrison are now using this sugar. I sold them seven barrels a few days ago. The demand is increasing. Perhaps this is the first time they have used free-labor sugar. The syrup is not our best specimen; it was the result of an attempt to make sugar. The lot of cane had been exposed too long at the mill, and we thought it best to convert the juice into syrup. Many of my Liberian neighboring farmers made much better syrup than I did this year.

The cotton is in its roughest state; some from trees one year old, and some from trees five years old. Two years ago, I encouraged the natives around to bring me cotton, intending to ship it. As they had no machinery for cleaning it, I offered them 2½ d.

in the seed. It soon accumulated on my hands, and having no market for it, and not knowing how to dispose of it, nor where to find a machine to gin it, I had to stop purchasing. As we have no gins in Liberia, except some old spoiled ones, sent to the Government several years ago (perhaps by yourself), I thought I would bring a sample of 100 or 200 lbs. to this place, and here have it ginned. I was informed that the Church Missionary Society had some here, and was about to apply for the use of one to the good and beloved Lord Bishop Bowen, of Sierra Leone, when his death suddenly occurred by the prevailing epidemic, which for the last two months has been sweeping off both the blacks and European population. I find that there are no gins in this city, but one or two up the rivers. Rather than throw the cotton away and spoil a good intention, I have shipped a little in the dirt and rough state, just as I have been buying it, because I know but little as to good or bad qualities of raw cotton. If this is a quality that will answer, we can obtain considerable quantities of such by paying a price sufficient to induce the native and American population to cultivate it more extensively. The natives interior from us, manufacture annually, thousands of country cloths, from one to two fathoms long, with which they overstock our market. They will sell the cloths or the raw material. The certificate of H. M. Consul, that these products were Liberian, was retained at this custom house; but that these specimens are African, I need only refer you to the Hon. J. J. Roberts, H. M. Acting Consul at Monrovia, or his Excellency S. A. Benson, our popular President.

I find that but few Englishmen here know the origin and history of Liberia; and I presume that such is generally the case with the British public. An American colony seems to presuppose that it is of necessity a colony begun, nourished and supported by the strong hand of the United States Government; but such is not the fact. The people of Liberia have never sustained any political relation whatever to the United States; and consequently have never received from the Government one shilling of pecuniary or other aid and support. Liberia is the offspring of American benevolence and christian philanthrophy [*sic*]. A few friends of the colored people organized a society at Washington city, in 1817, with the avowed purpose of assisting the free colored people of the United States in emigrating to Africa, and at the same time of founding an asylum for the slaves of the South who might be manumitted from time to time by generous masters. The first vessel sailed from New York about 1820. The first settlers landed at Sherbro; afterwards they removed to Monrovia; and after battling many years with the diseases of the climate and the savage natives, enduring all the privations and reverses incident to new countries, they at last established for themselves a government, civil and religious institutions, and at once extended these benefits to their heathen brethren around them. Like other civilized communities on this coast, they all at first engaged in petty trading with the natives; but finding from experience that trade in itself was precarious, and that the only means of securing permanent wealth and prosperity was in developing the agricultural resources of the country, they nearly all, for the past three or four years, have engaged in farming, and their success has begun to realize the most sanguine expectations of their friends in America. The national fairs of 1857 and 58 gave a new impetus to agricultural industry, and the farmers now vie with each other in producing any indigenous products which find a ready and accessible market. Last year I know of only one barrel of sugar being exported from the Republic to the United States. This year our farmers on the St. Paul's river, I think, have shipped not less than 80 or 100,000 lbs. to the United States, and I have disposed of about 6,000 lbs. in this market. I am confident that we shall have to find some other market instead of American for our sugar next year, and this will be the subject of my inquiries at present. These people have been plodding along slowly on their own little means, but they have not *failed*. I am personally acquainted with every man now growing sugar in Liberia; I do not believe there is more than one of them who had £100 capital to commence with; and I am quite confident that there is not one who has received to the amount of £100, either in goods or money, from America, England, or anywhere else, to invest in his farm-

ing operations. I except, of course, the two parties who have steam sugar mills from benevolent gentlemen in New York.

The American Colonization Society assist in sending them to the country, and give them six months' rations and support. There their connection ceases, and the emigrant becomes the architect of his own fortunes. In the event of any foreign difficulty or internal disturbance with the natives, they have enough of vegetable and animal food on their farms to sustain them one year without planting. Some of them now manufacture the cloth and clothes they wear. Liberia has no standing army, and needs none; her militia—her citizen soldiers—are sufficient for any emergency at home. The natives around us have a common interest in preserving peace. We pay their chiefs no stipends for keeping peace other than the protection and justice of our laws, the advantages of trade, and friendly and Christian intercourse. If they break the peace and assault us without cause, we flog them, and make them pay the expenses of being flogged. Liberia has not yet any foreign debt. If she fails, she will fail from nothing. Her citizens were all poor, seeking in Liberia what they could not obtain in America—life, liberty, and the pursuit of happiness. If they had only an amount of capital equal to that expended on St. George's cathedral in this city, or the amount expended on the army and defences of Sierra Leone for one year, they would turn the whole sum to the growing of sugar and cotton, and if they did not turn out some thousand hogsheads of sugar and as much cotton, they would bear with shame the imputation of having failed. But, sir, Liberia is not without her faults; they are many, and no man is more ready to reiterate them in the ears of her citizens than myself. But she has not failed as a Republic, and her people have not failed as citizens.

Liberia has four or five hundred miles of seaboard territory, thousands of acres of uncultivated soil at fifty cents per acre to Liberians and emigrants, and free to all the natives. She only asks that the natives of her country may remain at home, and grow cotton and sugar on their own soil, instead of being forced to French Guiana and Martinique;—that the world will give her a fair market for her produce, and that America and England will say to France, "Let us alone," as we never will consent to sell our brethren into emigrant bondage. We are expecting Messrs. Delany & Co. to visit the coast soon. We do not advise them, but we think that the Mercantile Association of colored citizens will eventually conclude, on examination, that some part of Liberia will be the best field for their enterprise.

I send you by this mail the *Liberia Herald*, the organ of the Government; the *Christian Advocate*, edited by the Bishop of the M. E. Church of Liberia, and two other clergymen; and the *Liberia Star*, an independent paper, all now published at Monrovia; also the *Colonization Journal* and the *Colonization Herald* of America; the *Era* and *African* of this city, and the Report of the last National Fair of Liberia, which was written by myself, as Secretary of the Committee, at the request of the Chairman of the Committee of Adjudication. While I have embodied the views of the committee, I have there fully expressed my own opinion on the growing of sugar and cotton.

With much respect and consideration, I am, sir, your most obedient servant,

AUGUSTUS WASHINGTON.

SIX THOUSAND DOLLARS
BETTER, 1863

Augustus Washington

The writer of the subjoined letter was born in Trenton, N.J., passed two years as a member of Dartmouth College and was widely known as an ingenious artist at Hartfort [*sic*], Conn. In 1854, he availed himself of the benefits freely offered to his race by this Society to reach Liberia; now, he represents, with others, Montserrado county in the Legislature of that Republic.

Mr. Washington remarks: "I am at least six thousand dollars better than I ever was in the States." Other Liberians could testify to the same effect and withal to their greatly improved social political and spiritual privileges. Emigration to Africa thus helps the emigrant and tends to propagate the blessings of the English language, free government, civilization and religion over a continent! Who can compute the value of the reflex influence in elevating those they leave in this country?

We have great faith that if the friends of the colored people will present to them the advantages of Liberia, a largely increased exodus thither would soon be witnessed. This idea we commend to the serious consideration of our citizens. Whenever a colored man can be helped to go to that Republic, it will be to his advantage. There never was a time in our national affairs when the mighty importance of efforts to improve the present and future of the people of color was so transparent and pressing.

[EDITOR'S NOTE: This letter from Augustus Washington first appeared in *African Repository* in March 1864.]

Monrovia, Liberia. Oct. 3, 1863.

Dear Sir.—Perhaps you would like to know what I have done. Well after being here nine years, I may simply state to you as a friend, without seeming to be egotistical or presumptuous.

After being here a year or more, I became convinced that the true interest of Liberia consisted in the development of her agricultural and mineral resources. Without any previous knowledge of farming, and surrounded by none that could instruct, I started into the forest, cut down the bush, planted a cane farm, and built the necessary houses. Then I had no capital, no mill, no cattle, no horses, nor means of turning my crops to profitable account, nor any friend here or elsewhere to help me. But I continued to plod along, acting as merchant at Monrovia, farmer on the St. Paul's and artist at Sierra Leone, the Gambia and Senegal. By carrying on so many branches of industry, I have lost a great deal, and yet this mode of procedure has been my success. I think I am at least six thousand dollars better off than I ever was in the States, and I believe that if I had remained there till now, I should have been so poor I could not get away.

Eight years ago my farm was forest; now we have growing sugar cane, coffee, rice, cassada, potatoes, and in our garden cabbages, radishes, turnips, tomatoes and many other vegetables. You can see here now our carts hauling bricks, rocks, wood, &c. Four yokes of the largest African cattle, milch cows and other cattle, two horses, six jacks, turkeys, chickens, ducks, pigeons, &c. You will see also fifty persons here who are fed, clothed and supported now in the rainy season, and who when the weather will permit, are engaged in various avocations. I reside at my farm nearly all the time, but I do not superintend in person any of the business on the farm. My own time is occupied with trade and domestic correspondence.

I have lately appointed an agent in New York, and if the war does not interrupt commerce, I shall export largely to that port, and order my American goods from that market instead of purchasing, as I have heretofore been doing on the coast, at an advance of seventy-five per cent, on the invoice. My wife and two

children brought from America and one born here, are all well.
We were expecting to come to the States last June, but you had
such storming times in New York, that we were afraid to venture.
  Yours faithfully,

A. WASHINGTON

Index

NOTE: In "The Looking-Glass," the Rev. Peterson listed the names of philanthropists and many other persons who may have been supporters, character references, or benefactors. Not all of these individuals are referenced in the index. The reader may find it helpful to consult the index and subheadings under Peterson, Daniel H., "reference letters cited" or "philanthropists praised," as well as pages 68–70 and 71–75.